STILL OURS
TO LEAD

Two corollary reactions to this narrative have emerged. Either America should ramp up its military and economic efforts to counter the rise of the new powers, China in particular.[8] Or America should turn inward, focus on its own economic troubles, and withdraw from a fracturing world.[9]

This book offers a very different narrative. It argues that while other powers have gained influence, the United States, buttressed by allies, is still the most influential actor on the world stage—and will be for some time to come. It also argues that the emerging powers are both a more diverse and a less threatening phenomenon than pictured, not least because they are sharply divided among themselves. And it argues that there are far more shared or overlapping interests between the established and the emerging powers than the narrative of disorder suggests.

I have spent much of the past decade watching the rising powers—principally China, India, and Brazil, but also Turkey, Indonesia, Mexico, and others engage the international system and struggle to alternately change it or adapt to it. Their first foray was at the United Nations, where, in the wake of the launch of the Iraq war, the emerging powers began to stake out a more determined claim for a greater share of influence in the international system—an effort I observed and tried to help shape as an adviser to Kofi Annan's effort to retool the UN to deal with modern security challenges. The emerging powers' play for influence in New York was paralleled by their ambitious initiative in Geneva, at the World Trade Organization, to rebalance the rules of free trade to accommodate their growing market power. I have tracked their campaign closely since, both in international bodies and in their capitals.

The renegotiation of power relations between the established and the emerging powers at the UN and the WTO was just prologue. As the emerging powers struggle to assert themselves and the United States struggles to recalibrate its leadership to new realities, bilateral and strategic relations are being renegotiated more broadly. This transition began to absorb U.S. policymakers when the global financial crisis thrust the emerging powers from the sidelines into the spotlight.

Tracking the efforts and strategies of the emerging powers over the past decade, and looking at the underlying dynamics, leads me to three conclusions.

INTRODUCTION

On the face of things, it has been a rough few years for the United States. America is only slowly winding down the second of two draining wars. Trying to avoid a third war, this time in Syria, has put the U.S. at odds with many of its allies in Europe and the Middle East, while Russian and Chinese intransigence has frustrated efforts to find a UN solution to that appalling civil war.[1] In the South and East China Seas, Chinese assertiveness appears not only to threaten America's long-time dominance in the region but also to risk a crisis with Japan.[2] America's European allies are mired in financial crisis and repeated recession. Global climate negotiations have repeatedly failed, in part because the emerging powers banded together to block agreement.[3] And all of this after the global financial crisis put a deep dent in America's treasury and reputation.

These events inform a narrative of the erosion of American leadership and a crisis in the international order. The underlying premise of that narrative is that a combination of declining American power and the "rise of the rest" (of the new economic powerhouses of China, India, and Brazil, in particular) is constraining America's leadership of the international system.[4] The narrative suggests that the power of the West to shape a secure and prosperous international system is in decay.[5] The result, it is argued, is that the United States faces a collapse in its ability to handle global crises and challenges and that global cooperation to solve problems is no longer possible.[6] The world might also face renewed cold war–style competition between the two great powers.[7]

PART III. HOW AMERICA CAN STILL WIN
FRIENDS AND INFLUENCE HISTORY

CONTENTS

To Wyatt
May you know a world at peace

ABOUT BROOKINGS

The Brookings Institution is a private nonprofit organization devoted to research, education, and publication on important issues of domestic and foreign policy. Its principal purpose is to bring the highest quality independent research and analysis to bear on current and emerging policy problems. Interpretations or conclusions in Brookings publications should be understood to be solely those of the authors.

Library of Congress Cataloging-in-Publication data

Jones, Bruce D.
    Still ours to lead : America, rising powers, and the tension between rivalry and restraint / Bruce Jones.
        pages   cm.
    Includes bibliographical references and index.
    ISBN 978-0-8157-2512-1 (hardcover : alk. paper)
    ISBN 978-0-8157-2597-8 (pbk : alk. paper)
    1. United States—Foreign relations—21st century. 2. World politics—21st century. 3. Globalization—Political aspects. I. Title.
    JZ1480.J66 2014
    327.73—dc23   2013043039

Printed on acid-free paper

Typeset in Sabon

Composition by Cynthia Stock
Silver Spring, Maryland

Printed by R. R. Donnelley
Harrisonburg, Virginia

STILL OURS TO LEAD

AMERICA, RISING POWERS, AND THE TENSION BETWEEN RIVALRY AND RESTRAINT

BRUCE JONES

BROOKINGS INSTITUTION PRESS
Washington, D.C.

One, America is an enduring, not a declining, power. Now and likely for some decades to come it is and will be the most influential actor on the world stage, buttressed by strong allies. The rhetoric of U.S. decline runs well ahead of the reality. There are newly important actors on the world stage to be sure, but some of them are U.S. allies, many of them are friendly to the United States, and even those whose drive is for autonomous power share core interests with the United States—and this includes China. Moreover, the rising powers are divided among themselves and often share as many interests with the Western powers as they do with each other. In short, the challenge these actors pose is less than has been asserted.

All the attention given to the economic rise of China has lessened the attention given to the important phenomenon of the economic rise of India and Brazil. Further, it has obscured the fact that other economies are rising too, among them Korea, Turkey, Indonesia, and Germany. And while some of America's long-standing allies (Japan, the United Kingdom, France) are experiencing a slump, so too is America's long-standing rival, Russia. The large majority of the most powerful economies remain U.S. allies. Thus the rise of the rest is a complex phenomenon and, correctly managed, offers U.S. leadership as many opportunities as challenges.

Two, the interest of the non-Western rising powers is not to break the order but to shape it and to gain more space within it.[10] Countries like India and Brazil—and also U.S. allies like Korea and Turkey—have repeatedly demonstrated that they do not seek to break the international order but rather to profit from it and to take a turn at the helm of major international institutions. This fidelity to the existing order is based on a variety of factors, not least of which is that the emerging powers rose precisely by integrating themselves into the global economic system. Only China arguably seeks to curtail U.S. leadership in some domains, but Beijing's incentives are hardly straightforward: in many aspects of foreign policy, China has no choice but to cooperate with the United States and its allies. It can challenge American leadership only if others will follow, and so far it has found few takers.

To be sure, this is hardly the whole story. The emerging powers also have a strong impulse to rivalry, or at least to autonomy, an impulse grounded in what I call the psychology of rise. This phenomenon comprises both their own first, devastating encounters with a globalizing West and the routine humiliations of their position in the postwar order. The psychology of rise is most evident in China's assertive stance in defense of its interests and influence in East Asia, but it is equally present in India's defense of its interests in the evolving climate change regime and in Brazil's aspiration for a bigger role in global security affairs.

But the emerging powers face a dilemma. They may have an impulse to rivalry and some interest in curtailing U.S. influence, but if they are too aggressive in their stance toward the United States they risk endangering their global interests. They have fundamental stakes in a stable global economy and in protecting the sea and air routes through which global trade and energy flow. This is particularly true of China, which needs to maintain very rapid growth both to sustain its domestic stability and to project international influence. But to grow, it needs to consume ever-larger quantities of energy (it has already surpassed the United States as the world's greatest carbon emitter). And to consume that much energy, it must import large quantities of it—along with food and other natural resources. These imperatives require three conditions: stability in the countries from which it can extract resources; stable markets, in which it can invest; and stable transmission routes, to bring resources into mainland China from its suppliers. And yet China's capacity to generate that stability and protect these investments is sharply limited and, in some cases (as in the Persian Gulf), is heavily dependent on American military power.

Thus while the rising powers strive for autonomy and demonstrate an impulse to rivalry, they also have incentives for restraint, even cooperation. This balance between the impulse to rivalry and the incentives for restraint is the most important dynamic in contemporary international affairs; and for now, the balance tips toward restraint.

The result of this is a continued ability to solve problems and to manage crises—at least, to do so at roughly the same rate as occurred when American dominance was unquestioned. Claims of an erosion in this ability, of the emergence of what has been called the G-Zero world (a world of no international leadership), are exaggerated. There is instead substantial cooperation on the global economy, if as yet inadequate to remove the risk of new crises, and on energy and the oceans (and even on the management of climate change). In spite of intensifying competition in the U.S.-China relationship, the world is a long way from a new cold war, and in important facets of the relationship there are restraint and even joint leadership. The management of crises and armed intervention—the most sensitive tripwires in international politics—includes a mix of cooperation and tension, success and failure. This is roughly the same mix that characterized the post–cold war era, during the height of American power.

From these arguments I draw the third conclusion: that the United States still has ample ability and opportunity to lead the international system. By *lead* I do not mean dominate. One implication of the analysis is that America's coalitional power (its alliance system, its ability to work with countries from all walks of international life, its facility in forging tools for multinational action) will be key to American foreign policy. For too long the notion of leadership has been narrowly equated with the option of unilateral military action. The United States retains that option, and military power is indeed a lynchpin of American power; but leadership is a broader concept by far.

The United States will undoubtedly face new challenges: allies torn between the security embrace of the United States and economic ties to China; new powers seeking autonomy, not alliance, on the international stage; and complex global issues that will test American diplomacy. All of this means that America will have to adapt its leadership to new realities. But it just so happens that this challenge plays to America's single most important asset in navigating the landscape ahead: that it is uniquely well placed to pull together broad and disparate coalitions for action. There is no other actor on the international stage, nor will there be in the near or medium term, with anything remotely like the range of alliances and relationships—including with several of the rising powers—enjoyed by the United States.

Hence the title of this book, *Still Ours to Lead*. The title can be interpreted in three ways. First, most obviously, is the reference to American power. No other actor, established or rising, has anything like the tools, the allies, or the relationships, coalitions, and institutions that the United States has. The ability to pull together coalitions for action is perhaps the most enduring feature of American power. True, the United States no longer enjoys the status of unrivaled hyperpower that it maintained after the end of the cold war. U.S. dominance is dulled. But it remains in a category of one in the international system.

Second, the stakeholders (the *Ours*) extend beyond Washington: there's a huge capacity in the international system to solve problems, to manage crises, and even to cooperate. Some of this is about the United States, but not all of it. *Ours* includes the emerging powers, even China, and actors capable of contributing to problem solving and crisis management. The United States should have the confidence of its position and welcome, not resist, other states' efforts to lead problem-solving efforts on specific issues.

Third, the phrase *Still Ours to Lead* deliberately echoes the phrase "still ours to lose." At an earlier stage I chose that as the title for this book—then rejected it as too defensive. But the concept of "still ours to lose" is an important one, because American leadership could still be squandered. Bad policy choices by the United States and by its allies could weaken its position, and miscalculation by the United States or by the rising powers could indeed propel the system toward more disorder.

One debate more than others has shaped the discourse over what lies ahead, a debate over the prospects for cooperation or conflict among the most powerful states. One argument emphasizes that the emerging powers' economic stakes in a stable order will drive restraint.[11] The counterargument is that a reading of the history of the rise and fall of great powers tells us that conflict, and even war, is inevitable.[12] Throughout this book, I argue that there is evidence to support the first claim but that it is incomplete; there is also an impulse to rivalry, and if it is underestimated, it risks being unleashed. At the same time, I point to evidence that suggests that the sense of the inevitability of war during periods of power transition is both too deterministic and misapplied.

The stakes are high. This debate is unfolding during the first period in contemporary history that is not predominantly shaped by tension between great powers.[13] Not accidentally, this era, following the end of the cold war, has seen astonishing economic advancement for hundreds of millions of people, a wave of progress against poverty. It is an era of sustained collaboration among states to tackle the great modern ill of civil war.[14] For most of the post–cold war era it has also been a time of growing freedoms, as dozens of countries moved toward democracy and as citizens challenged the economic and political constraints under which they live.[15] This historic progress could be eroded or undermined if the emerging powers underestimate the costs of American retrenchment or reaction; if America prematurely withdraws from the international stage; or if America fails to adjust its leadership style and diplomatic tactics to the realities of new actors on the international stage.

Now, debates about the international order often fail to define what this order is supposed to accomplish, except in the minimalist sense of avoiding great-power war—no minor thing, of course, given the horrors of the first half of the twentieth century. In this book, the concept covers tiered goals. First and foremost, yes, it is about avoiding great-power war, or tensions between the powers that run deep enough to forestall broader problem solving. Second, it is about maintaining and spreading economic prosperity. Third, it is about reducing the scope of tyranny, in part by encouraging development and democracy and, equally important, by checking tyrannical actors with force when ultimately necessary. And the international order is more worth protecting if it also serves, as it has for the past quarter century, to reduce poverty and internal war. Looking ahead, there's a further challenge: balancing the emerging powers' need to consume ever-growing quantities of energy with the impacts on a changing climate.

In the coming world, the options for American leadership will be shaped by three forces: the strength and vitality of America's established alliances will amplify or constrict the impact of American power; the attributes and attitudes of the rising powers will shape American options; and American leadership will be tested in complex global issues, like global trade and finance and climate change. In issue after issue, the tension will be between two powerful pressures: that of an impulse to rivalry, rooted in the histories and attitudes of the rising powers and the temptations of transitions; and that of deep incentives for restraint, bolstered where there are institutions or arrangements designed to allow the major powers to resolve their differences or limit their competition.

We should not be Pollyannaish; if we neglect the real risks of rivalry, we could unleash them. But nor should we overestimate them, lest we fear them into life. There are challenges ahead, but we are a long way away from failure and disorder.

For now, and in the most credible scenarios of what lies ahead, both the impulse to rivalry and the incentives for restraint will be present, and shaping the balance between these dynamics will be a central challenge to American foreign policy. Choices made by the emerging powers will shape that balance, to be sure, but the single greatest factor will be America's choices in wielding its power. In this most fundamental sense, too, it is still ours to lead.

PART I

A GREATLY EXAGGERATED DECLINE

The Fall and Rise of Major Powers

CHAPTER ONE

AMERICA'S
ENDURING POWER

In May 2006 the *Financial Times* published a survey of the most influential commentators in the world. Topping the list for the United States was Charles Krauthammer.[1] Krauthammer was cited for two articles he had written in the previous half decade: a manifesto for an ambitious program of American power projection titled "Democratic Realism" and an essay in *Foreign Affairs* magazine that defined the post-cold war moment as one of "unipolarity," or U.S. dominance.

Krauthammer was far from alone in reveling in a sense of American dominance. The launch of the wars in Afghanistan and Iraq and the start of the "global war on terror" occasioned a heady sense of the global reach of unfettered American power. A flurry of books and articles extolled the extent of American dominance and the merits of the American "empire." Issues for debate were whether the American empire was grander than that of Rome at its height, how long it would last, and whether America could sustain an imperial role while maintaining a liberal political character. Not questioned was the notion that America stood astride the globe, alone.

There was irony in the timing of the triumphalism. Just as Krauthammer and others were celebrating American dominance, a deep shift in the economic grounding of American power was beginning. The story is encapsulated by two numbers: 20 percent and 75 percent. Twenty percent is the proportion of the United States economy, measured by GDP, that the combined economies of China, India, and Brazil equaled in the year

2000. By 2010 that proportion was just over 75 percent. What a difference a decade makes.

The narrative has thus moved from debates about unipolarity and empire to ones about multipolarity and decline. Ever since the onset of the global financial crisis, it has become commonplace to refer to the fact that the world is now multipolar. Long, and fortunately, gone are the bipolar days of the cold war, when the two roughly equal superpowers stood eyeball-to-eyeball, backed by their respective blocs of allies or client states. But gone too is the brief moment of untrammeled U.S. power and with it, it is argued, U.S. leadership of the international system.[2]

This is not the only feature of the argument about declining leadership. The debate has been magnified, but also distorted, by partisan commentary about U.S. foreign policy choices. To liberals, the Bush administration's decision to expend U.S. treasure and blood in Iraq squandered American strength and sullied America's moral leadership. Mistakes of strategy in the long war in Afghanistan bled the U.S. Treasury. To conservatives, the Obama administration—or more precisely, Obama himself—has belittled America both by apologizing for its past errors and by failing to proclaim America's exceptionalism.[3] When the Obama administration chose to act with allies and through international institutions in responding to an imminent humanitarian crisis in Libya in March 2011, critics pounced on an administration spokesman who used the phrase "leading from behind" to characterize the U.S. posture: evidence, they argued, that the Obama administration no longer believed in U.S. leadership on the world stage.[4]

Nor has criticism of Obama's foreign policy been limited to Republicans. The civilian uprising in Syria in the spring of 2011 was met with a drumbeat of calls for tougher American action, from interventionists of both left and right. As the Obama White House steadily resisted calls for American military engagement, the criticism grew louder that the country had abandoned its leadership position. And looking at the Obama administration's policy across the broader sweep of the Middle East and Central Asia, the one-time State Department adviser Vali Nasr went so far as to reverse Madeleine Albright's famous injunction of American indispensability by arguing that the U.S. decision to draw down its military presence in the Near East, at a time of rising Chinese interest there, was set to make America a "dispensable nation."[5]

These lines of criticism blend together and sometimes conflate separate questions: about whether the United States is in a state of actual decline or in a state of relative decline (experiencing a shift in position between the leading and rising powers); about policy choices; and about whether the changing landscape of power means that the United States no longer has the capacity to lead. The essential questions are three. Is the United States actually in decline? And if pronouncements of unipolarity and empire were inflated, does it follow that the world has entered, or is entering, multipolarity? Is America genuinely becoming a dispensable nation? One analyst, whose own book on what he called a leaderless, or "G-Zero," world has helped shape this narrative, puts it this way: "Since midway through George W. Bush's tenure, there's been a steady hum from the pundit class that America's best days are behind it. An overreaching foreign policy, rising public debt, and a growing wave of outsourced jobs means that America will soon lose its status as the world's preeminent power. America was quickly on its way to becoming Rome."[6]

The narrative of decline is in part an inevitable corrective to the overwrought and often hyperbolic punditry about American imperial might that followed the 9/11 attacks and the start of the U.S. war in Afghanistan. Already, a number of correctives to this narrative have emerged.[7] Clearly, the United States no longer enjoys the unmatched dominance that it experienced for a very brief moment at the turn of the last decade. For all that, it remains an enduring power on the international stage, a power in a category of one in the international system.

Relative Decline, Economic Heavyweight

The debate on relative decline carries with it the residue of America's early mistakes in Iraq and the lingering war in Afghanistan. But it is driven more by global economic changes. Indeed, the economic growth of the emerging economies over the past decade truly is breathtaking.

Brazil entered the twenty-first century with an economy of just over $1 trillion and ended the decade with an economy worth almost $2.5 trillion, and in the process it overtook Canada, Italy, Spain, and the United Kingdom to become the sixth-largest economy in the world. India grew even faster, though from a lower starting point, beginning the century with an economy worth just under $500 billion; by 2012 it had become the eighth-largest economy in the world, just ahead of Russia and Canada, and worth just under $2 trillion. China's growth started earlier and reached breakneck speeds during the first decade of the 2000s, shooting from an economy worth just over $2 trillion to become by 2013 the second-largest economy in the world, at just over $8 trillion.

These economies' huge growth is reflected in global trade patterns; for every major trading region, the percentage of imports and exports to and from developing Asia (especially China and India) has skyrocketed. And on carbon emission, not only have the rising powers been catching up to the West, but China has overtaken the United States and India has overtaken Japan and Russia.[8] (These emissions are measured by country; on a per capita basis the United States is still by far the world's worst emitter.) This emissions growth is a decidedly mixed blessing for the emerging powers, given the problems posed by energy dependence and the international politics of climate change. But the numbers illustrate the scale of their economic growth and deal them a formidable hand in global economic and energy diplomacy. China is set to become a leading player on investment in green technologies. There is little doubt that where America's relative power has been most curtailed is in the realm of economics (figure 1-1).

But while figure 1-1 conveys one essential truth about the growth of non-Western economies, it is also misleading. For one thing, the U.S. economy is still the world's largest, and by a good amount.[9] But there is more than size to the influence of the U.S. market. The fact is that the United States has a dominant lead in innovation and high-end products. China, now the second-largest economy in the world, has grown rapidly in large part by becoming a low-cost manufacturer of goods that sell in the American market and other high-end markets, including Europe.[10] The result is that U.S. market power far exceeds what is suggested by a simple comparison of GDP.

Call this the Apple effect. Apple may use a China-based supplier to assemble many of the parts for its high-end products, but the richest share of Apple's activity—product design—happens in the United States. What market would Foxconn have if Apple did not exist? Apple has the option of shifting suppliers; Foxconn does not have a similar range of alternative, high-end producers. India's high-technology industry has blossomed

Figure 1-1. *Size of Economy, United States and BRIC Countries, 1990–2012*[a]

GDP in trillions of current U.S.$

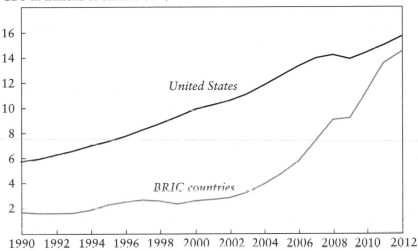

Source: World Bank, World Development Indicators Database.

a. The BRIC countries are Brazil, Russia, India, and China. South Africa, added in 2010 (and resulting in the term BRICS), is not included here.

largely by supplying low-cost supplements to America's high-technology industry. The same is true of dozens of other industries: the American share of the high-end market is simply too large to ignore.

Or call this the Walmart effect. When Walmart decided in 2006 to adopt compact fluorescent light bulbs as a standard part of its stock, the global market for manufacturing light bulbs was transformed. Walmart accounts for approximately 13 percent of the U.S. market for consumer goods, and the United States accounts for approximately 28 percent of the global market. No consumer goods manufacturer can compete on a global scale without selling to the United States—so when Walmart shifted gears, it created huge incentives for global manufacturers to adopt its standard. (Imagine if the United States used this power consistently to shape global incentives and standards for green energy technology.)

This market segmentation is only slowly beginning to shift, as manufacturers like South Korea's Samsung challenge American firms in design and technical edge. But it is relevant that the firms that can challenge their American counterparts in high-tech innovation are located in countries that are U.S. allies—and typically in countries that experienced their first wave of growth some decades ago. The U.S. economy may only be 20 percent of the global economy, but it is the richest and most lucrative 20 percent, with an outsize influence.

There is more. America's share of global GDP may be receding, but American economic influence is also a function of the size and the profit share and the role of its corporations, especially large, dominant, transnational companies. The vast share of the world's economic activity is transacted by large corporations, whether private or state owned. A 2013 study of the world's top corporations reveals a striking reality: namely, that U.S. firms continue to dominate in terms of profit share in critical sectors.[11] Indeed, in eighteen of twenty-five of the sectors tracked by Forbes, American firms have above 50 percent of the world's profit share, and that includes industries like aerospace and defense, computer hardware and software, financial services, media, and transportation. In several others (automobile, heavy machinery, and retail) the U.S. share is just below 50 percent. And in some critical sectors, U.S. profit share has grown in recent years.

The global financial crisis, and the American response, came replete with warnings that new efforts to put controls on Wall Street would lead to American financial expertise draining outward to markets like Dubai and Singapore and Hong Kong. What actually happened is revealing: whereas in 2006 American financial services firms accounted for 45 percent of profits from the global financial services market, by 2012 that number had risen to 53 percent.[12] And the 2013 study suggests that these numbers actually underestimate American influence, because there is a heavy imbalance in the extent of American ownership of overseas firms and overseas ownership of American firms. When transnational ownership is taken into account, American investors own a whopping 46 percent of the publicly traded top 500 transnational corporations. In other words, Americans own a far greater share of the world's wealth than the U.S. share of global GDP suggests (and 41 percent of the world's millionaires are American).

The same analysis reveals important structural weaknesses in the Chinese economy. Although China is now the largest exporter of electronic goods (a role long played by Japan), fully 90 percent of those exports emanate from foreign-owned firms. Chinese corporations have grown in three sectors, namely banking, construction, and telecommunications, sectors in which the sheer scale of GDP can drive expansion. But on the issue of competition in high technology and related areas, China has a huge distance to travel. As noted in the 2013 study, "Considering that it is uncertain whether China can catch up with Taiwan then South Korea then Germany then Japan, speculation on China being able to challenge the United States at the technological frontier in the foreseeable future is not credible."[13]

Indeed, China faces a deep challenge. To secure the next wave of its growth, China will have to overcome what economists call the middle-income trap; namely, the challenge of shifting from simple manufacturing to the more complex functions of engineering, design, and innovation. Below a certain income threshold (in today's global economy, economists roughly estimate that at between $4,000 and $8,000 per capita GDP), countries can grow by using cheap labor to produce low-cost exports to undercut high-priced manufacturers. But as the economy rises, so too do labor costs, and the advantage of cheap labor dwindles. Countries then have to be able to compete through innovation and to shift toward domestic production and consumption, which is a much tougher challenge. Many countries have started up this pathway of change, and failed. Put simply, the next wave of Chinese growth will be much harder to forge than the last. (China's systematic commercial cyberespionage is not surprising; the Chinese leadership grasps the challenge.)

Further, American service firms still dominate international finance, and to this date most of the world's economic flows are transacted in U.S. dollars and flow through Wall Street.[14] These are the traditional sources of American financial power, along with the capacity and will of the U.S. Treasury to rescue other economies during crises, that give the United States the de facto right to set the rules by which those states play the international financial game. Some of this influence was dented by the global financial crisis of 2008, of course; but for now there is no genuine alternative to America's financial role. (This is true even of the question, which China has raised, of the dominant role that the U.S. dollar plays as a global reserve currency. As we see in chapter 5, there is pressure on

America's role here, but not such that it seriously jeopardizes that role in the short or medium term.)

So in the economic sphere, there has been some degree of relative decline, or more accurately, a relative rise of others. But the United States remains an economic and financial powerhouse and will almost certainly retain its market-leading and dollar-reserve roles for some time to come.

And it is important to stress that these strengths will endure even if or when China's economy overtakes that of the United States in terms of GDP. If Chinese and U.S. growth rates mean that China overtakes the United States—most likely around 2025—there will still be a huge gap between American and Chinese per capita GDP and also huge differences in the nature of the two economies. China's economic managers are well aware of this fact: it is one of the reasons they work hard to retain unity among the major developing economies. As one of China's financial managers put it to me recently, "Unless things go badly wrong, we'll overtake the U.S. economy in size at some point in the next ten years or so. But even then, we can't go head-to-head with the U.S.; we'll still be a developing economy. We need others at the table to bolster our influence."[15] They need support from this broader set of countries to amplify their influence in the global economy: head-to-head with the United States, they are significantly weaker. But the central problem that China faces is that as its growth outstrips that of the other rising powers, there is less and less unity among them, even on core economic issues. And economic weight is far from the sole feature of power in the international system.

Military Giant, Regional Challenges

On March 17, 2011, the UN Security Council voted to authorize military action to prevent a humanitarian catastrophe in Libya. Two days later, 11 American warships, including guided-missile destroyers, attack submarines, and amphibious assault ships, joined forces with B-2 bombers, A-10 ground attack aircraft, electronic warfare aircraft, and a fleet of F-15 and F-16 fighters, deployed out of Europe. French and British forces were the first to strike, quickly followed by an American aerial assault on Libyan ground and air defenses, with 110 Tomahawk cruise missiles launched into Libya in the first hours of operations, while the U.S. and European navies mounted a sea blockade. The bulk of the early strikes were conducted by the United States, and the massive scale and global reach of American firepower were on vivid display. Within days, the Libyan air defense was dismantled, and a large Libyan assault force poised to strike rebel headquarters in Benghazi had been halted. The cost of the operation, at several hundred million dollars, was a mere rounding error in U.S. defense calculations.

Two years after the global financial crisis, which spurred the confidence of the rising powers, the Libya operation reminded them of the scope and reach of American power: that the United States remains the only power with the ability to act globally in military, intelligence, diplomatic, political, and economic terms.[16] Libya was not a major challenge to the United States in either military or geopolitical terms, but the simple fact that the United States could mount the Libya operation without it taking on much significance in terms of the military budget or military capacity pointed out the fundamental differences between the United States and other actors in terms of global military reach.

A simple measure of the chasm between the United States and its potential competitors on military matters is defense spending. In 2011 the United States spent just under $700 billion on its military; Russia and China combined spent just over $250 billion (though the Chinese number may well be somewhat larger, given the opacity of Chinese military accounting).[17] Those numbers underestimate U.S. military dominance, though, because they do not depict three additional American strengths: military spending by its allies; a substantial technological and experience gap between the United States and its competitors (a gap that by most accounts grew during the past ten years as a function of innovation and field testing in Afghanistan and elsewhere); and the accumulation of assets during almost a quarter century of post–cold war spending.

The financial and technology gap between the United States and its putative competitors means that any one of them could substantially increase the quantity of its military assets—as both China and India are doing—and still come nowhere near to having the capacity to compete with the United States militarily at a global level or to perform the global security functions that the United States does. And even to do this, a competitor would have to devote huge shares of its GDP to military expenditure over the next two decades or more—and then it would only reach a stalemate, at best. Under some credible scenarios, Chinese military spending will not match American military spending until sometime after 2050. For now, only Russia comes close to the United States in military capacity, and that is solely due to its nuclear arsenal.

Still, it is important not to underestimate Chinese military spending. Over the past decade, sharp—if opaque—increases in Chinese military spending mean that China has clearly moved into the second slot in global military spending. At the same time, though, the United States retains a major legacy advantage. One forthcoming book on U.S.-China relations notes that the United States had almost a quarter of a century to accumulate high-end military assets with no major competitor—and that it retains most of those assets.[18] Overall, the estimate is that the United States has a ten-to-one advantage over China in terms of high-quality military assets. But China is now clearly in second place in terms of defense spending.

What might motivate rising powers to challenge the U.S. militarily? During the cold war, the primary purpose of American military power was to contain the Soviet Union and deter a nuclear war. But this was never the only function of the American military. While the United States has never aspired to be nor acted like the world's policeman, it wields its power in ways that deter conflict between major powers, limit or contain regional conflict, and stop terrorist organizations from disrupting the functioning of the global economy.[19] It provides a security guarantee to allies in Asia and the Middle East, helping to avoid regional arms races. At times the country has wielded its power to defend the essential principles of the international system: in 1991 it led a military coalition to halt Saddam Hussein's illegal invasion of Kuwait, an invasion that violated the bedrock principle of sovereignty and the foundational rule of the United Nations Charter, that a state should not use force against another except in self-defense. The United States has used its power to tackle the hydra-headed organization that is al Qaeda and its affiliates—so far with important if incomplete success.[20] Its navy protects critical shipping lanes, through which travels the vast majority of the world's supply of oil and gas; and its navy patrols the high seas against piracy.[21]

Governments in all mature economies recognize that the security of their trade rests heavily on American power.[22] For nonallies, that is often an uncomfortable recognition, but most officials would privately acknowledge that a shift away from American security dominance would come with a greater risk of conflict—conflict that, for now and far into the future, these countries have no certainty of winning. Not only do the major rising powers have little to fear from American security dominance, they have vital interests in the United States continuing to perform a set of global security functions.

These security functions kept the emerging economies, before the 2008 financial crisis, content to rise in the slipstream of American power. In 2007 a Brazilian politician told me, "We don't want a collapse of American leadership. We want a long, slow soft landing for American dominance."[23] In Beijing, an official was even more blunt: "We know that our growth is dependent on American security power. It's very convenient for us."[24] America has long complained about the fact that its allies free ride on American security spending, but the great irony of the American global security subsidy is that some of its greatest beneficiaries are putative rivals.

This being said, few states are entirely comfortable subcontracting their security to another. Doubts about long-term American intentions fuel rising states' sense of insecurity. So whether or not they have the intent to challenge the United States at a global level, there is a logic of self-defense and self-reliance that pushes rising states with the option to do so toward either developing the military capacity to defend their interests or at least curtailing U.S. dominance in their region. The trajectory of this is uncertain; in the capitals of the rising powers, including Beijing, there is a debate about whether to invest the considerable resources necessary to develop a global military capacity.

The rising powers, however, compete with the United States only in their own backyards, not on a global level. Region by region, therefore, a smaller military capacity can rival what the U.S. can credibly deploy. Of course, the United States, which maintains a global military presence, can move assets around the globe, so a regional challenger has to contend with that fact. But balancing this out is the reality that any clash is likely to be much closer to the rival's border—the huge gap in capacity between the United States and any potential challenger is lessened somewhat by the difficulty of deploying those capacities across vast distance.

For now, this matters most with respect to China, which is trying to close the gap with the United States in two ways, both relying on technology rather than scale.[25] One, in terms of its regional security and its regional role, China has begun investing in new technologies that could dent U.S. naval superiority in the seas surrounding China—so-called anti-access, area-denial (A2/AD) capabilities. Two, China has been investing heavily in cyberoffense. The basic purpose of cyberwarfare, in this setting, is to level the playing field, at least temporarily, by undermining U.S. computing capacity to manage its far-flung war assets. It is a tool built around the recognition that in a general conflict between the United States and China, American military capacities would be far superior—to say nothing of its nuclear dominance. China's ploy would be to curtail that superiority by striking at command and control systems.

These asymmetric technologies could substantially limit America's military options in Asia and challenge America's military alliances in the region. The United States seeks to maintain a global military footprint, while so far China only has to compete in one region. And China is exporting some of these technologies, which will complicate America's choices elsewhere.

However, even as China attempts to challenge the United States at a regional level, it confronts two complicating factors. One, for every step that China takes to weaken American security dominance in the region, other states take corresponding steps to strengthen it. Japanese defense spending has increased, U.S.-Korean diplomatic and joint military activities have increased, and the U.S.-Australian military alliance in the region has been refurbished. These are not minor factors; the Japanese navy is a serious competitor of China's, for example, and Korea's land army is also a force to be reckoned with.[26] And slightly further afield, China has to contend with India, which has developed a substantial and growing military capacity.[27] Even Russia and Japan have pursued closer ties.

Two, even if China could successfully challenge the United States at a regional level, it would have to face the fact that America's global security presence—with which it cannot compete for decades—can seriously

Figure 1-2. *Global Military Spending, 2012*

Expenditures in millions of 2011 U.S.$

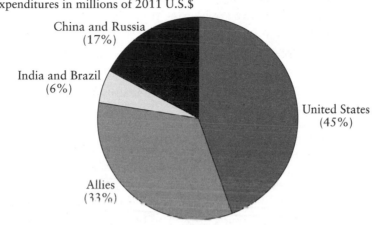

Source: Stockholm International Peace Research Institute (SIPRI), Military Expenditures Database, 2012 (www.sipri.org/research/armaments/milex/milex_database).

compromise its interests. Most important, U.S. military superiority is such that, given a war scenario, the United States could choke off Chinese economic and energy imports. In other words, Beijing is still heavily dependent on American forces to provide security in the oil-producing states of the Middle East and on the U.S. Navy to secure the free flow of trade and energy through the Strait of Hormuz and the Strait of Malacca. The majority of Chinese imports flow through the latter.[28]

American military power is also not limited to its own assets; those of its allies count as well (figure 1-2). When I was writing the first draft of this chapter, I received a mass email from Lockheed Martin, an advertisement for their new version of the F-35, the so-called Lightening II fighter jet. More impressive than the hyperbolic promotion or even the product itself (the program has been riddled with contracting and production problems) was the list of countries that are partners in the production and use of the aircraft: the United Kingdom, the Netherlands, Italy, Turkey, Canada, Australia, Denmark, Norway, Japan, and Israel. That's a pretty good list of America's core fighting allies, to which could be added America's Persian Gulf allies. And this still does not capture America's

Asian allies. Total defense spending by America's European and Gulf allies adds roughly another $400 billion, or about twice what Russia and China spend combined.[29] Even as Europe trims its military spending, it still retains substantial military assets.

Furthermore, among the rising economies, both Brazil and India have defense agreements with the United States, and neither could be considered friendly to Russian or Chinese military expansion.

The Multiple Tools of American Power

Economic and military strengths might be the foundation of American power, but they are hardly the only elements, as the following story makes clear.

In the predawn of May 2, 2011, two helicopters from the 160th Airborne take off from an airbase just inside the Afghan border, fly toward the border, and enter Pakistani airspace, undeclared and undetected. Minutes later they swoop down into a compound in Abbottabad in northeastern Pakistan. One of them crashes on landing, but the Special Forces teams in the helicopters have prepared for this, and they swiftly adapt. They secure the outer buildings in the compound, then storm the main house. What happened next is now well known: within an hour, they leave the compound and signal back to the Pentagon: Geronimo EKIA (enemy killed in action). Osama bin Laden was dead.[30]

Though this was an operation of modest scale, the ability of the United States to project lethal force, with secrecy and pinpoint accuracy and halfway across the globe, conveyed the impressive reach of the United States. But peel back the curtain on this episode and it reveals another critical feature of American power: its intelligence capacity. American intelligence efforts have frequently been derided, especially after its failure to foretell the capacity of al Qaeda to conduct the 9/11 attacks and its incorrect assessment of Saddam Hussein's nuclear and other weapons of mass destruction programs in the lead-up to the 2003 Iraq war. But no country can begin to match the scale of American intelligence gathering (some portion of which was revealed by leaks from an ex-NSA contractor, Edward Snowden) or the ability to twin this intelligence with special operations of the kind demonstrated by the Bin Laden raid. Only Britain, Russia, and Israel are in the same league in terms of human intelligence capacity; and two of these three are America's closest allies. And even these countries cannot compete with the United States in the use of signals intelligence. None of the emerging powers has even the beginnings of an intelligence infrastructure capable of supporting global power projection. Of course, as with the Snowden leaks, perceived abuses of that capacity can create reputational problems for the United States.

The scale of American power is evident also in U.S. diplomatic strength. Most diplomatic services of large Western countries like Britain and Canada maintain a staff in the several thousands. The United States has around 18,000 diplomats and other members of the foreign service.[31] Size does not equal influence, of course, but it helps. To give a sense of comparative scale, in 2007 the Indian diplomatic service, at about 900 diplomats, was more than twenty times smaller than the U.S. diplomatic service.[32] The Indian diplomatic service is fewer in number than the number of Americans serving in the U.S. Embassy in Delhi. Granted, this balance is starting to shift. Brazil has one of the world's most professional foreign services and is expanding it rapidly, particularly in Africa.[33] Conversely, some of America's allies are facing budgetary cuts and shrinking the scale of their diplomatic service.

Size matters because of the range of bilateral and multilateral issues that are constantly being negotiated on the international stage. At any one time, a leading power has to maintain intensive bilateral relations with two dozen or more powerful countries (France has a diplomatic staff of almost 500 for its relations with the United States alone). In seventy to a hundred countries a diplomatic presence matters both for bilateral relations and for global negotiations. In a further thirty to forty weak states, a leading power will want to play a role in conflict management and reconstruction. At the same time, there are ongoing negotiations on disarmament and various forms of arms control; multiple, country-specific issues will be up for negotiation in the UN Security Council; there are ongoing climate negotiations, trade negotiations, and intellectual property rights negotiations; development issues are being negotiated at the World Bank and any one of twenty UN agencies; and so on and so on.

Just having enough diplomatic capacity to be present in these negotiations is a challenge, let alone having the diplomatic muscle to lead them.

But size is not the only source of U.S. diplomatic power. The country also has built-in privileges and powers in critical global institutions. Although there are institutions in which the United States has less influence, still there is a direct relationship between how important a body is and how much power the United States wields within it. In bodies with real power, like the UN Security Council and the International Monetary Fund, the United States has a huge influence—and a veto. In bodies whose actions are symbolic, like the UN General Assembly, its power is more diffuse, but then the stakes are not as high.

All of this combines to give the United States an enormous amount of "gravitational pull" in the international system.[34] Some of this is positive pull, which leads officials from a wide range of countries to want to be close to the United States (and to want to be seen to be close to the United States), because there are enormous military, diplomatic, and institutional privileges available to those in the American orbit. Some of the gravitational pull is defensive, as any president or foreign minister or senior official deciding whether to support or not support the United States on an important issue has to make the calculation, Is it likely that I will need U.S. support on some economic, political, intelligence, or diplomatic issue down the road? The opportunities that the United States has to help its friends and punish its opponents are tremendous, and this situation amplifies America's political and diplomatic influence. No other power, established or rising, comes close to this level of influence.

Then there is the appeal of American values. The depth and character of American alliances is not limited to security arrangements; those arrangements are often premised on shared democratic values.[35] When these shared values ring true, America's most enduring alliances have weathered divergent economic interests and even sharp disagreements over matters of war and peace. And this is true even when America's own political system is in a moment of introspection and gridlock.

These values are not just about America's political system; they are also about America's willingness (albeit episodically) to act against tyranny. That does not mean going to war for every democratic movement or opposing every authoritarian regime; but it does mean being willing at times to lend American power to fight against extreme examples of tyranny and oppression and supporting democratic movements that challenge those forces. (Of late, there has been too much of a blending of the concept of defense against tyranny with the wider notion of promoting democracy.) Historically, it has also meant standing for opportunity, in terms of both the opportunity provided to immigrants and to investors in the American market and the willingness to see other economies grow. The fact that the American-backed system has facilitated enormous global economic growth is part of what gives American leadership its appeal—or at the least it is part of why many countries welcome or accept (rather than chafe at) American leadership.

And that matters, because to carry the day in diplomacy or the economy or military affairs is easier with the support of allies and friends. And here, America is spectacularly well endowed. Indeed, perhaps the single most important feature of American strength is that it has more than fifty allies—over a quarter of the world's states—and of those, two dozen are strong, close, effective allies with which the United States shares military technology and intelligence and works diplomatically, while providing them a guarantee of security. These allies are found on every continent and are part of almost every regional or diplomatic grouping. From Australia to Britain, from Israel to the United Arab Emirates to Japan, America's allies give it force multipliers around the globe. British listening stations in Cyprus amplify the United States' massive signals intelligence edge in the Middle East; Diego Garcia, leased from Britain, extends American naval capacity in the Indian Ocean; Japanese bases extend the U.S. naval reach in East Asia; bases for air and sea assets in Qatar and Bahrain facilitate the U.S. security role in the Persian Gulf. The United States also has diplomatic allies in global institutions, extending its options in those bodies.

The scale and strength of America's alliances are unprecedented in the modern era. And American allies are not minor actors, simply seeking protection from a dominant power; America's closest allies include the vast majority of the world's largest economies and military powers, almost three-quarters of the forty wealthiest countries in the world. It is a reality that should give pause to anyone seeking to analogize from past shifts in power alignments to the contemporary moment.

Granted, some of these allies have growing economic links to China, links that may produce, over time, the phenomenon of torn allies. Former Australian foreign minister Bob Carr once argued that Australia's greatest foreign policy challenge was to avoid having to choose between its security relationship with the United States and its economic ties to China. Such tensions may be a growing phenomenon. Still, the political character of many of these alliances makes it likely that if push comes to shove, these countries would side with the United States. Moreover, even in those countries with growing economic ties to China, economic links to the West often remain strong. And for now at least, China is doing its level best to ensure that these countries stay solidly in the U.S. camp (see part 2 of this volume).

Moreover, the fact that these torn allies want to avoid that choice is likely to generate substantial diplomatic energy from these middle powers to help the United States and China manage tensions and avoid confrontation. Middle powers are largely overlooked in international politics, but they can make a substantial contribution by serving as honest brokers between major powers, helping to find pathways to ease tensions and deconflict interests.[36]

The phenomenon of the Arab Spring—the revolutionary and counterrevolutionary dynamics that continues to roil North Africa and the Levant and to threaten the Persian Gulf—is likely to complicate aspects of America's alliance system, namely America's relationship with the Gulf Sunni monarchies. In the first days of the Arab Spring, the U.S. decision to dump its longtime ally Hosni Mubarak caused shock waves among other Arab allies, notably the Gulf monarchies that rely on U.S. support for their rule.[37] Tensions continue, as these monarchies resist any form of democratic change, whereas the United States sees change as necessary to avoid crisis. And the recent—albeit interim—initial nuclear deal between the United States and Iran has further complicated the relationship, because America's Gulf allies perceive Iran as a regional threat, perhaps to their security and certainly to their dominance. The Gulf allies' reaction to the interim deal doubtless exaggerates the extent of U.S.-Iranian rapprochement, but it is a complication for U.S. leadership in the region.

There is another dimension of this that is interesting. Ask this question: Which of America's putative rising rivals profits from an erosion of the

U.S. security role in the Gulf? The answer is none. China and India (as well as Turkey and Korea and Japan and Europe) are heavily dependent on the U.S. role in the Gulf to secure the free flow of oil from that region into global markets. If anything, instability in the Middle East has amplified the emerging powers' awareness of their dependence on this American role.

The Fundamentals

Quite apart from questions of rising rivals, there has been a chorus of arguments that America is decaying from within.[38] Even President Obama has argued that we need to focus on nation building at home.[39] Obviously there are many factors here, some of them dependent on domestic politics.

One factor is U.S. indebtedness—and even more, the cost structure embedded in the country's debt service and entitlement spending. Many argue that these pose a threat to the long-term health of the U.S. economy and thus to the U.S. role in the world.[40] This problem has become a point of convergence between the two otherwise polarized U.S. political parties. There is still a gulf between the Democratic and Republican parties over the questions of when to tackle the debt (immediately? or after extending fiscal stimulus to stimulate employment growth?) and how to tackle the debt (that is, where should spending cuts fall? and who should pay more taxes?). Short of a sharp political turn, though, the country can bring its debt under control one way or another. And the scale of current debt is not unprecedented: it is about a third lower, as a percentage of GDP, than it was in 1945, when the United States exited the last great global crisis. In the years that followed, the country rapidly lowered its debt/GDP ratio, as the American economy grew steadily in the 1950s and 1960s. Now, both household and corporate debt are being paid down faster than in previous crises, easing the overall situation.[41] And the Congressional Budget Office estimates that the United States has a dozen years before the debt will start to rise significantly—likely time enough for even today's divided Washington to find a pathway to long-term balance.[42]

The fact that the debt has been paid off before does not mean that it can be done again, or as easily. Concerns about the debt and the possibility of a default (Greek style) have been subjects of commentary since 2009. But there has also been another important and steady trend: the

United States has eased the pressure of its debt burden by moving from short-term to long-term bonds, a majority of them not due until 2018.[43] This gives the country time to get its fiscal house in order and reduces the odds (already low) of default. Indeed, there is still a substantial body of economic thought that the country should now increase its debt load to further stimulate growth.[44]

Debt default is not the only challenge; so too is financial regulation. In the aftermath of the global financial crisis, the U.S. Treasury proposed a series of reforms that would have restored regulatory health to U.S. markets; but only a portion of these reforms was passed in the still-controversial Dodd-Frank law. There are also growing concerns about weaknesses in the Chinese financial system that could generate a new round of financial instability.[45]

Putting this in context, though, is every bit as important as the debt itself, and this context is very strong fundamentals, even when compared to the country's rising competitors. The United States has a huge middle class, a comparatively young population, political stability, a good balance between production and exports, and huge advantages in its higher education sector. For example, American universities continue to dominate global rankings of the top performers.[46]

Could the United States languish in a "lost decade" of the kind that dulled Japanese growth and engagement since its stock market collapse in 1997?[47] The answer is, perhaps—if political gridlock and political dysfunction are allowed to block the measures necessary to right the economy. But just as feasible is that the country reverts to reasonable growth— despite gridlock—within a modest time span and that it continues to grow in the coming decades. That the U.S. economy began growing, albeit at a sluggish pace, merely a year after the greatest financial crisis in three generations—one it spent nearly $5 trillion containing—speaks to its underlying strengths. And as we see below, its competitors are slowing.

This positive scenario is likely to be bolstered by demographic trends. The demography of most rich countries, as well as of India and China, is graying—that is, their populations are rapidly getting older, which means that their economies will have to bear a growing retirement support burden with a shrinking productive and tax-generating base. The United

States does not face this problem. Over the course of the next forty years, between domestic birth rates and immigration, the U.S. population will swell to over 400 million.[48] In other words, it will add the population of a whole country roughly the same size of France, and a young country at that—adding hugely to its productive and economic power. Estimates of the economic impact merely from legalizing existing (currently illegal) immigrants range as high as 5 percent of GDP over two decades.[49]

Another factor is America's geographical advantage.[50] Whereas China and India have a common, tense border, as do China and Russia, the United States has large oceans separating it from potential threats. Only Mexico, on its southern border, presents a form of insecurity through drug-related violent crime, but that is a modest challenge compared to the border and territorial conflicts confronting emerging powers.[51]

Added to this advantage is America's huge energy and resource endowment. Not only has regulatory and technological innovation unleashed massive natural gas reserves through shale gas, it is unlocking what is known as tight oil at a tremendous rate.[52] In addition, the United States is rapidly becoming a major coal exporter. According to the International Energy Agency, the United States is on a course to overtake Saudi Arabia as the world's largest energy producer,[53] This underlines the fact that the United States has domestic supplies to provide the energy required for advanced growth well into the future. By 2030 the country is likely to be able to meet 100 percent of its import needs from the Americas. No other power but Russia has anything like that degree of energy security, and by contrast China and India have enormous energy import needs, which is a major stumbling block to their economic growth.

Finally, the United States has economic as well as military allies. When China's growth, or that of India and Brazil, is depicted against American growth, the argument about catching up is warranted. But if we portray America's economy as well as that of its close allies against that of the major rising powers, things look rather different (figure 1-3).

Compared to the überdominance of the mid-1990s, this comparison might look like relative decline, but in absolute terms, the United States and its allies still dominate the global economic landscape. And there is no good reason to put India's and Brazil's growth in the same category as China's or Russia's. Let's take the opposite assumption for the

Figure 1-3. *Size of Economy, Various State Groupings, 1990–2012*

GDP in trillions of current U.S.$

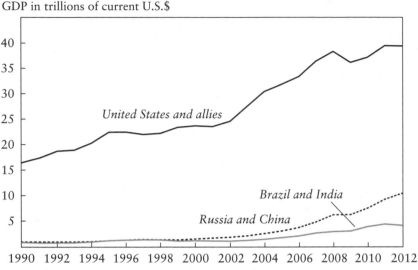

Source: World Bank, World Development Indicators Database.

moment: that on major strategic and global issues, Brazil and India are closer to the United States than to China. At the very least, if we assume the worst about both China and Russia—that they are genuinely aiming at damaging the international system (and I do not believe the evidence supports this claim)—it is a reasonably safe assumption that Brazil and India would not support them in that role; to say nothing of other rising economies like South Korea, Indonesia, and Turkey.

And this reality will deepen as the United States implements two initiatives, the Trans-Pacific Partnership (TPP) and the Transatlantic Trade and Investment Partnership (TTIP), two free trade initiatives to deepen U.S. economic integration with Europe and with its East Asian allies. One Russian analyst describes these U.S. moves as creating a "lord of two rings," noting that, once established, the TTIP and TPP would put the United States in the driver's seat of two overlapping trading blocs that, collectively, account for more than 70 percent of global trade.[54]

It is not a world that should be reassuring to Chinese or Russian strategists. And that is the sting in this tale: the deepening of U.S. trade ties in

Asia risks solidifying Chinese perceptions that the United States is bent on stymying its rise, and that has consequences for a critical relationship still in formation. We return to this theme in chapter 7.

The United States as an Enduring Power

To describe an enduring power is not to describe an absolute one. In the economic realm, the United States now has something approaching peer competitors and a complex playing field. China's economic growth, combined with the costs to the U.S. economy of the global financial crisis, has fueled the debate about American "decline."

There is no question that America has for some years now been transitioning from dominance to a lessening of its economic influence and even, though to a far lesser extent, its political influence. But none of its potential competitors can even begin to rival it in intelligence, diplomatic, military, or alliance capacities; none has anything like the suite of tools of power at America's disposal. That being said, there are some facets of the new landscape of power that play to the strengths of these competitors, and their influence is certainly rising relative to the past two decades. Not all of this erodes U.S. strength in the world; for example, the economic and diplomatic growth of Korea, a close U.S. ally, strengthens the U.S. position, not the other way around. Over the longer run, India's growth likely will help the United States more than hinder it.

In his book *The World America Made*, Robert Kagan points out that, historically, the United States has had a strong peer competitor in the form of the Soviet Union, so the fact of competing powers is nothing new.[55] Indeed, as he argues, if we compare the relative power of the United States now to its relative power in the mid-1970s, when it stood eyeball-to-eyeball with a more genuinely equal Soviet Union, U.S. relative power is greater now.

This is an important insight. Much of the narrative of U.S. decline, in describing the dynamics of contemporary global geopolitics and geoeconomics, uses as its implicit reference point the immediate past fifteen or so years, years of unparalleled dominance. From that peak to the present, the United States has moved onto a more complex global stage. But that brief and exceptional moment in a longer history of U.S. leadership ought not to be the sole reference point. That the economic ground has shifted is more a function of other countries' growth than of U.S. decline. The phrase *relative decline* comes closer to defining the shift; this is the argument that the United States has less relative power than it did, say, a decade ago. That phrase still misses the multiple characteristics of U.S. power and influence, though, and the reality that some of the rising powers are likely to cast their lot with the United States or at least with the system the United States has built. There is certainly a redistribution of power in the international system, but only a portion of it is antagonistic to American power or purposes.

And most of these features of strength are likely to endure. Of course, some of this depends on scenarios. I am very sympathetic to John Maynard Keynes, who famously warned, "The long run is a misleading guide to current affairs. In the long run we are all dead." But because there is so much speculation about this, it warrants a discussion.

In 2012 the U.S. National Intelligence Council (NIC) garnered headlines for a projection that showed the Chinese economy overtaking the U.S. economy, in size, in 2030 (one of several scenarios the report depicted). Critics noted that similar warnings about Japan overtaking the United States in the 1980s had never materialized. Much depends on assumptions about the rate of growth. If China sustains an 8–10 percent rate of growth, and the United States a 2 percent rate of growth, then 2030 is indeed the symbolically important date. It could come sooner: optimistic Chinese estimates put it at 2020. But if, as many economists believe is likely, Chinese growth slows to 5–6 percent (and breaking with historical precedent, suffers no recessions or intermediate crises, unlike any major economy in modern history), and if U.S. growth restores to 3 percent (slightly above where it is in 2013 and slightly below its fifty-year average), then the date at which the two economies cross goes out much longer. Even at 2030, the period between now and then is longer than the period between the fall of the Berlin Wall and the fall of the Twin Towers.

This reaffirms the point that when the role of the U.S. economy is considered, it is important to look at not just U.S. dynamics but also comparative dynamics. In the debate about the U.S. economy, there is an assumption that the next decade or more is set in a comparative context

of a continuation of the astronomical growth of China and India and Brazil—that is, growth rates between 8 percent and 10 percent for better than
a decade. But economists who track the emerging markets closely are skeptical about that. And market analysts are even more so. Ruchir Sharma,
a market analyst and author who has been prescient about short- and
medium-term trends in emerging economies, outright rejects the notion
that we should pay much attention to projections past about half a decade.
But he also takes a position that more and more economists are coming
around to: that several of the emerging economies are set to experience a
significant slowdown in the next few years.[56] Brazil has already slowed to
a mere 1 percent growth, and India to 5 percent. The big debate is whether
China will be able to sustain 8 percent growth rates; Sharma argues that
China will be fortunate to sustain 5 percent growth rates in the short term.
And in the short to medium term, he insists, China faces serious challenges
in the form of inflation and other structural obstacles to growth.

When Sharma compares U.S. fundamentals—market position, currency, energy, reviving manufacturing base, population—to those of the
emerging economies, he concludes that the most likely prospect is a U.S.
economic renaissance. In a similar vein, Ian Bremmer and David Gordon,
among the first analysts to warn of an erosion of global leadership capacity, have come around to the conclusion that the United States is a rising,
not a declining, power.[57]

And because the issue gets so much attention, it is worth reiterating
this point: even if the Chinese economy overtakes the U.S. economy in
size in the next decade or so, it will still be less influential than the United
States even in economic terms, let alone other forms of power. If that happens in 2030, when the NIC predicts, that is more than fifteen years from
the publication of this book: during a similar time span, the United States
entered, fought, and won World War II, forged the Bretton Woods institutions, built the United Nations, and helped rebuild postwar Europe.
China in 2030 will have less innovation, less freedom, less economic influence, more pollution, and fewer allies than the United States. The notion
that China will be a more influential peer competitor over a decade from
now should hardly deter America from believing in its capacity to lead—
a capacity that, I argue, will endure well beyond the point that China
catches up in economic size.

Gideon Rachman, the *Financial Times* correspondent for global issues, has argued that "America will never again experience the global dominance it enjoyed in the 17 years between the Soviet Union's collapse in 1991 and the financial crisis of 2008."[58] True enough; but America is still, and will be for some time to come, in a category of one in the international system. Reports of its decline are, like Mark Twain's death, greatly exaggerated.

CHAPTER TWO

THE TRILLIONAIRES' CLUB

Though America is an enduring power, there is no question that there are other actors on the international stage, some of whom are rising in influence. If any single event illustrates the rise of these new actors, it is the international response to the global financial crisis in 2008.

The financial crash started with ripples in the U.S. housing market in 2006. It rolled through the British, Irish, and Icelandic banking sectors, swelled into the bailout of the American Insurance Group (AIG) and the bankruptcy of Lehman Brothers in September 2008, and then crashed on September 29 with a 777-point drop in the Dow Jones, the biggest one day drop in its history. This was followed by Wall Street's worst week ever, by the end of which the Dow Jones had lost 40 percent of its value from its record high in 2007. The effects of the crash instantly spread outward, causing a global financial crisis, signaled by dramatic drops in the U.K., German, Chinese, and Indian stock exchanges. Even though the long waves of the global financial crisis have not yet exhausted themselves, there is already much to learn about the changing landscape of power.

The response was swift—and global. The participation of key Western allies like Japan and Germany, financial powerhouses like the United Arab Emirates (UAE) and Switzerland, and the rising powers, including China, India, and Brazil, illustrates the new landscape of international economic power. One way to see the response is as evidence of erosion of America's financial power.[1] The G-20—the grouping of the world's twenty largest economies—was called together to orchestrate the global response.[2] China, India, and Brazil were an essential part of this response, as were Mexico, Turkey, and Indonesia. Also in attendance were the International Monetary Fund and the World Bank, international bodies used by the major powers for the management of the global economy.

But if the composition of the group points to a redistribution of economic power, it also points to the reason why members of the group participated in the response: all of these countries were affected—and threatened—by the economic crisis. The scale of American influence in the global economy and in global finance and the extent to which these countries are knitted together in a single global financial system meant that the rest of the world was instantly affected by the American-born crisis. For several years before, many economists had argued that the emerging economies had "decoupled" from the United States, that their growth was no longer connected to the U.S. market. This argument was an important part of the story line of the rise of a separate group of challenging powers. The global impact of the crisis shattered that myth.

So there is quite a different way of looking at what happened other than the erosion of America's financial power. The response was marshaled by American leadership, and at the outset in particular, Washington's role was crucial. No actor other than the United States could have orchestrated the kind of global financial response that followed the collapse of Lehman Brothers or convened the leaders of the world's twenty most powerful countries with merely a few days notice. Core U.S. allies were the first and most critical partners: when Lehman Brothers collapsed in September 2008, President Bush's economic advisers orchestrated a collective international action starting with Japan, Germany, Switzerland, and the UAE.

The emerging powers also, by and large, went along with U.S. leadership and made important contributions to sustain, rather than upend, the existing system. One instance is a decision made by Brazilian president Lula da Silva in September 2008. Brazil had been chairing the annual negotiations among the finance ministers of the G-20, a role that would have put Brazil in the position of leading the international response to the financial crisis at a time of presidential transition in the United States. Modesty is in short supply in international politics, nor is it normally associated with the bombastic former Brazilian president; but at this critical juncture, Lula recognized that Brazil did not have the tools to lead the international response. Meeting in a basement room at the United Nations in New York just days after Lehman Brothers collapsed, Lula suggested to the prime minister of Great Britain, Gordon Brown, that Brown, who had been scheduled to take over later that year, take the reins early. London not only had the manpower and financial resources to orchestrate the global response but also had the behind-the-scenes relationships in Washington that allowed it to help the United States play its own role—particularly while the newly elected president, Barack Obama, was assembling his cabinet and financial team.

Prime Minister Brown led the response to the crisis heading into the G-20 summit in London in April 2009, where crucial steps to bolster the global economy were taken.[3] The International Monetary Fund was instructed to pump money into key economics to shore up their financial positions.[4] During that same period, President Obama made a decision to launch a massive economic stimulus package in the United States, which anchored the global response. He then led negotiations heading into a third summit, in Pittsburgh, where two things were done: a new round of stimulus measures was agreed upon to shore up the response to the crisis, and work began on new tools to help prevent a recurrence of a crisis of this magnitude.[5]

In short, America played a decisive leadership role, America's key Western allies bolstered its leadership, the rising economic powers played constructive roles, international organizations performed as they were designed, and tools for cooperation were adapted to suit the critical needs of the moment. The result was a series of bold financial and economic moves. By the time the G-20 leaders met in Pittsburgh, a global depression had been averted. It was one of the most important episodes of American and collective leadership since the end of World War II.

The episode lends credibility to an important argument about what lies ahead: that the emerging powers are seeking to shape but not to break the international economic order. The argument is that because the U.S.-led economic order is open to participation by others, they will not seek to overturn that order but to profit within it.[6] The reaction of the rising powers to the financial crisis (that is, not to use the moment to shatter U.S. leadership but to actively bolster it) is important evidence in support of this argument. Governments from Beijing to Delhi to Abu Dhabi to Brasilia took an active and responsible part in the series of coordinated actions, led by Washington, that constitute the response to the global financial crisis.

The argument for the decline of the American-led order and the emergence of a post-Western world is strongest if there are significant powers that do not see themselves as part of the West or do not seek to align themselves with the order led by the West.[7] The argument would even be strong if there were Western powers in decline, or if the West were not unified, or if the rising powers were unified. There is evidence against each of these propositions.

The Trillionaires' Club

That the landscape of power is changing is by now widely recognized, through both concern about China's rising military clout and recognition of the role of the G-20 countries in the global economy. Much of the attention goes to the original BRICs—Brazil, Russia, India, and China. But the focus on these countries has obscured the ascendance of other countries.

One way of thinking about the countries that matter most in international economics is the idea of a trillionaires' club, that is, countries with a GDP of a trillion dollars. The evolution of this club is revealing. In the early 1980s only two countries were members: the United States and the Soviet Union.[8] By the end of the 1980s, five additional members of the G-7 (Japan, Germany, the United Kingdom, France, and Italy) were in the club, and the troubled Soviet Union had dropped out. China joined in the late 1990s, to surprisingly little fanfare, a reminder of the fact that China's economic growth has been a reality for some time. Then in 2004 Canada and Spain met the requirement. At this stage, the club largely resembled the G-7 (plus China). Then in 2006–08 the club's mix shifted distinctly. Russia rejoined in 2007, buoyed by global oil and gas prices. Four new members joined: Brazil, Mexico, India, and South Korea. Australia joined in 2008. The rankings within the club are shifting, too: India is now in the top ten; Brazil has overtaken Britain for the number-six slot; and in 2010 China overtook Japan to become the world's second-largest economy. And just outside of the club are three countries relevant to global dynamics: Indonesia, the Netherlands, and Turkey, each with an economy above $750 billion.[9] (At least, the Netherlands was close until the eurozone crisis slowed growth across the continent.)

Together, the fifteen members of the trillion-dollar club (plus the three almost-rans) account for an astonishing 75 percent of the world's economy and roughly 90 percent of its population.[10] China, India, Brazil, Indonesia, and Turkey alone have a combined population of over 3 billion people. For decades, these countries languished at a low level of economic development, the vast majority of their populations poor. Two decades of intensive globalization have transformed this picture. These countries now have a combined middle class of almost a billion people, growing rapidly. The next twenty economies combined make up a mere 13 percent of the world's economy (with just under a billion people), with the remaining 12 percent of the global economy split among more than 150 countries, with a population of more than 2.3 billion people.

Membership in the trillionaires' club corresponds pretty closely to the membership of the G-20. For archaic reasons, Argentina (twenty-seventh-largest economy in the world) has a seat in the G-20 that its economic size does not warrant.[11] South Africa (twenty-ninth) is in the G-20 for political reasons; South Africa is, for now, the largest economy on the African continent (with Nigeria hot on its heels). Spain, the Netherlands, and Switzerland have the awkward distinction of being the only top twenty economies in the world not to have a seat in the G-20, a source of deep angst in Madrid and The Hague when the G-20 was established (and a reason they got to attend under the EU umbrella at the pivotal November 2008 G-20 summit).

Of course, a trillion dollars is not what it used to be, and there is a substantial difference between the countries at the top rung and those at the bottom. Still, any country with an economy at or approaching the trillion-dollar mark wields a degree of influence in the international system, and it is as good a list as any to reference the top powers. And whether we use the trillionaires' club or the G-20 as a reference, these two facts remain. First, and widely acknowledged, there are several more countries in the top tier of world power now than there were merely a decade ago. Second, and widely ignored, the majority of them are U.S. allies or friendly to the United States.[12] Depictions of a post-Western world neglect this essential fact.

The Big Three

Of course, China, India, and Brazil matter a lot. The acronym BRIC came to be shorthand for the concept of the emerging economies and, more recently, the broader phenomenon of emerging powers.[13] Lumping in Russia, though, is odd in economic terms, since Brazil, India, and China have a radically different relationship to the global economy than does Russia; and it is odd in geopolitical terms, too, since Russia had long been a player in geopolitics when the term was coined, and, if anything, its power is waning. So for now I dispense with the BRIC notion and look at Brazil, India, and China—the big three non-Western powers on the rise.

China is obviously furthest along of the three. It has substantial economic clout within its region (and unlike the other emerging economies, beyond it). It has a large, sophisticated, and growing military and is a force to be reckoned with in its neighborhood. Its phenomenal economic success has, for developing countries, lent credence to its model of mixed state-market capitalism. It also has human capacity to spare, evidenced in the scale of its diplomatic operations, intelligence apparatus, and burgeoning universities. And for now, it profits from the shadow of the future, as other countries anticipate its further rise. From Asia to Africa, business people and government officials talk about China's rise and how it shapes their calculations.

But that may begin to change. Constraining China are formidable internal and external difficulties.[14] It has limited cultural affinity with countries beyond its immediate neighborhood, and its model of semiauthoritarian politics does not have widespread appeal. The appeal of its mixed state-market model has been contingent on rapid economic growth, but that growth is slowing. Its military history within its own neighborhood also means that it confronts powers that are suspicious of China or even hostile toward it. These include India, Japan, South Korea, and Australia.[15] Moreover, its economic rise is dependent on its integration into an economic system still managed and underpinned first and foremost by the United States. Its continuing growth can only be fueled by energy supplies from regions secured by the United States and that are imported via transshipment lanes protected by the U.S. Navy. And for all of its regional strength, China has minimal capacity to project power beyond its neighborhood. Domestically, it faces substantial tensions between an increasingly open market and its still largely closed politics, all while it confronts regional poverty, intense pollution, and political dissent. Not for nothing has China been referred to as a fragile superpower.[16]

Brazil occupies a very different space from China, with per capita GDP three times bigger and a far smaller population. Brazil wields substantial economic clout in Latin America and, in some instances, has turned that into diplomatic leverage. Like China, it has generated some ill feeling among its neighbors, which resent being bullied by Brazil, just as, in an earlier era, they resented being bullied by the United States. A Brazilian diplomat, at a Princeton conference in 2011, said that Brazil is rapidly discovering that the only thing its neighbors like less than being bullied by "the big father" of the United States is being told what to do by the "big brother" of Brazil.[17] Brazil also has negligible military capacity, even in regional terms.

On the positive side, Brazil's diplomatic service is among the world's most professional, and it is expanding rapidly. Perhaps Brazil's greatest strength internationally, however, is the appeal of its model: it has grown as rapidly as China but in concert with genuine democratic progress. Although it has grown through integration with global markets, it has a good balance of domestic production. All of this adds up to its ability to exert economic influence and to claim a stake in global diplomacy. Still, it is well short of being a power with global reach. And it still has to grapple with domestic poverty as well as high levels of corruption, inequality, and domestic discontent. Widespread middle-class and working-class protests against the government in 2013 revealed lingering social tensions and new dissatisfactions with the highly unequal nature of Brazil's economic growth.

India lies behind China and Brazil in its economic development and between them in its military power. It has a huge population (which will soon exceed China's), a rapidly expanding middle class, reputational appeal as a multiethnic and secular democracy, and a wealthy and influential expatriate émigré community, especially in the United States. As with China and Brazil, India's integration into global markets has been key to its growth.

India faces five major challenges.[18] First, everywhere India would seek to extend its influence, even on its immediate northern border, it finds China working just as hard to counter it by the same means. Myanmar, Nepal, and Bangladesh may all be zones of traditional Indian engagement, but in each of them China rivals India for diplomatic and economic influence. Second, that a large swath of India's territory is contested by Maoist or other rebel groups and not under the full control of its central government does not actually disrupt its economic growth, but it certainly distracts its government and military. India also has to deal with the realities of a populous, dangerous, and badly fractured Pakistan on its western flank. In Afghanistan, India is deepening its economic activity and its political influence, but in every step it takes, it competes with Pakistan.

Third, beyond its own neighborhood, India's foreign policy has long been built around its leadership of the Non-Aligned Movement, a movement for which the raison d'être has come and gone, even if it still operates in vestigial fashion.[19]

Fourth, its economic model is less appealing than Brazil's or China's, as it remains riven by corruption and marred by government inefficiency and a dysfunctional energy sector.[20] Corruption is present in China and Brazil as well, of course, but not to the same degree as in India, with its Byzantine system of bureaucratic overregulation. India's tourism industry's media campaign uses the term "Incredible India," but India's chamber of commerce has called for a campaign to build a "credible India" through anticorruption measures and similar reforms. As of 2013, the lack of such reforms was causing India's growth to slow substantially.[21]

Fifth, India has a very shallow pool of elites on which to draw for the intellectual, political, and diplomatic functions of global power status. Just as Brazil has done, India has extended its diplomatic reach and certainly its influence in global policy; but it has neither the economic model nor the military and intelligence capacity to project influence beyond its region. Shyam Saran, a diplomat from a storied family who rose to the rank of foreign secretary, calls India a "premature power."[22]

All of these countries—Brazil, India, and China—still have enormous populations of the desperately poor. Even after having risen quickly for a decade, it matters that these countries are still, in per capita terms, far, far poorer than their Western peers. Indeed, the per capita GDP gap between the United States and China has actually grown in the past decade, even as the gap between China's total GDP and America's has shrunk.[23] A recurrent theme in these countries' own narrative about their contemporary strategy is the need to focus on domestic consolidation.[24]

None of these rising powers have so far been able to consolidate the full tool kit of global power. But that is not to say that their influence isn't growing; it is. For example, the major emerging economies are now, as a group, almost as large a source of foreign direct investment as the Western economies.[25]

This trend may grow, and many have pointed to it as a likely source of future Chinese political influence. But that oversimplifies. The rise of the emerging powers as sources of investment does not mean that the United States or major Western economies have no remaining standing in the economic or political realm. In every region, the United States or close Western allies remain the number-two or number-three source of investment even where China or India or Brazil has taken the number-one position. Taken together, the United States and its core allies are often still the largest source of investment.

A similar story emerges if we look at political and military weight within the regions. The emerging powers' influence in their own backyards is greater than global rankings suggest. This enables them to complicate U.S. initiatives on major geopolitical questions. U.S. military capacity dwarfs India's, but India's political relationships in Iran are a factor that America must grapple with (or learn to use), as it must with Brazil's in Venezuela and Bolivia and China's in North Korea. And as shown in the next part of this book, China's military expansion and attempts at energy acquisition in Asia constitute a significant challenge to American policy.

Each of these three rising powers is also investing in regional organizations, in a bid to institutionalize its increasing influence. China has invested both in established forums like the Association of South East Asian Nations (ASEAN) and in less known and more restricted groups like the Shanghai Cooperation Organization (SCO). Brazil led the establishment of a new regional mechanism, the Union of South American Nations (UNOSUR), in which it has a leading diplomatic role. India has fewer options but has put new diplomatic energy into the traditional

South Asian Association for Regional Cooperation (SAARC). The United States does not belong to any of these organizations.[26]

This new influence is not uncomplicated, though. One of the most interesting dynamics in contemporary international politics is that some actors, traditionally resistant to the U.S. presence in their region, now see it as balancing that of the regional power. In South East Asia, Vietnam has called for sustained U.S. engagement in the South China Sea to combat Chinese assertiveness there.[27] When Vietnam of all countries is calling for U.S. political and military engagement in its region, something is afoot. India's neighbors look at its rise with similar trepidation.

Finally, the big three have been profiting from the phenomenon of the shadow of the future. States devise their strategies by assessing not only the present but also their perceptions of the future influence of the great powers. Accurate or not, the dominant international perception is of an America past its prime and of emerging powers whose time is coming. The scramble is on to get into their good books and investment strategies. This is not only true of smaller states that are recipients of aid or FDI but also of the larger economies, including Germany, the United Kingdom, and Canada. It is illustrative that when U.K. prime minister David Cameron was elected to power in 2010, his first major foreign trip (after the traditional obeisance to Washington) was to Delhi. Chancellor Angela Merkel has made no effort to mask Germany's intent to gain closer commercial ties with China. Prime Minister Stephen Harper, of Canada, still America's largest trading partner, has dropped his original China skepticism for an all-out effort to win energy and trade contracts in Beijing.[28]

But this is slowly beginning to change. Washington's pivot to Asia and the launch of free trade projects in Asia and Europe are signaling to the world that the United States has no intention of fading away. And as shown in chapter 5, states have a growing awareness of America's renewed energy endowment. An illustrative moment: Anne-Marie Slaughter, a former head of policy planning at the U.S. Department of State, together with Brazil's foreign minister, Antonio Patriota, attended a 2013 Munich Security Conference. She watched as Patriota listened in on a discussion about America's energy renaissance and renewed alliances. Patriota, she says, reflected that the emerging powers have to remember that "the established powers are not sinking powers."[29]

The Rest of the Top Ten

Of course, some of the established powers *are* sinking, but only temporarily. And it is not just Brazil, India, and China that are rising. There are myriad changes in the distribution of power, and all of them matter—such as the rest of the top ten. Beyond the United States and the big three rising powers, the ranks of the top-ten economies of the world are filled out by Japan, Germany, France, the United Kingdom, Italy, and Russia. Of these six, five are core U.S. allies. Now several of those allies are in some form of short- or medium-term difficulty. But so too is Russia.

First in the allies-in-trouble category is Japan, only now gradually escaping from its fifteen-year-long "lost decade." Japan's internal politics are still dysfunctional, one indication of which is that in 2012 the country appointed its seventh prime minister in as many years. Japan has consistently grown more slowly than the United States and Europe since the mid-1990s.[30]

Still, even slumping powers matter. When the global financial crisis broke, the first phone call by the secretary of the U.S. Treasury was to Tokyo, and Japan's $250 billion stimulus package was essential to the global response. And China's increasingly assertive behavior in Asia has awakened Japan from its slumber. In late 2012 Shinzo Abe was returned to the position of Japanese prime minister five years after an unsuccessful first stint on the basis of two pledges: to (finally) reinvigorate the Japanese economy and to stand up to Chinese aggression over islands in the East China Sea. Further, Japan has a sizable military and navy; while Japan's constitution confines it to self-defense, defending Japanese territorial, maritime, and energy claims in the sea between China and Japan fits that definition.

When it comes to the four big European powers (France, Germany, Italy, and the United Kingdom), there are both bad news and good. Italy and France are mired in debt and fiscal crisis, while the United Kingdom is, in 2013, in its third bout of a post-financial-crisis recession. France and Italy look set for a rougher ride and a longer recovery. Down is not out, though, and over the medium term it is likely that both France and Italy will remain among the top-ten players in global markets—and with the diplomatic and military capabilities to match. Britain's slump looks shallower than France's and Italy's, and Britain is not burdened by the euro, though of course its economy is closely tied to Europe's. And even amid a short-term slump, the United Kingdom retains one of the most effective and tested militaries in the world, a first-rate diplomatic service, a large intelligence service, the soft power that accrues from its global television, newspaper, and magazine presence, and a wide diplomatic network forged through university, cultural, and colonial ties.

Of the four European powers, Germany looks most like a rising power. Its economy has grown even in the immediate aftermath of the financial crisis, and its centrality to European and global financial markets has been demonstrated by its role in the eurozone crisis. It has a large army, though, until recently, not a very effective one, with the bulk of its troops fixed in position to defend against a Soviet tank attack rather than deal with contemporary threats. However, this has begun to change, as Berlin modernizes its force posture. It still faces constitutional constraints on deploying its troops but has begun to find ways to contribute constructively to international operations like Afghanistan (though it chose to stay outside of NATO's operation in Libya, to the chagrin of its allies). Most important, its economy is the engine of Europe and a major force in the global economy. Frankfurt is a critical center for global finance and banking; in Europe, it is second only to London.

The membership of these four countries in the European Union is both a blessing and a curse.[31] Collectively, the twenty-eight states that form the EU are the world's largest economic group, with a GDP larger than that of the United States. Even without the big four, the EU constitutes the world's third-largest economic unit, just shy of China and just larger than Japan. By comparison to any other region, the EU constitutes an economic and cultural bloc unlike anything else on the globe. It enjoys enormous cultural appeal and enviable standards of living. Its national and unionwide aid budgets are among the most generous in the world—and allow it both to export its model and to influence developing countries and global policy debates.

On the other hand, Europe's military capabilities, including its contribution to NATO, are diminishing.[32] During the cold war, Europeans accounted for roughly half of NATO defense spending. By 2001 they spent less than 40 percent. They now spend less than 25 percent. European diplomacy has become entangled in incessant internal coordination and processes, much of which forces European policy to lowest-common-denominator positions and hobbles it as a diplomatic force in global negotiations. On major policy questions, moreover, like the Middle East, Russia, and Afghanistan, Europe continues to operate as America's lesser cousin and to rely on American firepower, a source of irritation in the transatlantic relationship. Still, compared to India, Brazil, and China, Europe is a substantial power in international politics. It should not be conceived as an alternative pole of power, as it continues to define its interest as closely tied to that of the United States.

Of course, by 2010 the EU was mired in a major economic crisis. This is a genuine crisis, and it is likely to deal a significant blow to European cohesion and capacity in the short, and perhaps the medium, term. There is a worst-case scenario here, in which the EU actually unravels. If this manifests, then the geopolitical and geoeconomic strength of the West and of the Western-led order will have to be recalculated. But it is only a worst-case scenario, not the likely scenario. There is also a scenario of rapid exit from the crisis, though that seems equally unlikely.[33] The most likely scenario is a long, slow stumbling, with the core of the EU surviving but with its energy sapped. This has significant ramifications. I return to this question at the end of the book, but it is worth noting three points here.

First, even at the peak of the crisis, the EU is still a major player economically. Second, the decision of the Obama administration in 2013 to launch negotiations for a transatlantic partnership (a U.S.-European free trade area) could give the EU countries new economic energy as they emerge from the crisis and would signal that the U.S. economic team has confidence that they will. Third, even at the peak of the crisis, and while substantial military assets were deployed in Afghanistan, the United Kingdom and France both put significant military assets into the Libya campaign; France mounted a unilateral mission (with UN encouragement) to counter an al Qaeda affiliate in Mali; and both the United Kingdom and France have put substantial air assets in bases in the Gulf to bolster the U.S. military presence there, preparing for the threat of an acute crisis with Iran. The European Union is the world's top economic grouping, and even bowed it is a major factor.

But if the West's tally in the global scorecard seems threatened because of Europe's slump, it is more than evened out by the deep troubles facing

Russia. It may sound odd to argue that Russia is in a slump, or in decline, given that Russia is treated as part of the group of rising powers. It depends on where you start looking. If we start from the low point, in 1999, Russia's economy has grown stratospherically since then: in 2011 it was nine times larger than it was a dozen years earlier, reaching $1.8 trillion. But go back a decade farther and things look different. Just before its collapse, the Soviet Union had an economy valued at somewhere between $775 billion and $1.15 trillion, roughly $2.9 trillion in 2010 dollars. The collapse of the Soviet Union and economic crisis in the late 1990s led to a total devastation of the Russian economy. So seen in perspective, Russia's rise of the past several years is less remarkable; by 2010 it had grown back to roughly two-thirds the size of the Soviet economy in 1989. At present, Russian GDP is one-quarter that of China and the same size as Canada's, despite it having four times Canada's population (even though Russia lost roughly half of its population when it shed the former Soviet states).[34]

Of course, Russia retains from Soviet days some of the trappings of global power, including a huge nuclear arsenal and a veto-wielding seat on the UN Security Council. But it has few allies left. By 2011 its only military base outside of the former Soviet Union was in Syria, hardly a solid basis for international power projection. Nor does Russia's trajectory since the early 1990s present much evidence that Russia will be able to adequately cope with globalization's challenges. The Russian political system remains sclerotic and generally unresponsive to societal demands, and while Russia's conventional military capabilities will likely remain strong, its cohesion and discipline are hard-hit by political and social dysfunction. It remains heavily dependent on energy exports and shows few signs of adapting to a rapidly changing global energy market.[35] A factor in international security dynamics it is. The pole of an alternative bloc, or a rising rival to American influence, it most certainly is not. The Eurasia Group, a political risk assessment firm, rates Russia as a "submerging power."[36]

The Rest of the Trillionaires

The shape of the global landscape is set not only by the top ten powers. The history of geopolitics might be written from the perspective of great powers, but for each of those powers there are several second-tier powers that matter to their economies and strategies. For the United States, Canada is still its largest trading partner, Australia still a critical security partner, and so on. For China, Indonesia and South Korea matter both economically and in the political and security dynamics of Asia. Turkey is a pivotal power in the Middle East.[37]

The rest of the trillionaires' club (or the rest of the top twenty, either way) encompasses several of these consequential middle powers, and eight of the ten are close U.S. allies or partners. Canada, Australia, Spain, the Netherlands, Korea, Turkey, and Saudi Arabia are U.S. allies; the others, Switzerland, Mexico, and Indonesia, although not U.S. allies, are not remotely hostile to the United States. Not all of these countries are serious military actors, but then, that is not the only criterion for global influence. As Secretary of State Hillary Clinton acknowledged, "For the first time in modern history, nations are becoming major global powers without also becoming global military powers."[38]

That being said, the military contribution of these countries is far from negligible. When the United States looks at the fighting coalition in Afghanistan, of its allies that rank among the top-ten world powers, only the United Kingdom can credibly be said to have carried its weight. Much of the rest of the load was carried by countries in the second economic rung, including Canada, Australia, and the Netherlands.

Meanwhile, Turkey has been a close ally in the Middle East, as has Saudi Arabia in the Gulf. That is not to say that these two relationships are not complicated for the United States or that neither has relations with the other powers. Turkey in particular has become a very complicated regional player, as its relationship with Israel deteriorated dramatically in the first phase of the Arab Spring.[39] But Turkey remains a NATO ally of the United States and has played important roles (often in close coordination with the United States) in Libya, Syria, and Iran. It is also taking on other roles, such as helping to stabilize Somalia, alongside American Special Forces.[40]

Saudi Arabia is another complicated ally. The U.S. decision to walk away from long-time ally Hosni Mubarak in the early days of the Arab Spring badly strained relations, already complicated by growing U.S. awareness that wealthy Saudi families and charities fund terrorist movements or affiliated charities. As Saudi Arabia sells more and more energy to China, the ties between them deepen, and an American trend toward energy independence might eventually shift Saudi Arabia's place on the global chessboard. Saudi Arabia also faces serious internal challenges, both political and economic. Its rising middle class consumes a great deal of electric power, and within a decade (unless solar or renewable technologies make a substantial leap), Saudi Arabia will be using large amounts of its own oil to generate electricity. The issue of Iran may deepen divisions between the United States and Saudi Arabia, but the Saudis face a dilemma because there is no alternative to the U.S. for power projection in the Gulf—the idea that China could step up to fill the vacuum is a delusion. For now, and for the medium term, the U.S. is the only state capable of guaranteeing its security. (And the Saudis should know this; until now, they've been very impatient about China's unwillingness to press Iran about its nuclear program.)[41]

Mexico is not a defense ally of the United States, but it is a free trade partner and a growing actor on the international stage. Although there is a long history of U.S.-Mexico tensions, there are also close economic ties; and there is nothing in Mexico's economic rise that challenges U.S. leadership. Some argue that internal instability in Mexico could become a security threat to the United States, if Mexico becomes a failing state; but that is a worst-case scenario. A more likely scenario is that Mexico develops in a pattern similar to that of India, where national growth and a stable center are combined with violence in peripheral regions.[42]

Indonesia's arrival on the global stage has been both less dramatic and less commented on than others, but its transformation is remarkable. Indonesia was a one-party state that underwent a major financial crisis in 1997 (out of which, in fact, the G-20 was born, as a finance ministers' mechanism) and a major security crisis in 1999, with the separation of East Timor. Since then it has become a democracy, has settled major internal conflicts, has survived the Christmas 2004 Indian Ocean tsunami, and has seen its economy more than quadruple in size. With a population of 242 million, it is the largest Muslim country in the world and an increasingly influential actor in global politics. It hosts one of the region's key organizations, the ASEAN, and has been the diplomatic host for important global negotiations on climate change. When UN secretary-general Ban Ki-moon was looking for the leader of an emerging power to cochair an important UN process on the future of development, he turned to Indonesia's ambitious (and term-limited) President Yudhoyono. None of this makes Indonesia a powerhouse in a continent chock full of them, but it does mark Indonesia as a rising player both in Asia and increasingly on the global stage.

As is the Republic of Korea, which is given perhaps the least attention among the rising players. Korea's strong economic performance since the financial crisis led some analysts to argue that it should be added to the BRIC group, as South Africa has, but as a close U.S. security ally it plays a very different role. It has become a powerhouse of high-end manufacturing and is on course to become richer than Japan in per capita terms (at purchasing power parity) within the next five years.[43] Faced with a rising China, Korea has responded by strengthening its alliance with the United States and embarking upon controversial defense cooperation with its old enemy, Japan (though both parties continue to give in to the temptation of nationalist ploys). Korea has also taken an active role in upholding the international order: hosting the G-20 summit in 2010; pushing that group, against some resistance, to take up the topic of international development, at a crucial moment; hosting a nuclear security summit in March 2012; and successfully placing its candidate in the position of secretary-general of the UN.[44]

None of these actors individually reshapes the balance of power in the international system. But collectively, they are a factor. Most of them add economic and military assets to the U.S. sphere of power, but just as important, they are all countries that matter, economically and diplomatically, in international negotiations and strategy.

This is one of the undertold stories of international politics. Analysis focuses, understandably, on the biggest powers. But there is no great power whose economic, security, and political situation is not shaped, sometimes heavily, by its relationships with influential middle powers. These countries matter as trading partners, as neighbors, as security partners, and in global negotiations. Middle powers do not have the tools, either economic or military, to shape an unsettled world, so they rely on international stability and pressure the great powers to contribute to that stability.

No account of the new landscape of power would be complete without touching briefly on four niche powers, powers that combine small size with outsize finances. The established niche powers, Norway and Switzerland, have a reputation for neutrality (in Norway's case, despite being a NATO ally). These two countries play important roles in peace negotiations and global diplomacy. The other two niche players, Qatar and Singapore, are newer in this role. Qatar has weighed in heavily into Middle East crisis diplomacy, and Singapore has played an important role in pressing the G-20 to engage in a wider process of consultation and deliberation on global financial regulations. These four countries, in their activist diplomacy, do not always precisely align with U.S. positions; but it is notable that three of the four are U.S. allies.

Beyond the State

Of course, global power also is affected by private actors and the civic sphere. It is a complex topic, one I cannot do justice to in this book. But a few important points are worth covering here.

It is clear that a number of private actors play a substantive role in global economics. We might call them the billionaires' club. The world has roughly 1,400 billionaires, with a combined worth of $5.4 trillion, placing them, as a group, in the trillionaires' club.[45] But of course these are individual actors, not a group, and come from all over the globe. When Mexican billionaire Carlos Slim topped the list of the world's richest individuals, it was widely cited as an indicator of the reach of the emerging markets.[46] But the full list tells a very different story. The United States has vastly more billionaires than any other country, with 446 (30 percent of the total). China does claim the number-two spot, with 121 billionaires, but the net worth of those billionaires is less than a quarter that of the American set.

Of course, as other economies grow, they may come to compete with the United States in privately held wealth. More particularly, the argument is that as Chinese trade and investment grow, so will its political influence. But this simple equation ignores the fact that when Chinese trade and investment grow, Western trade and investment are not at a standstill. If trade and investment generate political ties, then what they are generating are two-directional ties. Think of this from the perspective of an economic elite in a given country. Say that 30 percent of the trade ties of this elite are with China and 25 percent are with the United States. This does not necessarily suggest elite pressure on that country's politics to side with China over the United States. Rather, it suggests that these countries will pressure the United States and China to maintain stable bilateral relations so that they are not forced into an impossible choice between them.

The link between private trade and political influence makes private trade an important stabilizing influence in great power relations. So it is also important to remember that America's private sector is the largest in the world: as mentioned earlier, 46 percent of the world's top transnational corporations are owned by Americans. And this produces an important political fact: in every major market, the global investor class profits when the U.S. economy is strong.

That the private sector is, broadly, a force in support of open global economic ties is important, but it is not the whole story. In some trade sectors there is a downside, in that the private sector is opposed to the kinds of regulation that can stabilize a given sector. In the United States, regulation of the financial services industry has been resisted by the private sector. Similarly, private sector actors were influential in watering down efforts to forge a stronger regime for dealing with biological weapons and materials, concerned that regulations aimed at malfeasance and military concerns would end up restricting legitimate economic activity. Thus we need to look beyond the notion that the private sector, narrowly defined, is necessarily a force for stability.

And there are limits to the influence that private trade and investment brings. What is the leverage that China or the United States can wield in a country where there are strong trade ties? Withdrawal of the relationship? Perhaps, but at costs on both ends. And in a globalized economy, there are very few places where a country like China is going to be able to withdraw a trading commodity that cannot be replaced elsewhere. A striking example of this is with rare earth minerals, like flourcerite and synchysite, that play vital roles in high-tech and defense production. China had a dominant supply of these, and when China and Japan came into a confrontation in the East China Sea (see chapter 7), China suspended exports of these minerals to Japan. Within three years, however, Japan was able to replace most of these rare earth imports from domestic sources and from U.S., Canadian, and Australian suppliers. Other countries, concerned about supply security, followed suit. So there are limits to the influence of punitive measures.

Finally, in the world of global action, we should note a growing role for cities. In most countries whose economies are growing, this growth has been combined with rapid urbanization.[47] U.S. diplomacy has already begun to recognize the importance of urbanization in the effort by the Bush and Obama administrations to move U.S. diplomats (political and economic) out of capital cities and into major population and economic hubs.

Urbanization may have important implications for a range of global issues, notably energy and climate change. The role that urban centers play in carbon production and emissions is striking. One statistic tells much: New York City emits as much carbon as the whole of sub-Saharan Africa, excepting South Africa.[48] When it comes to forging more effective patterns of cooperation or governance of global problems, the role of cities may thus loom large. For example, in tackling climate change, a new organization called the C40 Cities Climate Leadership Group (composed of the executives of forty large cities committed to green growth) may become an unimportant global actor.[49]

Conclusion

The landscape of global economic power is complex. The United States does not confront a pliant international order: it confronts allies grappling with their own economic difficulties; a declining but still influential Russia determined to maintain its place in international security politics; rising powers striving for autonomy; and a huge array of private sector actors competitive for profits and influence. But the West has hardly been eclipsed, and fully two-thirds of the top twenty economies are U.S. allies. And even among the nonallies, there are more shared interests with the West, and more divisions among the rest, than commonly supposed.

CHAPTER THREE

NO MORTAR
IN THE BRICS

If global power is dominated by the trillionaires' club, then two questions follow: What do the members of that club want from the international order (and from the United States)? And how unified are the various groupings within it—specifically, the BRICs and the West?

The discussion starts with the rising non-Western powers.[1]

The World They Want: The Psychology of Rise

The narrative of the post-Western world does not just refer to the who of rising powers; it refers also to what they want. A post-Western world is usually described as an alternative to the current Western-led order, and one that displaces the West's leading role. While several of the rising powers are aligned with the United States, or lean toward alignment, most of them resent the Western domination of the international system and the major international institutions. They thus share an agenda in challenging that domination. This resentment is partially about core economic and security interests, and it is partially about the psychology of rise.

Consider this. In the early 1800s, India and China comprised just shy of 50 percent of the world's GDP, Europe just under a quarter, and the newly independent United States only 1.8 percent.[2] This scale is often cited when looking to the economic potential of China and India, which, along with Turkey, have begun to refer to themselves as re-emerging powers.[3]

These powers' economic past, however, is more or less irrelevant to their economic future.[4] But it is relevant to the strategic psychology of the rising non-Western powers. As major powers through the mid-1800s, they were brought low by their encounters with the West. The decaying Mughal dynasty in India was subjugated to and then dismantled by British imperial might; China's Ming dynasty, also decaying, was bent and eventually broken by the British, with French and a bit of American help; and the Ottoman Empire, too, was picked apart.[5] As the interactions between the new cast of powers unfold, it is important to remember that this is not the first go-round.

For China, the first free trade treaty with the West, the Treaty of Nanking, was ratified in 1843, at the end of one in a long series of opium wars. The British navy had waged war against Chinese ports in order to open them to trade, particularly in opium and Indian tea. The Chinese refer to the Treaty of Nanking as the first of a series of "unequal" treaties, as it placed no requirements on the British. The treaty's signing was the start of what contemporary Chinese history records as a "century of humiliation."[6] So too with India, both during the imperial age and the postwar era: its experience with free trade backed by Western power was one of subjugation, humiliation, and unequal treatment.

The psychological residue of this resentment lingers in the foreign policies of the rising powers. Resentment is hardly, of course, the only theme: these countries are struggling to form a coherent identity as major powers in a system they once resisted but in which they now have vested interests. But the residue of humiliation is real, even for those rising powers that see their interests aligning more and more with the United States. The intervening period of decline is often viewed as "a historical mistake that should be corrected."[7]

Think of how the world must have felt to young Chinese or Indian or Brazilian elites just a few years ago. Think of a young Chinese finance official being sent to Washington to encounter the reality that Canada, with 35 million people, had an International Monetary Fund (IMF) board seat with as much influence as China's. Or a young Brazilian diplomat sent to the UN to discover that a country like Norway, with a population of 4.7 million, is able to exert more influence in that body than Brazil, with nearly 200 million. Or an Indian strategist who watches Italy participate in the decisionmaking of the G-7 on an issue like counterterrorism—an issue in which India has a vastly bigger stake than Italy.

Small wonder, then, that a common thread in the policies and practices of the reemerging powers is that they seek to dispel this sense of subjugation. They seek to be, first and foremost, autonomous. They are not looking to be part of someone else's alliance or to be led by another power but, rather, to find their own space and their own voice on the international stage. As they find their power and voice, though, they discover the costs and consequences of that new role. As Sanjaya Baru, a former Indian "sherpa" to the G-20, puts it: "Indian foreign policy will have to grow up, leaving behind its days of innocence and adolescence. India will have to learn to take sides, offer security to others (especially in our region), and address new challenges in the field of nuclear diplomacy. As a maritime power, India will have to bring its foreign policy in line with its national security policy: winning new friends without losing old ones."[8] But for now, the ambition for autonomy remains; this theme runs throughout this book.

The emerging powers also want to have the freedom to pick and choose which parts of the system to participate in meaningfully, a freedom they see the United States exercising and want to replicate. When American officials call on the emerging powers to be responsible members of the international order, emerging power officials tend to respond: We'll be exactly as responsible as you are, implying a certain freedom to ignore the rules when they are inconvenient.[9] Moreover, they seek to undo what they view as unjust treatment from international bodies or treaties forged at a time when they were powerless. One way they can make such change is to have greater weight in these institutions, especially the governing board of the IMF, the governing board of the World Bank, and the UN Security Council.

One way to think about this ambition is that these are bodies with genuine power in international affairs. A far more accurate formulation, however, is that these are bodies through which states with power wield influence. And so the rising powers' demand for seats and voting weight in these bodies is motivated by two concerns: to be in the room when influence is being wielded and to be recognized as a state that warrants being in the room. This concern is embedded in the psychology of rise and the desire to no longer be subject to unequal treaties, even though the fact of their new power means that the rising states are no longer as subject to these bodies as they once were. The concern is also about their interests. They have a stake in the rules of international finance as these are debated and negotiated by the major powers at the IMF; they have a stake in the World Bank's financing of energy and infrastructure; and they have a stake both in the Security Council's stabilization operations (for reasons discussed in chapter 4) and in the efforts of some of the Western powers to redefine the boundaries between sovereignty and intervention (chapter 6).

It is no surprise, given how multilateral institutions work, that the rising powers are making more headway (albeit still with obstacles and headaches) in the international economic institutions than in the UN Security Council: they have actual power in the international economy, but those that do not already have permanent seats in the Security Council have sharply limited power in international security (for now). Further, the rising powers are unified on reform of the international financial institutions, but they are deeply divided on UN Security Council reform, with the two that have seats (China and Russia) actively working to block those without seats (India and Brazil) from gaining them.

This matters for more than just the governance of international institutions. While China, India, Brazil, Turkey, and other rising powers are situated very differently in many respects, they share an aspiration to be more influential players on the international stage.[10]

This search for autonomy is particularly important for India. Squeezed between a globally dominant United States and a regionally assertive China, India is struggling to forge an internal consensus for its foreign policy orientation. China's increasingly assertive posture in Asia has convinced many in India's strategic community that India's long-term interests lie with the United States. But India cannot afford to alienate China, either. To be relieved of these pressures, India is trying to assert its autonomy.[11] Although India has significant shared interests with the United States, it is not at this stage willing to be treated as an ally, in a narrow sense, or to do America's bidding in the region. When President Obama traveled to India in 2010 to consolidate deepening ties, he was given a warm welcome—but he was also given a clear message: we will be strong partners, but do not take us for granted or expect us to become a traditional ally.

Brazil has a similar philosophy, though it is not similarly squeezed. The old joke about Brazil was that it was so nonaligned that it didn't even join the Non-Aligned Movement, a 1960s-era grouping of states that were neither NATO nor Warsaw Pact members (Soviet allies) during the cold war. Brazil retains this sense of its wholly autonomous foreign policy identity and seeks to match it with autonomous influence. Brazil is perhaps the emerging power that most resembles the United States in its foreign policy in this one sense: unlike the others, which have realist policies oriented around their interests, Brazil has a broader conception of its role in the world. (It helps that Brazil has never had to fight a war and that it is so much larger than its neighbors that it feels no threat from them.) Brazilian foreign policy echoes the American sense that it is supposed to serve a larger purpose than just self-interest, narrowly defined. That sense of broader purpose tends to align Brazil with the UN Charter, and the core precepts of the charter happen to align with Brazil's core interest.

The Shifting Landscape of Economic Power

Are the big three emerging powers—Brazil, India, and China—seeking to overturn the existing international economic order? The irony for many rising powers is that, to the extent that they are reemerging powers, the pathway back to power has been premised on profiting from the existing order. For the first forty years of the cold war, Brazil, India, and China stood apart from the two main groupings, seeking to insulate themselves from the superpower rivalry. That strategic decision coincided with and reinforced an economic decision to stay outside of the global financial and trade system. (Turkey, of course, took a different path, joining the NATO alliance in 1952; even then, Turkey has had a troubled relationship with the main European economic structures.) The consequence was that their economies stagnated while those of the West (and of Western allies like Japan and South Korea) took off. In the 1980s, variously under pressure from the IMF and as a consequence of changing domestic politics, India, China, and Brazil and, later, Indonesia and Turkey chose to shift their economic orientation and jump headfirst into global trade and the global financial system. The result was the largest wave of poverty eradication in modern history and startling growth. So it was precisely by joining the very system they resent that this new group of powers began to reemerge.

During the period roughly from 1980 to 2000, the basic story of the global economy was one of more and more countries entering globalization. China, India, and Brazil made decisions in the late 1970s and early 1980s to liberalize their economies, deregulate their markets, and open up to international trade. These decisions took these three large, insular, semisocialist economies into the global economy. Several smaller countries, such as Vietnam and Mexico, took similar steps. This phase of globalization has been referred to as the extensive phase—that is, the geographical scope of globalization was widening. A symbolic illustration: between 1990 and 2000 McDonald's more than doubled the number of countries in which it had a restaurant, from 50 to 116. A more technical measure: during the 1990s, 135 countries completed the process of joining the World Trade Organization (WTO), the body through which states negotiate the rules of free trade—and thus also the defining symbol of contemporary globalization.[12]

But since 2000 McDonald's has opened restaurants in only seven more countries.[13] And the WTO has added only twenty-two members. These numbers track what is referred to as intensive globalization—that is, a shift from further spread of globalization to more trade and financial interactions between countries already in the global marketplace.[14]

The important consequence of these interactions is that the leading players among the rising powers—with the partial exception of Russia— are enormously dependent on overseas growth for the health of their economies. The weight of trade in their GDP is striking. For China, that figure reached 59 percent before the global financial crisis and still hovers around 55 percent. For India, the share, around 54 percent, is similar. The figure for Korea is a stunning 110 percent. (The shares are still higher for niche operator Singapore—391 percent.)[15]

The emerging powers' numbers are familiar to the major European economies. The average European economy has a trade dependence of around 60 percent. But there is an essential political difference between China, India, Indonesia, and South Korea, on the one hand, and Europe, on the other. While large portions of both sets of countries' trade, both imports and exports, go to the advanced Western economies, the political difference is that, for Europe, this translates into trade dependence on neighbors and close allies. For China and India, it means trade dependence on the West, as well as on each other. Analysts who talk about the economic rise of China and India as reflecting the rise of the "post-Western world" neglect this essential fact.

Of course, there has been a shift toward trade within the non-OECD countries. For example, China-Brazil trade has grown, as has trade within Asia. Still, Western trade and investment still loom very large in both the global economy and the individual economies of emerging powers. Take Brazil: the fact that China has become the number-one destination of Brazilian exports has generated a lot of attention, even though the United States remains its number-one source of imports. However, the United States and its core European allies, combined, are substantially larger than China as a source of both imports and exports.[16] The idea that trade integration between emerging powers sidelines the West is simply not borne out by the facts.

And it is important to highlight that the emerging powers are not the only countries for which trade is a growing percentage of GDP—it is true as well for the United States. The current U.S. trade/GDP ratio is 25 percent. From one vantage point, that looks like a country much less integrated into the global economy than the rest of the trillionaires' club. But here is another vantage point: in 1989 that number was 15 percent—so there has been a 60 percent rise in U.S. integration into the global economy over the past two decades. And there are strong indications that that number will continue to rise.[17] This deepening trade dependence creates shared incentives, to protect the health of the global economy and restrain competitive tendencies. In spite of the fact that countries seek to adapt globalization to their interests, they are constrained by their deep integration into it.

The tension accompanying the rise of the emerging powers explains a number of apparent contradictions in how these countries behave. Both their aspiration to great-power status and their muscle memory of subjugation cause these actors to behave in contradictory ways on the international stage. They are gaining power but, at the same time, are shaped by historical resentment.[18] Although their goal of autonomy is overarching, they are caught between the impulse to rivalry and incentives for restraint.

Strategic Divides within the BRICS

Does a shared interest in redressing the balance within international trade and finance regimes mean that the emerging powers are indeed a unified bloc, focused on challenging the U.S.-led order?

The annual BRICS Summit has become a symbol of the challenge to Western dominance of the international order. The BRICS countries meet and make joint statements about the international order and about their claims for a greater share in its governance. This behavior stokes fears that the rising powers are indeed a bloc and do indeed seek to constrain the United States. And when during the humanitarian crisis in Libya in 2012 the BRICS—all of which happened to be in the UN Security Council at the same time—actually caucused together, these fears were deepened.

The members of the BRICS do in fact have good reason to get to know each other better. They have a common desire not to allow the United States or the West to dictate the terms on international issues without consulting them. They have a common motivation to be heard in international debates. They have a common agenda in wanting greater representation and voice and votes in the major global bodies. They have a similar need to find new sources of financing for development—they are too rich at a national level to receive Western development aid but still have to find a way to help a combined 750 million citizens out of poverty. So they are likely to act together to establish new tools for development, including a planned BRICS bank and a BRICS investment fund.

The one thing they do not have is shared strategic interests. M. K. Narayanan, who was India's national security adviser from 2005 to 2010 (and who thus was present at the creation of the BRICS mechanism) describes India and China as natural adversaries.[19] After all, China and India have fought three wars against each other since 1950, and leading Indian security scholars still spend their time planning strategies for the next war.[20] India's current national security adviser, Shivshankar Menon, told a meeting of scholars in New Delhi that the biggest threat that India currently faces is Chinese cyberattacks. India, while still struggling to deal with almost 600 million poor people in its country, is pouring resources into its navy for one reason only: to balance China's naval buildup. The more China rises, the more the Indian strategic community sees India's interests being best served by a deepening relationship with the United States. India made a major pitch in 2008 to become a member of the Nuclear Suppliers Group, a small group of states that have the self-appointed right to monitor and block exports of nuclear materials. One major obstacle to India's joining? Objections from China.[21] As I was finalizing this section of the book, Chinese forces actually moved into contested territory along the disputed border in Ladakh, on the Chinese-Indian "line of actual control." Several rounds of tense negotiations were required before the situation was resolved. The episode did nothing to strengthen the hand of those in Delhi—including senior officials in the current government—who believe they can build a more stable relationship with China.[22]

This tension, however, should not be overstated. India and China are hugely important to each other economically—and will remain so. The India-China relationship is set to look a lot like the China-U.S. relationship—and, to a certain degree, like the India-Russia and Russia-China relationships. In all these relationships, economic ties compete with strategic tension. None of them fit neatly into classic categories of rivalry or partnership. This ambiguity is central to what lies ahead.

There are other schisms as well. China regularly suggests shifting away from the U.S. dollar as a reserve currency, and it has badgered various BRICS summits into issuing joint declarations on the issue. But when China first raised this issue, in the immediate aftermath of the global financial crisis, the proposal was met with deafening silence, and not just from the United States and Europe but also from India. For policymakers in India, strengthening China's hand at the expense of America's hardly seems to be in India's interest. Only Brazil has seriously considered the proposal, and in 2011 China and Brazil began to denominate some of their trade in their own currencies—up to $30 billion a year, according to a 2013 BRICS Summit agreement.[23] That sounds impressive, but considering that total BRICS trade now exceeds $300 billion a year, the $30 billion is roughly 10 percent. And their overall trade is $1.7 trillion a year; against that, the $30 billion shrinks to insignificance.

Rebalancing global institutional arrangements also means a seat at the table—especially at the UN Security Council. Brazil and India have made the pursuit of permanent Security Council seats top priorities of their foreign polices. But the main obstacles to their ambitions are not Washington or London or Paris (though none of those capitals are exactly in a hurry to reform the Security Council); instead, the obstacles are Moscow and Beijing, which are keen to retain their privileged permanent seats. Brazil's pursuit of a Security Council seat has grown into a major irritant between that country and Russia and China. Not for nothing has Brazil actively kept alive a forum for the emerging democratic powers, the IBSA (India, Brazil, South Africa) mechanism. As China increasingly asserts itself on the international stage and Russia's behavior is more and more truculent, Brazil has become more attuned to the differences between the IBSA and the BRICS.

Does it matter if the BRICS are not united? China clearly thinks so. It spends a great deal of diplomatic energy and finance shoring up the BRICS process (along with the larger developing world grouping, the G-77). In economic terms, China is by far the largest of the BRICS. But in a trade-based economy there are limits on how much China can reshape rules unilaterally. In global negotiations at the IMF, in the UN climate process, and at the UN, the United States and the West still have huge institutional advantages, so it is only together that members of the BRICS can challenge current governance arrangements. It matters in strategic terms, too. When it comes to non-Western strategy on military intervention, or to maritime security arrangements, China would be in a much stronger position vis-à-vis the West were it engaged in a strategic alliance with India. But it is not.

The strains are beginning to show. Take climate negotiations. In 2009 China, India, and Brazil worked together to resist a major European push on climate negotiations. These three forged a bloc (termed BASIC, which for political reasons also included South Africa) to negotiate in the Copenhagen climate change conference, and this one instance of cooperation came to symbolize the ability of the emerging powers to work together to block global negotiations. The BASIC group was tactically useful, but it masked hugely important differences among the members. Climate negotiations are about reducing per capita carbon emissions, or narrowing these differences among countries, and here members of the BASIC group have huge differences. China has reached European levels of emissions, at 5.8 tonnes per capita; India's are 1.6; Brazil's, 1.9. (U.S. emissions, for comparison, are 17.3.) The huge difference between China's and India's positions has Indian negotiators worried that India's international reputation is suffering from its relationship with a country with which it increasingly does not share energy or climate interests.[24]

Does the West Still Matter?

Of course, how much BRICS unity or disunity matters depends a bit on the relative unity on the other side of the equation. How unified is the West?

For the forty years between the erection of the Berlin Wall and its fall, the cold war was not just the defining but the overwhelming feature of international politics. It shaped every aspect of domestic and foreign security policy for the United States and its allies in Europe and Asia; it shaped every aspect of domestic, security, and economic policy in the Soviet bloc; and it dominated the realities of the so-called third world, which was caught in between. During the cold war, to talk about international politics or the international order was to talk about the West and its rivalry with the Soviet bloc.

The dominance of the Western alliance in foreign policy thinking continued through the first years after the end of the Berlin Wall, through the presidencies of George H. W. Bush and Bill Clinton. There were moments of tension, especially between the United States and the European powers over the European response—or more precisely, the nonresponse—in the Balkans. (Or from the European perspective, the issue was the two-year delay by the Clinton administration in responding to the Balkans problem.) There were tensions in the Security Council between the United States and France over Iraq.[25] And there were policy differences in global bodies on issues like development—and the beginnings of what would eventually be deep differences on climate change. Nevertheless, the pattern of U.S.-European cooperation, consultation, and joint action is deeply woven into foreign policy on both sides of the Atlantic.

This pattern survived the strain that arose from European distress and divisions over the 2003 war in Iraq. This history is recent and widely known and needs no recounting here, other than to recall the sense among European policymakers that the U.S. actions in Iraq not only destabilized the region but actively undermined the international order on which European stability and prosperity rests.[26] Moreover, broad rhetorical attacks on multilateralism and the UN in the early George W. Bush years alienated European foreign policy elites and publics (and had the effect of driving them, along with much of the rest of the world, into a strong pro-UN stance). America's rejection of the Kyoto climate deal and its selective approach to international humanitarian law further aggravated anti-U.S. sentiment. It should be noted, as relevant to the present day, that even Democrats who opposed Bush's war strategy found some of the anti-U.S. rhetoric that emerged from Europe in this period—as well as many European states' wan stance in Afghanistan—hard to swallow.

Afghanistan became an important feature in the alliance dynamics—a source of both unity and division. European allies joined the fight against the Taliban after 9/11, which helped reaffirm the strength and relevance of the alliance. But it was thus shocking to the European allies that when they offered to invoke article 5 of the NATO Charter—the "one for all, all for one" clause that commits NATO members to joining forces with any member that faces an attack—their offer was spurned by the Bush administration. As the war progressed, the U.S. attitude fluctuated between denigrating the Europeans' fairly flabby military performance, admiring the exceptions to that norm (particularly Britain, Denmark, Poland, and the Netherlands), and recognizing the U.S. need for cooperation from Europe on everything other than the narrowest of military objectives. That fluctuating attitude was as true of the Obama administration as of Bush's; officials in both administrations shared a suspicion that much of Europe is ultimately unwilling when push comes to shove; and officials in both administrations also understood that, on the civilian and economic dimensions of Afghanistan strategy—and for the overall legitimacy of the mission—Europe is essential.[27]

In Bush's second term, his administration was distinctly more cooperative with Europe. It repeatedly turned to the UN Security Council for peacekeeping, counterterrorism, and counterproliferation support. Condoleezza Rice's move from the National Security Council to the State Department consolidated the changed approach. Later, diplomatic reengagement on the Israeli-Palestinian issue further mollified once-alienated allies in Europe and the Arab world, and the transatlantic alliance seemed back on track.

By then, however, the rising powers were well into their phenomenal growth spurt of the first decade of the 2000s, Russia was recovering economically, and the United States had begun to notice the emerging economies, especially China and India. Relations with these economies became a source of tension between the United States and its allies in both Europe and the Pacific.

The First Pivot

The Bush administration's relationship with China had a rocky start when, in April 2001, an American spy plane collided with a Chinese military jet over China, killing the Chinese pilot. The relationship changed, however, after 9/11. With the al Qaeda attacks on the Pentagon and the World Trade Center in New York City, U.S. policy priorities shifted rapidly and decisively to terrorism, specifically Islamic terrorism. And there, the Bush administration discovered, the United States was on common ground with China, Russia, and India. Each of those countries was grappling with an Islamic terrorism threat in its own neighborhood—Russia in Chechnya and the former Soviet countries, China with the Uighurs in western China, and India with Pakistani militants across their highly insecure border. This focus on Islamic terrorism, however, began to drive wedges between the United States and the European flank of the Western alliance. In particular, the fact that the United States would often side with the emerging powers (and the other way around) on the human rights and justice aspects of the fight against terrorism left the Europeans feeling isolated. In debates about the post-Western world, the view is often presented that the issues of democracy and human rights are important barriers between the West and the rising powers; but in practice human rights and international law questions have as often divided the West.[28]

The Bush administration, as part of its shift in focus on the emerging powers, opened a new phase of relations between the United States and India. A rapprochement had already begun under President Clinton, whose deputy secretary of state, Strobe Talbott, had started negotiations with his Indian counterpart on a range of normalization efforts. The Bush administration took this a large step further by offering to strike a deal with India on the issue that most symbolized the wedge between the two countries—India's nuclear program. This issue, however, would drive a wedge between the United States and Europe, which wanted much stronger guarantees about India's nuclear program before relaxing the rules by which India could acquire nuclear fuel and technology. There were different strands of thought within the Bush administration about the U.S.-India nuclear deal, some viewing it as a step toward building a defensive alliance to contain China. But overwhelmingly, the factors that drove the shift appear to have been two: the growing prominence and influence of the Indian émigré business elite; and the sense within the administration, felt more acutely after 9/11, of the value of building relations with another giant democracy threatened by Islamic terrorism—and one whose rise intrinsically balances China's. And in practice, once the U.S.-India deal was approved by the U.S. Congress and the Indian Parliament, the European countries that had to sign off did so—and then rushed to be first in line for nuclear contracts.

The Obama administration has also been frustrated by what many see as Europe's sense of entitlement when it comes to the question of global institutions. Many European foreign policy officials had anxiously awaited the Obama administration and an anticipated return to multilateralism. Abstractly, many of these officials acknowledge that the process of revitalizing international institutions and the collective management of global problems necessarily involves shifting around the chairs so that the emerging powers have seats. But most of these officials appear to have deluded themselves into believing that this process could occur without Europe giving up seats. They were sorely disappointed on this score by the Obama administration.[29]

The election of President Obama to the White House in 2008 was accompanied by signals of a major break in foreign policy between the two administrations, notably over Iraq and Afghanistan. But on relations toward emerging powers, there was initially more continuity than break—despite outsize expectations.

On China, there was initially not just continuity but an effort to deepen ties. The U.S. relationship with China is heavily shaped by the reality of economic and financial interdependence. That interdependence was amplified by the 2008–09 financial crisis; by spring of 2009 China held over $2 trillion in U.S. debt. China's role in the G-20 solidified its status as a major economic power. Controversially, the Obama administration decided that the first trip for its secretary of state, Hillary Clinton, would be not to one of the traditional Western allies' capitals but to Beijing. During that trip, both countries agreed that traditional and nontraditional security threats were becoming increasingly interlinked and that fostering economic recovery was a shared goal. Clinton provoked a minor scandal in the United States when she said during the trip that human rights—traditionally a dividing issue between Washington and Beijing—would not be a major factor in the relationship with China, which would be put on a new strategic footing.[30]

With India, there was continuity as well. The Obama administration continued to deepen U.S. engagement on both strategic and economic issues. With the U.S.-Indian civilian nuclear deal—finally, if painstakingly, resolved in 2008—political space opened up for a broader strategic dialogue. Secretary of State Clinton, in her summer 2009 trip to Delhi, stressed that she and her counterpart had begun discussing all matters of importance and that these discussions would continue with the dialogue's commencement in late 2009. Then, in 2010, President Obama traveled to Delhi for a prominent state visit, designed to cement ties and launch new business investment. President Obama also used the visit to make a public declaration in support of India's permanent seat in the UN Security Council (much to the annoyance of Germany, which had received no such public declaration from Washington).

There was even more of a break between Obama and Bush regarding Russia. Although the Bush administration had enjoyed a period of good relations with Putin's Russia, by the end of Bush's (and Putin's) second term these had deteriorated badly. Putin complained about American missile defense plans, aggressively challenged U.S. foreign policy in a speech at the 2007 Munich Security Conference, and fought a short war with Georgia (whose government was friendly to the United States). The Obama team, coming into office, believed that some of this deterioration had been driven by policies and rhetoric that unnecessarily highlighted divergent rather than shared interests. Hence the "reset" concept in the administration's early overtures to Russia, a concept designed to lessen the long-standing antagonism in the relationship and create the possibility of cooperation on such issues as Iran. The reset concept was far from popular in Central and Eastern Europe, where many of the states that integrated into the EU after 1991 have strong suspicions of Russia. This suspicion has only grown since 2012, with the return of Vladimir Putin to the presidency; and following his return, there was a sharp deterioration in U.S.-Russia relations.

All of this irritated the allies, which were feeling taken for granted both in global negotiations and in Afghanistan. And some were more than just irritated. When Hillary Clinton referred to the U.S.-China relationship as "the most important bilateral relationship," the Japanese reaction could be described as apoplectic.[31]

Still, while much of this strained relations among U.S. allies, none of it eroded them. And as the emerging-power dynamic deepened, America's attitude began to shift—back toward its core allies.

The Second Pivot

A turning point came in late 2011. In November, President Obama took a twice-delayed trip to the Pacific. The destinations said a lot about the new texture of the global playing field: on the itinerary were visits to Indonesia, a rising player in Asia and globally, and Australia, one of America's most enduring allies. Obama used the trip to stress an old theme—a theme that, if not lost, was certainly displaced during America's entanglements in Iraq and Afghanistan—the theme of America as a Pacific power and a leader in Asia. As Obama told the Australian Parliament, "Our new focus on this region reflects a fundamental truth—the United States has been, and always will be, a Pacific nation."[32] He also used the trip to Indonesia, which hosts the major Asian regional body, the Association of South East Asian Nations (ASEAN), to stress America's recommitment to that body. This was a response to a growing chorus of concern in the region that, in the absence of a visible U.S. commitment to ASEAN and the region, China was beginning to dominate.

More significant was Obama's announcement, made alongside Australian premier Julia Gillard, that the United States was going to be deploying a contingent of marines to an Australian base in Darwin, on Australia's northern coast. For the first time since the end of the Vietnam war, U.S. combat troops were to be back on Australian soil.

Over the long run, perhaps the most important outcome of the trip was an American decision to intensify negotiations over a free trade zone linking the United States with key Pacific economies like Japan and Korea (which had already signed a bilateral trade deal with the United States in 2012)—the Trans-Pacific Partnership.

The diplomatic language of the trip bears careful scrutiny. Obama was meticulous: at no point did anything he said imply or even hint that the United States was now shifting to a strategy of containing China's expansion. His stress was simply on leadership and continuity: America had been, was, and would be a Pacific power. National Security Adviser Tom Donilon was even more careful: this was not about a dramatic shift in priorities but about a rebalancing of focus and of forces, back toward America's traditional broad global focus, which had always incorporated a Pacific presence. But Secretary Clinton used a different phrase; this was a "pivot to Asia," she said, and the phrase stuck.

The phrase also confused. If you are pivoting toward something, you are necessarily pivoting away from something else. And such were the insecurities of America's European allies—feeling unloved by the Bush and Obama administrations, with their focus on Asia—that many in Europe assumed that what America was pivoting away from was Europe. The American foreign policy commentariat reached much the same conclusion, many excoriating the Obama administration for neglecting its transatlantic friends by refocusing on Asia.[33] But this missed the key dynamic. The rebalancing in question was not away from Europe but from excess U.S. entanglement in Central Asia and the Middle East. There was not to be a pivot away from Europe. In fact, at the same time, the United States had begun implementing a series of moves designed to reinforce unity in the West and to develop a shared strategy in dealing with the rise of China and other new players.

An important signal for this were two back-to-back summits of the G-8 and NATO, hosted by the United States. These meetings were held in May 2011 on symbolically resonant ground: at Camp David, the U.S. presidential retreat, and in Chicago, Obama's home turf. Together, they were a powerful symbol of America's continued orientation to the West and to its Western alliances.[34]

Neither the issue of the West and its alliances nor the question of China and the emerging powers was on the formal agenda of either summit. The G-8 meeting focused on global economic issues, particularly the eurozone crisis. The NATO summit focused on Afghanistan, where the West was fighting against an adversary, al Qaeda, that found no friends in any of the rising-power capitals. But topics and purpose are not always the same, and the underlying purposes were quite different. In the G-8 meeting, the real purpose was to put concerted Western pressure on Moscow to shift ground on Syria (which it did not). In the NATO meeting, the purpose was to strengthen the ties between the transatlantic allies, NATO members, and Pacific allies like Australia and Japan. Behind the scenes, the United States used the G-8 meeting to reinforce to its core European allies the need to work together to deal with the challenge being posed by China and Russia. This was the West saying "enough."

Strange Bedfellows

As much as the Obama administration has worked to reinforce the sense of unity with its allies, especially in the Pacific, the result of this has not been a BRICS-versus-West dynamic, for this reason: in addition to the basic dynamics of intra-BRICS ties and tension, there is another dynamic among the trillionaires: the recurrent phenomenon of strange bedfellows.

Take, for example, the eurozone crisis. This was a tragedy foretold: as early as late 2008 U.S. Treasury and White House officials were warning their European counterparts that the euro was going to come under pressure and that European debt ratios were unsustainably high. But there was a divide within Europe and beyond it about the remedy, a divide that illustrates the complex coalitions that are going to be characteristic of the world ahead of us. The coalition that lined up to deal with the eurozone crisis through stimulus included the United States, China, Brazil, and India. Lined up against using stimulus were Germany, the United Kingdom, and Australia. In other words, faced with the dangerous second wave of the global financial crisis, U.S. policy was closely aligned with the non-Western rising powers and at odds with its closest allies.

It is characteristic of the present narrative that during this period, most of the public debate and commentary on international economic issues focused on the tussle between the United States and China over China's practice of keeping its currency artificially high. This was a genuine cleavage between China and the United States, to be sure, but it overshadowed the equally important alignment between China and the United States—and India and others—over stimulus.[35]

Nor is this the only place where these odd bedfellows alignments occur. We see it when the United States brokers a deal to downgrade Europe's representation on the IMF by two seats in order to make room for China, India, and Brazil. We even see it around crises and intervention. But there is an important qualification to this: while the West is often divided on policy issues, it remains a group with shared values and systems and one that will unite in the case of genuinely impactful issues and certainly in the case of threats. The strange bedfellows phenomenon allows the United States to cooperate with the emerging powers but with no real loss of unity with the Western allies.

This matters, because the myth of a post-Western world is the notion that the views and interests of the United States and the West will be pushed aside by a non-Western bloc. But there is no such bloc, and the views of several of the rising powers on key strategic questions are closer to the views of the United States than they are to one another's views.

Global Electoral College Math: America's Enduring Advantage

To return to the beginning: Does the changing international landscape result in a multipolar world? Today, the answer is no. Nor do current patterns suggest its inevitability. Instead, the picture is complex and one not evidently threatening to U.S. interests.

An image can help. Think about the way that American electoral strategists watch the electoral college map to see where there are states that are "solid" for their candidate, states that "lean" toward their candidate, and "swing" states. For the Democratic Party, California, New York, and large swaths of the Northwest and Northeast are essentially solid, while for Republicans Texas, the South, and much of the interior

West are solid. The early election is fought to shore up "leaning" states (such as Michigan and Pennsylvania for Democrats and North Carolina and Missouri for Republicans, in recent elections). Later phases are fought in a handful of swing states (Ohio, Florida, Virginia, Colorado, among others).

This map changes over time for two reasons: changes in where people live, how they vote, and whether their state "matters" in electoral college outcomes; and the politics of the candidates, which can make leaning states into swing states. (It is rare for a state to move during one electoral cycle from being solid for one party to being a swing state.)

An international map can be depicted in something like these terms, with the two parties being the West and China. Think of forty or fifty countries on the electoral college map, America's core allies, that are solid for the West—including the largest prize of all, the United States. That is a very reassuring start, though the United States has to be worried about the fact that the net scale of this solid block is gradually shrinking, as these countries slowly lose population and thus lose rank in the electoral college tally. However, there are another thirty or forty countries (from Singapore to Thailand to Mexico to Morocco to Jordan to Ethiopia to Ghana to Chile) that lean toward the West.

There are then fifty or sixty countries categorized as swing; they comprise large numbers of small to medium-size African and Asian states. Quite a few of these are starting to lean toward China, though not irreversibly; it has been a long time since the West offered them anything other than highly restrictive aid and pressure to comply with American counterterrorism interests, and they are not sure they can trust either an unbound United States or an arrogant and aging Europe. China and India look like easy sources of money, while Brazil looks like a very sympathetic source of genuine development investment. On the other hand, their early experience of Chinese campaign tactics leaves them questioning.

The countries that are solid for China are China, North Korea, Cambodia, and perhaps Pakistan. That's it. One could say that Russia leans toward China, in that (publicly) it is less nervous about China's rise than it is about America's continued dominance. But, in fact, Russia is at best unreliable for China.

And China's electoral college math has recently gotten worse. Ten years ago, China launched a major project to consolidate its influence over its large neighbor Myanmar. Myanmar has for decades been ruled by an authoritarian oligarchy with close ties to China. And while Myanmar was internationally isolated and marred by several simultaneous civil wars, that did not stop China from focusing on Myanmar's three major strategic assets: it is one of the world's largest producers of rice, a staple of China's diet; it has huge mineral and energy reserves; and most important, it has a 1,200-mile coastline on the Indian Ocean and the Andaman Sea. For China, Myanmar's coastline could solve its greatest dilemma: dependence on trade and energy that flow through the narrow Strait of Malacca, making these flows vulnerable to Western blockage. With this access in mind, China has invested in major infrastructure projects in Myanmar.[36] But what has happened is quite different. Instead of Myanmar being solidly for China, its long-time ruler has reformed the country's governance and economy and has opened the country to foreign investment. In the process, the country has gone from a solid pro-China stance to one that leans heavily toward the West—a significant strategic loss for China.

On the other hand, increasing economic integration between China and countries like Thailand could mean that these countries could go from being in the lean-West category to the lean-China category. This, however, is where implementation of the Trans-Pacific Partnership might balance China's growing economic influence in the region.

Among the key emerging powers, two—Turkey and South Korea—are in the solid camp for the West, though Turkey is starting to show signs of drifting toward the leaning category. Indonesia is too close to call between leaning and swing. Brazil is still a swing state, but the fact that in 2010 it signed a defense agreement with the United States says something important about its overall position. And successive visits to Brasilia by Susan Rice, Joe Biden, and John Kerry, all in 2013, did a lot to build a positive image of the United States among Brazilians—though this work was eroded somewhat by the Snowden revelations about NSA spying on Brazilian politicians.[37] India, which matters more in strategic terms, is starting to show signs of leaning pro-West. It will not declare for the West, because it needs to maintain good ties with China; but more and more it sees its future linked to American strength and to cooperation on issues like maritime security.

This image hardly suggests that the world has become post-Western. In fact, in strategic terms, the situation looks pretty good for the West and pretty rough for China. Political scientists will notice that this image does not account for one trend: in votes in the UN General Assembly and the UN Human Rights Council, some analysts have noted a trend whereby the West has lost more votes of late than it has during previous decades.[38] That is true, but two factors may explain it. First, most of these votes are of a symbolic nature, and a vote against the United States or its Western allies is sometimes a useful "safety valve" for states that are not aligned with the West but are nevertheless quietly cooperating with Western countries. When he was Kofi Annan's senior adviser on UN reform, Stephen Stedman raised this issue with a senior Western counterterrorism official—the context was the difficulty of getting enough states to support strong counterterrorism language in the UN General Assembly. The official's response was, in essence, that those countries were quietly providing the United States with a lot of cooperation in terms of sharing intelligence about suspected terrorists, and if the choice was between cooperation on real counterterrorism at the cost of resistance to symbolic measures, or the other way around, the choice was clear.

Second, after 9/11 the Bush administration adopted a much tougher posture on issues like human rights in the Middle East—guaranteed vote losers in UN bodies—and was more willing to push issues to votes, for symbolic reasons, than it had been previously. The Obama administration has been equally assertive on human rights issues in the UN, and in other domains like LBGT rights—tough fights to have in the UN.[39] So the trend line may be capturing something other than shifting alliances.

Of course, more important, the image is simplistic. Countries are not individual voters. There is no quadrennial vote count or anything that resembles it. Instead, countries' relations are complex and are made to balance their regional ties and their global interests. Still, the image of a global electoral college should give pause when the narrative of a post-Western world is told.

Can We Avoid a War? The Part 1 Answer

Against the backdrop of rapid changes in the world, one question looms large: Can war be avoided? It is a question rooted in the argument that when one power rises and another fades, war is inevitable.[40] I hope that part 1 of this book has sown some doubt that the United States is a falling power. Still, this question looms over much of the contemporary debate about rising powers.

There is an optimistic counterargument: that there is something new in the contemporary period— something specific to the exercise of American power—that changes the equation. More precisely, the argument is that because the United States has used its power to back a system of free trade and global finance that any state could choose to join, new powers can rise within the system (as Brazil, India, and China have done) and therefore do not need to challenge the established power. Renegotiation and competition may be inevitable, but war is not.

It is certainly the case that the rising powers grew by participating in the established international system. There is little doubt that this gives them a powerful incentive to cooperate within that system, even as they negotiate to change its contours to meet their interests. That is an important claim of the more optimistic argument about what happens next.[41]

The central tenet of this argument, that the emerging powers will seek space within the existing order, not challenge it, has several core elements. One clear point is that there is now substantial pressure to reallocate authority within the international system. We have seen that that is true, and we'll see more evidence of it in part 2. There is also quite a lot of continued support to sustain core aspects of American hegemony, understood as leadership within a set of rules and institutions, to sustain the international order. Of course, there is no question at all that the global financial crisis which emanated from Wall Street, and which the U.S. Treasury failed to foresee or prevent—eroded international support for U.S. hegemony. But what is the alternative? Even China has to confront the limits of the alternatives. Even in the area where the emerging powers' weight is greatest, international finance, when they propose to weaken the role of the U.S. dollar as a reserve currency, they have few if any takers. They may succeed but only at the margins. Furthermore, no one else is interested in a decisive shift away from American leadership. The "we want a long, soft landing for American power" argument still holds.

Then, more controversially, some who hold to this line of argument also assert that the fact of nuclear weapons and economic integration means that we have seen, in effect, the disappearance of the option of great-power war, and that this sharply limits the option of a rising power forging an alternative order. And thus, for all of these reasons, we are likely to see the continued existence and growth of the liberal international order—defined, in essence, as the avoidance of war between the great powers and as a sustained international economic system in which they all participate.

Part 2 of this book is an empirical account of the interactions between the powers, examining patterns of competition, cooperation, deconfliction, and the management of energy, climate, economics, and security issues. The evidence strongly supports the hypothesis that economic stakes in the current system create incentives to continue to participate in it and to protect it from crises; to negotiate *within,* not against, the system. That being said, the argument that this removes the risk of great-power war is overstated. Alongside incentives for cooperation, I see evidence of strategic tensions and competition and a psychology of rise that will complicate things and create risks. The bottom line is, both the incentives for restraint and the impulse to rivalry are alive and well in the current system; and the balance between them is central to the question of whether we will live in a stable or unstable system in the period to come.

PART II

OF RIVALRY AND RESTRAINT
The Persistence of Cooperation

CHAPTER FOUR

OVERLAPPING INTERESTS

Transnational Threats and the Security of Globalization

In part 1 of this book, I make the argument that the attitudes of the rising powers are characterized by a balance between the impulse to rivalry, on the one hand, and on the other, incentives for restraint and cooperation. The essential argument is a simple one and has been made elsewhere: because the rising powers rose within the established economic system, they have interests in protecting and expanding it. I find a lot of evidence to support that claim.

There is more. As members of the trillionaires' club rise in power, their global reach spreads, and their stakes in protecting those interests rise. But their reach exceeds their grasp. While China, India, Brazil, Turkey, and even smaller players like the United Arab Emirates are reaching further afield, their power to shape outcomes and prevent threats becomes more limited. This leads to two phenomena: substantial increases in their diplomatic and developmental engagement and investment in far-flung corners of the world; and an expansion of cooperation with Western powers to stabilize fragile states, limit terrorism, and prevent threats. Cooperation with the West takes the form of emerging powers' participation in both existing institutions and new institutions, both those formed by the BRICS themselves and those formed by the West to combat terrorism and arms proliferation. This is not perfect cooperation, of course; there is rivalry for status and resources. But overall, there is evidence of surprising levels of cooperation, which are vividly illustrated by the arrangements to tackle threats to global trade in the Indian Ocean.

Protecting Globalization: Counterpiracy in the Indian Ocean

In 2009 I began to study an interesting experiment taking place off the coast of Somalia, where several nations' navies were patrolling together to protect their trade interests from piracy. What made the story particularly interesting was the participation, alongside American and European ships, of not just other American allies, from Pakistan to Bahrain, but also Russia, China, and India. This was just as the aftershocks of the global financial crisis were beginning to turn people's attention to new challenges to American leadership, to the risk of a G-Zero world, to the coming disorder. So it was intriguing to hear a different story line, of unusual partners cooperating against a common threat.

Somalia's 3,300-kilometer coastline, the longest in Africa and the Middle East, undulates along the shores of two bodies of water, the Indian Ocean and the Gulf of Aden, off the southeastern edge of the Arabian Gulf. It is one of the most beautiful coastlines in the world and under different circumstances would be replete with resorts and hotels catering to tourists. But as Somalia is one of the poorest countries in the world and wracked by decades of internal war, its coast is home to a quite different kind of traveler. From villages scattered along the shoreline, hundreds of crews practice one of the world's oldest professions: piracy.

In 2005 the International Maritime Organization in London started warning of an increase in piracy attacks in the Gulf of Aden.[1] There had been a handful of attacks in the previous decade, but then there was a sharp rise in 2005, to more than ten. That year, and in each of the subsequent two years, there were roughly a dozen attacks. Concern about them was amplified by the fact that Yemen, on the northern shore of the Gulf of Aden, is one of al Qaeda's strongest footholds. (In fact, by 2010 al Qaeda would control three out of five Yemeni provinces.) An al Qaeda affiliate, al Shabab, was gaining a foothold in Somalia's anarchic soil.

In 2007–08 three things happened that amplified international attention to Somalia's pirates. The number of attacks spiked to 51 in 2008 and then to 111 in 2009. The attacks spread from the Gulf of Aden out into the Indian Ocean. And in 2008 Somali pirates attacked a ship that was part of a World Food Program convoy bringing food to relieve the crisis in Somalia—where an estimated 2 million to 3 million Somalis were facing starvation. It sparked a unique response. The response started with the UN Security Council calling for governments to take swift action to protect the World Food Program's ships and to tackle the mounting problem of piracy.[2] This had international lawyers in New York scrambling to figure out one of the oldest domains of international law, the law of piracy, largely a series of legal arrangements between the European powers from the eighteenth century. The council then took two other important steps.

One of the bedrock principles of contemporary international order is that state sovereignty extends into the seas—specifically, every state is granted a twelve-mile zone of exclusive sovereignty into what are called its territorial waters. Other countries can sail through those waters through a provision known as innocent passage, which (rare for an international legal concept) actually explains the principle at stake: other states' vessels can pass through a sovereign state's territorial waters if their presence in no way threatens or harms the sovereign state. In all other cases, the consent of the state is required. In the case of Somalia, the Security Council waived that provision, giving any state willing to participate in the fight against piracy the right to enter Somali territorial waters for that purpose. And the council gave those states the right to use "any and all means" to repress the pirates—that is, they gave them the right to use force.[3]

As it happened, there was already a set of ships patrolling in the Gulf of Aden. In the wake of 9/11, the United States had established what was known as Combined Task Force 150 (CTF 150) to guard against terrorist activity in the Gulf. That force was a visible manifestation of America's alliance reach. It contained more than two dozen nations, drawing from NATO allies, non-NATO allies, and others, including Bahrain, Saudi Arabia, Malaysia, and Pakistan alongside core NATO allies like Germany and the United Kingdom.[4]

In response to the Security Council's call for action, part of this combined force was repurposed into CTF 151, with a counterpiracy mission focused on the Gulf of Aden. But the spread of the attacks into the Indian Ocean and the attacks on the World Food Program called for a broader response. And in a further demonstration of the breadth of Western capability, the EU stepped into the ring, agreeing to deploy its own naval task force, the European Union's Operation Atalanta, or CTF 465. Twenty-six European nations have participated in Operation Atalanta.[5]

The United States has spent years complaining to its European allies that they should take on more of the burden of maintaining European and international security and rely less on U.S. defense forces for that function.[6] So it is slightly puzzling that the U.S. reaction to the EU decision to mount Operation Atalanta was to launch the separate, U.S.-led NATO Operation Ocean Shield. Five NATO allies make up the core of Operation Ocean Shield: the United States, Denmark, Italy, Turkey, and the United Kingdom. Other countries—Ukraine, for example—have participated in the force through alliance partnership arrangements.

But what really makes the maritime operations off the coast of Somalia interesting is that several of the rising powers have joined in: the Republic of Korea and Turkey in Operation Ocean Shield, the United Arab Emirates in CTF 151, and the navies of India, China, and Russia patrolling alongside NATO forces.[7] In short, operations off the coast of Somalia were a kind of tableau of the changing international distribution of power.

There is only one problem with the operations: they did not work. In the two years after the deployment of these forces, piracy attacks stayed steady at just over 200 attacks a year.[8] The reasons why this was true, and what has happened since, tell us a lot about the prospects for cooperation among members of the trillionaires' club. We revisit this story at the end of the chapter.

China's "Go Out" Strategy: Rising Powers and Far-Flung Interests

As noted, the emerging powers' growth is not just accompanied by, but actually driven by, their participation in global trade. China is the number-two country and India is the number-eight country ranked by imports.[9] Even smaller emerging economies like South Korea, Singapore, Mexico, and Turkey have entered the top twenty in terms of their volume of imports. This growth has put the emerging powers into relationships with the suppliers of a wide range of commodities, from food to bauxite to natural gas, and on every continent of the world.

Emerging powers' interests are increasingly affected by instability in places well beyond the scope of their established relationships—and well beyond their own regions. Within their regions, the emerging powers—certainly the big three—have built influential diplomatic and commercial relationships and have invested in regional organizations for the purposes of helping to maintain stability. But beyond their regions, their interests are growing and their options are more limited. Part of India's drive to greater influence and status in the World Bank, for example (and part of the logic of creating a supplementary institution like the BRICS bank), comes from this realization. An example: India has important energy stakes in bauxite, and among its major suppliers is Bolivia. The creation of a sufficient infrastructure in Bolivia for the export of bauxite is subject to financing by the World Bank and to environmental conditions on that financing. India has limited means to influence the outcomes of the Bolivia–World Bank negotiations on infrastructure financing, even though its has a great stake in the outcome.[10]

It is too simple to say that this produces unified interests with the Western powers, but it does produce overlapping ones. Specifically, what it produces in the emerging powers, broadly speaking, is a strong interest in stability. Normally, the Western powers profess an interest in stability, too—but there are different trade-offs here, involving humanitarian interests and concerns about democracy. For example, these were dividing lines when the UN Security Council was debating whether to authorize a humanitarian intervention in Libya (when in 2011 Muammar Qaddafi was cracking down on a domestic uprising against his autocratic rule). India had developed substantial interests in Libya, largely to do with subcontracts to the oil industry. In its official statement explaining its vote to abstain on the question of deploying force, the Indian government pointed to its commercial interests in contracts in Libya's oil fields. (India's experienced UN ambassador, Hardeep Puri, had the good sense to excise that passage before India's text was presented to the Security Council.)[11]

India had similar concerns about intervention in Syria, too, although its more powerful global economic interests eventually swung it in a different direction (chapter 6). In both cases, India had to face the reality of having important interests in the country with no capacity to protect those interests. Nor was India alone. When the situation deteriorated in Libya, China, which also had major investments and a substantial number of people in the country, was left scrambling for commercial leases of aircraft to fly its personnel out of harm's way.[12] Brazil's challenge is slightly different, in that it is a supplier, not an importer, of natural resources; yet it too recognizes that protecting its interests requires more than just regional diplomacy. In the words of its defense minister, "Brazil's abundance of energy, food, water, and biodiversity increases its stake in a security environment characterized by rising competition for access to, or control of, natural resources. In order to meet the challenges of this complex reality, Brazil's peaceful foreign policy must be supported by a robust defense policy."[13]

In short, the emerging powers' reach—for now—exceeds their grasp.

One aspect of this phenomenon that has been given substantial attention is China's decision to shift away from a stance of being very careful about overseas investments. The Chinese authorities were conscious of their huge import needs for energy and food and launched what was termed a "go out" strategy, whereby they encouraged Chinese companies, including Chinese nationally owned companies (which go by the awkward acronym CNOCs), to venture into overseas markets to procure supplies of energy and other resource needs.[14] The basic model was a mercantilist one; that is, the CNOCs were in the business not simply of trading in the global market but also of trying to lock up original source supplies—by buying mines, buying shares in national oil fields, and buying land, especially in Latin America and Africa, for the production of food to import to China. India's investments in land in Africa, and its overall foreign direct investment in Africa, are just shy of China's. Korea and Singapore are also investors. (The list of investors is still topped by the Western powers: overall, the largest investor in these deals is the United States.) Brazil is now the largest foreign investor in Mozambique, the United Arab Emirates is one of the largest development players in Somalia, while Turkey has launched stabilization efforts in Somaliland, which has just found substantial energy reserves off its shores.[15]

This process and the business practices that accompany it—paying bribes to corrupt officials, using imported labor rather than hiring locally, extracting energy concessions in exchange for aid—have been roundly criticized in the Western press and by governments and civil society organizations.[16] Some of that is well deserved; some of it is hypocritical, even by the low standards of international politics. For forty years the West backed some of the world's most corrupt, kleptocratic, and abusive rulers in that region—like Mobutu Sese Seko, who amassed a corrupt fortune worth almost $5 billion, while ruling a country with a GDP only slightly higher than that figure. (I am sympathetic to arguments from Western civil society organizations that aim their criticism at Western actors as well. The West has improved its aid practices and even its policing of corruption practices, but only very recently, and there are myriad examples of Western mining and energy companies engaged in highly dubious practices, in Africa and elsewhere.)[17]

What might slow this race to the bottom between the West and the rising powers is the progress made by the countries in which these investments are being made. The fact is that over the past twenty years they have experienced important levels of growth, substantial reductions in civil war, and increases in democracy.[18] The result is that many of the world's developing countries now have governments and civil societies capable of pressuring outside investors—whether from the big three or the West—to comply with basic anticorruption and accountability standards. Regional organizations play an important role here, too: even when an individual government is too weak to stand up to Chinese or Indian (or French or American) investors, the regional organizations to which they belong are able to fight for those standards and to exert diplomatic leverage as well. China and India have learned this the hard way. As countries with major stakes in various global negotiations, members of the African Union can sway global negotiations—a reality that the United States has used to its advantage in, for example, climate change negotiations (see chapter 5). China, India, and to a lesser degree Brazil all claim the mantle of leadership of the developing world and invoke that claim routinely in global institutions. But to sustain this claim they can be at odds with only so many African or Latin American developing countries at one time.

What investment by the emerging powers has done is imbue their investment decisions with the same calculation that the West has been making since the end of the cold war: that while some degree of instability in developing countries may simply be a cost of doing business (and for some emerging powers' companies, it is a comparative advantage in their competition with the more risk-averse West), conflict and collapse are absolutely bad for business.[19] Some minimum stability is a prerequisite even for mineral extraction, let alone for more costly investments in oil or gas production, which have decades-long payoff schedules. Emerging powers have thus launched efforts to stabilize states far from their immediate neighborhoods.

Investment also exposes the emerging powers to risks in the transport of materials from their overseas suppliers to their domestic markets. Most of this trade is by sea and vulnerable to disruption from piracy. Given the scales involved—roughly 90 percent of all world trade travels by sea, and trade comprises on average 55 percent of the emerging powers' GDP—this is no minor interest; it is a vital one. Interest in development follows from this need to secure other investments in these countries. Of course, this interest in development leads to competition with the West, which has dominated the development game through the Organization for Economic Cooperation and Development and the World Bank. The downside of this is even greater confusion in development standards and models; the upside is greater economic flows to developing countries and their access to the development models employed by the emerging powers themselves, which may be more suitable to them than a Western model.[20]

Exposure to unstable countries at the frontiers of their investment has also reinforced in the emerging powers their fear of radicalization and terrorism, especially Islamic terrorism. And in this they find common cause with the United States.

Terrorism and Its Proliferation to Nonstate Actors

Terrorism has been a focus of cooperation and aligned interests among the emerging powers since 9/11. This cooperation of strange bedfellows perfectly illustrates the beyond-blocs theme. Ever since 9/11 there has been substantial cooperation and policy alignment among Washington, Moscow, Beijing, and New Delhi. All of these capitals see a threat from Islamic terrorism to their domestic stability and to their networks of globalization and have been willing to cooperate to tackle it. This cooperation includes intelligence sharing and also domestic action to hinder the operations of al Qaeda cells or affiliates or financiers.

Sometimes the policy alignment between these powers has caused some of them to turn a blind eye to human rights violations by their counterparts. These include the pursuit of al Qaeda by Washington, of Islamist terrorists in the North Caucasus by Moscow, of Muslim Uighurs in western China by Beijing, and of Pakistani terrorist organizations by New Delhi. The policy alignment also includes participating in political and military stabilization efforts. Turkey, for example, is committed to supporting the complicated effort to stabilize a fragile peace in Somalia (where the United States deployed its Special Forces to counter an al Qaeda–affiliated group, al Shabab).[21] China has contributed armed peacekeepers to Mali, where another al Qaeda–inspired group, al Qaeda in the Maghreb, has attacked Western energy interests. China had previously deployed civilian peacekeepers (engineers) to a stabilization mission in Lebanon—one of whose mandates is to help the government of Lebanon control Hezbollah (a mission that has been failing, it should be noted).[22]

There has been policy tension, of course, but it is primarily among the Western powers. The United States and Europe have been divided over legal issues, in particular—the question of rendition and the legal procedures for listing and delisting suspected terrorist figures by the UN Security Council and other bodies.[23] The United States, India, Russia, and China have taken a legally minimalist view on these issues, while Europe has sought to expand legal protections.[24]

The United States has even been able to translate these shared interests into a new institution designed to generate cooperation on counterterrorism, the Global Counterterrorism Forum—an informal, multilateral mechanism established to help countries share lessons and strategies on counterterrorism strategy. It is a nice illustration of the new dynamics of global diplomacy. Although the negotiations to create the forum were strongly led by the United States, State Department officials in charge wisely brought Turkey—an American ally and a Muslim-majority one—into the leadership of the process. Here is the list of governments that have joined the forum: Algeria, Australia, Canada, China, Colombia, Denmark, Egypt, the European Union, France, Germany, India, Indonesia, Italy, Japan, Jordan, Morocco, the Netherlands, New Zealand, Nigeria, Pakistan, Qatar, Russia, Saudi Arabia, South Africa, Spain, Switzerland, Turkey, the United Arab Emirates, the United Kingdom, and the United States.[25] This is not the cast of a post-Western or post-American world; it is the list of allies, partners, and willing contributors pulled together by the United States around common interests—and a compelling illustration of what I call America's coalitional power.

There has been a similar experience in efforts to prevent nuclear materials getting into terrorists' hands. Here too the United States led in pulling together what was initially meant to be a one-time summit to galvanize states' efforts to secure their loose nuclear supplies—but that has rapidly evolved into the Nuclear Security Summit (NSS). Membership in the NSS is similar to that of the Global Counterterrorism Forum.[26] The NSS is also an example of a new style of multilateral effort. Its mode of operation is more similar to private ventures like the Clinton Global Initiative than to staid bodies like the UN Conference on Disarmament. That is, rather than coming together to negotiate dry texts that are often then not implemented, the mode of the NSS is that countries come together each year to report on actions they have taken over the previous year. This creates a kind of moral pressure on participants to take substantial actions—it is embarrassing to have to stand in front of forty-five of your peers and paper over your inability to get anything productive done in the year past.

It is another example of American coalitional power. However, here it is important to be clear that there is a difference between, on the one hand, the shared interests that the Western and rising powers have in preventing nuclear material from getting into the hands of terrorists or organized criminal groups and, on the other hand, cooperation on proliferation issues more generally. The latter is a more mixed picture.

Cooperation on terrorism extends to America's war in Afghanistan. Of course, here the issue is complicated by the fact that America's objectives are not limited to that country: its presence there has important implications for Pakistan and even Iran. The start of the U.S. war in Afghanistan occurred before the emerging powers had begun their rise and has continued during the entire period of it. It can be argued that the American focus on the long war against the Taliban, and even more so the decision to pursue nation building in one of the world's poorest countries, distracted the United States from paying sufficient attention to the important phenomena of China's and India's rise and Russia's (perhaps temporary) rebound. Seen through the lens of the Afghan war, the emerging powers are modest players, largely regional in their outlook, and—notably—broadly constructive.

At the outset of the war, the emerging powers joined the broader international reaction in supporting American action. Quite apart from the shock and the sympathy that followed the 9/11 attacks, the emerging powers had their own reasons to support American action in Afghanistan: Russia, China, and India share with recent American policy a strong opposition to Islamic terrorism. Pakistani terrorism in India, Muslim Uighur uprisings and terrorist attacks in western China, and Chechen terrorism in Russia have the same political and psychological effect on those countries that the al Qaeda attacks had on the United States.

Even Russia, which arguably had most to lose from a NATO presence in its backyard, has played a largely constructive role in enabling U.S. operations in Afghanistan, by facilitating transportation routes that make the United States less reliant on Pakistan and by supplying aviation fuel for America's extensive air operations in Afghanistan—two forms of logistical cooperation without which the U.S. presence in Afghanistan would have been enormously more complicated.[27] At times, Russia has used these supports as a source of leverage in other negotiations—but only to a modest degree, and never to the point of genuinely complicating U.S. strategy in Afghanistan.[28] That being said, a large U.S.-NATO presence in its backyard has been a concern for Russia, and Russia has been leery of ending up with permanent U.S. bases in its neighborhood. Russia's mixed interests and mixed motives were summed up for me by an exchange I witnessed between a Russian official and an American official (long-time friends) during a regional workshop I hosted on Afghanistan. The American teasingly challenged his Russian counterpart: "I've never quite been able to decide what your strategy is. Is your objective to get us to destroy al Qaeda for you? Or to see NATO bleed itself dry in Central Asia?" The Russian official smiled wryly and responded: "Why not both?"

China's motives are probably similar. These were summed up by a Chinese official (in a discrete U.S.-China exchange I hosted) who wondered why the United States would spend close to a trillion dollars in Afghanistan and Iraq and then allow China to vacuum up much of the oil and natural gas supplies in the region. Still, in the immediate sense, China supported

U.S. and NATO military action in Afghanistan, has strong interests in seeing the defeat of Islamic terrorism in the region, and has been willing to use economic and diplomatic tools to foster a stable Afghanistan. Some Chinese participants have privately floated the idea of being part of a UN-backed coalition to provide stability after NATO withdraws. The potentially massive mineral deposits in Afghanistan create strong incentives for China to invest, as it did in 2007 (putting $3.4 billion into copper mining in the Aynak deposit in Logar Province).

For India and Turkey, both key players in the region, the motives are more straightforward, but the reaction is also mixed. Both have strong interests in the outcome of events in Afghanistan, and neither seeks the erosion of American military strength. However, both, with strong interests and long-standing ties in the country, have had grave doubts at times about American strategy.[29] More to the point, as the United States prepares to draw down to a minimal presence in Afghanistan, it is leaving behind a turbulent and fragile peace, which if it collapses—as it could—would have serious repercussions in the region.

That should be a cause for concern for the United States itself (though not necessarily a cause for keeping a large troop presence there longer—that would be sensible if and only if a sustained troop presence over another several years would make a substantial difference to the prospects of long-term stability in Afghanistan, and that is far from evident). Under any circumstance, as the United States withdraws, it should surely be preoccupied by the risks that this poses for an ally like Turkey and for India. I am surprised at the very limited extent of U.S. interest in the Turkish and Indian analysis of the situation and concerns regarding strategy—a lack of willingness to pay attention to allies and friends that will increasingly prove costly to the United States.

Afghanistan, by the way, is another example of the astonishing coalitional reach of the United States. Not only was the United States able to pull NATO into the fight, despite having scorned NATO's offer to invoke its all-for-one, one-for-all clause, it also managed to pull in several other allies that were not NATO members, among them Australia, the United Arab Emirates, Jordan, Malaysia, and Singapore. Even neutral Switzerland contributed a small force. This inclusion has given rise to the notion of a global NATO or at the very least a NATO Plus—which could serve as a coalition of democracies (and a few allied nondemocracies).[30]

Counterterrorism and stability interests are even strong enough to start a dialogue between the United States and China about Pakistan, each country's erstwhile ally. China has a long-standing alliance with Pakistan.[31] It is even alleged that China supplied some of the technology and know-how for Pakistan's nuclear weapons program. It is a very unusual situation in that Pakistan is also a U.S. ally—albeit perhaps the ally with which the United States has the most tortured relationship. China and the United States have different interests in Pakistan, to say the least. But they overlap on one important point: neither desires, nor can afford, the descent of Pakistan into internal collapse and turmoil. The consequences for regional security and for global terrorism would be tremendously negative. In the summer of 2012 Beijing went so far as to reach out to Washington to suggest that the two capitals, very quietly, have a dialogue about what each could do to stabilize Pakistan (including by enhancing their cooperation on Afghanistan).[32]

Indian Ocean, Revisited: Getting It Right

With these shared interests, why do the Western powers and the emerging powers not succeed with something as comparatively simple as preventing the piracy based in Somalia? There are two problems. First, with four separate sets of naval assets, there were pretty substantial coordination problems—especially with the emerging powers' navies, which were not operating under U.S. or EU coordination. Second, there was a policy gap. The basic story is that pirates were being captured reasonably efficiently but then released. Why? Because the powers could not agree on what to do with them: sink their ships or capture them for trial. But here is the interesting point: the policy fight was not between the United States and the rising powers or between the West and the "rest." Instead, it was between the United States and the Europeans. The United States shared with India, Russia, and China the attitude that the use of force was a perfectly acceptable response; the Europeans were insisting on due process, the application of international law, and human rights. In other words, the Europeans were insisting that pirates be tried and, if convicted, held in jail.[33] But whose jails? The Europeans' insistence on human rights provisions did not extend so far that they were willing to have Somali pirates jailed on their own soil. In the absence of an answer on the legal questions, pirates were being released—and going right back to attacking ships.

Debates in the UN Security Council among the powers participating in the Somali response led to the UN secretary-general appointing a special adviser to look into how to get better results and, in particular, how to cut the legal knots. In short, a number of governments donated money to Kenya, the Seychelles, and Mauritius in exchange for them agreeing to try Somali pirates in their courts and keep them in their jails.

And the coordination problem was largely resolved as well by the establishment through NATO of the SHADE (Shared Awareness and Deconfliction) mechanism, an informal coordination mechanism in which all participating navies share information about pirates and their operations.[34] Remarkably, China, India, Russia, and all of the other nonallied navies participate in NATO's SHADE mechanism.

There were other steps as well. Efforts on land included the United States sending Special Forces into Somalia to deal with al Shabab, and the UN and the African Union mounting a joint operation to maintain security in Somalia's major port, Mogadishu. The EU sent naval patrols up Somalia's rivers to attack pirate villages on land. A political process got under way, too, with support from the United States, the United Kingdom, and Turkey. Turkey and Sweden mounted a joint initiative on economic development in Somalia, and the UAE's largest maritime business, Dubai Ports World, invested $200 million in private sector funds in Somalia.[35] The net result: piracy attacks plummeted from 286 to 99 between 2012 and 2013.[36]

The international response to piracy in Somalia is a Rorschach test of the international order. There are those, particularly in the security community, who see it as trivial: What sort of threat do pirates pose? This stance neglects the huge economic stakes: a huge volume of the world's container trade flows across the Indian Ocean, worth about $1 trillion every year. Even in a postglobal financial crisis world, $1 trillion is real money. Then there are those who see in the response dysfunction and inefficiency—does it really take several of the world's navies, and four separate operations, to deal with Somali pirates? There is obviously room for improvement here; but it is striking, too, that much of the inefficiency comes from the American alliance: three of the four operations sailing along Somalia's coast are composed exclusively of U.S. partners and allies. The fourth operation, run by emerging powers, participates in the NATO-led coordination meeting. No less a figure than Admiral Mullen, commander of the U.S. Navy during the start of the operation, has said that coordinating with the Chinese navy off the coast of Somalia has been a useful confidence-building exercise.

And thus there are those—myself included—who see in the Somali operation the upside of the current international moment. It is messy and inefficient—multinational action always is, even just with allies. This is not some false ideal of cooperation, or global governance, or the ability of the major powers, established and emerging, to cooperate for the common good. There are tensions, inefficiencies, and dysfunctions, but none of them is debilitating. And the following points all hold. The major and rising powers expressed a common objective through a common tool, the UN Security Council, which mandated the operation. The powers, both established and rising, all agreed to assume a share of the burden because they have a shared interest in protecting globalization. Other actors with growing influence, like the United Arab Emirates, are contributing as well, since they have stakes in the free flow of shipping. There were differences of policy, but these were among the Western powers and were amenable to resolution. There is scope for improvement, to be sure, but all in all the operation proved the merit of realistic, interest-based cooperation to tackle a common problem—showing that such approaches can help to build confidence and shared threat perception, as well as enable the powers to de-conflict their interests (that is, to find ways for each to pursue overlapping interests without interfering in the others' interests) a lesson that we'll come back to later in this book. And all of this, notably, is under the leadership of the United States.

Looking Ahead: Forging Deeper Ties

The United States has started down the right path on bringing the emerging powers into international efforts to tackle transnational threats and threats to globalization, building both patterns of cooperation and, where useful, multinational arrangements to structure and deepen these patterns. This cooperation is important for its own reasons but more for its function as a confidence-building measure. Deeper efforts on transnational threats do three things. They reinforce a sense of overlapping interest. They create peer-to-peer relationships among diplomats and military officers. And they help protect globalization. This could prove important as the terrorist threat evolves, as it inevitably will.

The most important place that action against transnational threats can be deepened is in the maritime domain. There are several ongoing efforts here, from Somalia to the Niger Delta to the Malacca Strait to the Indian Ocean. But the need will grow as the threat mutates. And there would be value in linking these disparate regional efforts to generate shared lessons, networks of expertise, and confidence-building measures. The United States could lead efforts to pull together an informal mechanism that brought together counterpiracy, sea-lane security, and search and rescue agreements. This would be an important step, not incidentally, in providing a global context within which to tackle the fraught maritime disputes in the East and the South China Seas (chapter 7).

One transnational threat not touched on yet is deliberate terrorist use of biological materials, and also naturally occurring infectious disease epidemics. The biological arena is often presented as the ultimate transnational, or global, issue, but in fact it also touches on core national sovereignty concerns, especially for the emerging powers. Forging an infrastructure that can deal with biological situations could be a critical test of American leadership. The United States already has one crucial piece of this infrastructure: its Centers for Disease Control and Prevention, a world-leading medical center, operates globally to help governments respond to outbreaks of infectious disease. It is in effect a global public good. But more tools will be needed.

Changes in the international distribution of power—the phenomenon of rising states—will not make the terrorist challenge harder for the United States; to some degree, these changes should make it easier. At least there are more states to share the burden. As long as the emerging powers remain wedded to globalization—and with above 50 percent of their economies deriving from international trade, they have no choice but to be—they will have important overlapping interests with the United States to secure the infrastructure of globalization. This is likely to be an enduring feature of the evolving international order, one that creates important incentives for cooperation. In this chapter, I highlight one example of that—counterpiracy cooperation. It is an easier challenge than some but illustrates both important overlapping interests and potential approaches to building on them. It involved using the UN Security Council to create both a legal basis for action—including actions that override sovereignty—and the political space to allow non-Western powers to contribute; flexible multinational instruments that combine burden sharing with genuine military heft; and U.S. coordination and leadership. It is a model whose major elements are worth trying to replicate in other areas.

And there are similar lessons to be learned from other seas. One of them is the Arctic.

CHAPTER FIVE

SHAPING IT,
NOT BREAKING IT

*Economics, Energy,
and Climate Change*

A different sea, and again the established and emerging powers encounter one another—in this case, with divergent interests and potential rivalry. During the cold war the Arctic was a zone of tense cold war rivalry. As the cold war receded, so too did the strategic significance of the Arctic.[1] In recent years, though, new tensions arose. Rapidly melting Arctic ice has meant two things: new prospects for extracting energy resources from the Arctic waters and a new passageway for sea-borne trade.[2] These changes have created a complex and, to some, a worrying political picture.

Control of Arctic navigation confers important economic, energy, and military advantages. China is set on gaining access to the Arctic's sea routes, as is India. There are also concerns that competition for energy reserves could become militarized. Russian saber rattling has aroused the greatest fears. In 2007 the Russian explorer Arthur Chilingarov led an expedition that planted a Russian flag on the Arctic seabed. Russia also has fired cruise missiles over the Arctic, resumed regular patrols of the region for the first time since the breakup of the USSR, and announced plans to augment its naval surface capabilities and submarine force for Arctic patrols. A Washington-based think tank, the Center for a New American Security, quips that "the only thing in the Arctic melting faster than the northern ice cap is the international comity."[3] In 2006 U.S. maritime strategy identified the potential for "competition and conflict for access and natural resources."[4] In 2008 the head of the Russian navy saw the potential for a future "redistribution of power [in the Arctic], up to armed intervention."

Is the Arctic emblematic of the risks inherent in the interlinked topics of economic growth, the search for energy, and climate change—or are there other lessons here?

Economic Growth, Interdependence, and the Rules of the Game

Five years after the onset of the global financial crisis, there is a bewildering array of opinion about the state of economic play. Leading economists do not agree. These are differences of diagnosis, but there are also glass-half-full, glass-half-empty debates. The implication for our understanding of the role of American leadership in the world can already be discerned.

Backdrop: The State of Economic Play

No one disputes that there has been an important degree of recovery since the global financial crisis, but assessments diverge on the pace of that recovery.[5] There are different assessments about the prospects for the emerging powers—especially the big three—to resume the fast-paced growth that characterized the past decade. Already Brazil's growth has slowed dramatically, largely due to slowing imports from China, and new questions abound about the pace of Chinese growth over the next few years, and India is facing a serious slowdown.[6] Economists also debate the pace at which the high-income economies will return to full health, especially as the eurozone crisis lingers.[7]

There is a glass-half-full, glass-half-empty debate, too, about the international financial reforms that have been put in place by the G-20 and its subsidiary bodies since the 2009 crisis. As noted in chapters 1 and 3, the major powers, the G-20, and international financial institutions did in fact perform well, and collectively, to stem the global financial crisis. Since then, the pace of performance has been slower, and however you look at the glass, it is pretty clear it is not full. Despite the range of debate among economists writing about the topic, all of them agree that there is a large amount of work to be done among the leading economies to coordinate or deconflict their macroeconomic strategies in the years ahead and to more deeply reform the financial sector to prevent another financial crisis.[8]

There is more consensus on the issues that relate directly to the topic of this book: the interaction between the rising powers and the established ones and the impact of those interactions on the future of the global economy.

First, it is clear that, if anything, the global financial crisis resulted in closer integration among the world's major economic actors.[9] That might not have been the case: the shock of the crisis might have meant a turn to nationalism and protectionism, and that has been mostly avoided. And the shock might have made for diversification of trade away from the relationships that existed before the crisis. To a mild extent that has happened, in that, as the emerging economies recovered faster than the United States and Europe, trade among the emerging economies grew faster than trade with the United States and Europe. Still, interdependence between the United States and the big three has grown, not receded, in the past five years. For example, in 2010 the growth in trade between the United States and China occurred at double the rate of trade growth between the United States and other partners.[10]

There is some evidence that there has been a degree of what economists call decoupling between the West and the rising economies.[11] That is, growth in one is not wholly dependent on growth in the other. But even those who make this case acknowledge that the decoupling has been partial and that the emerging powers' economies are still closely tied to the West when it comes to short-term growth and regular business cycles. The old saying was, "When America sneezes, the world catches cold." That is still true. What has changed is that the reverse is also true: if China, India, and Brazil catch a cold, America will begin sneezing.

Second, some of the emerging powers, and particularly China, are now facing what is known as the middle-income trap by pessimists and as the middle-income transition by optimists.[12] The point here is essentially this: if countries put the right basic policies in place, growing from real poverty to middle-income levels is not that hard. They have a big advantage in cheap labor, and they do not need to do complex things like innovate in high-tech industries; they just need to manufacture low-cost goods in low-tech industries (like agriculture and clothing). As long as there are high-income customers out there (especially in the rich West), they can grow by selling them consumer goods and agricultural goods more cheaply than those customers can produce such goods themselves.

The trap/transition is this: as these countries grow, and the incomes of their populations rise (to levels roughly in the $4,000- to $8,000-a-year range), the supply of cheap labor declines. They encounter something called structural inflation, which simply means that laborers demand better wages and better conditions, and it becomes more costly to manufacture.[13] These countries must shift to high-end manufacturing, and that means innovating in high-end technologies, with a better-educated population. It is not an impossible transition—Singapore and Korea and Japan made that transition some decades back. But it is not an easy one, either, and a lot of countries don't make it: they get stuck in a middle-income trap.[14]

Now, the big three currently have advantages that countries trying to make this transition earlier did not have.[15] There is globalization itself, which means that countries can simply import and adapt technology, rather than having to invent it—or, in the case of Chinese cyberprograms, simply steal it. There is also scale: the big three are each large enough (and collectively certainly large enough) to realize economies of scale in innovations and medium-tier industries. Further, the middle-income transition has been tried a number of times, and there is now a history of success and failure and lessons to be learned. Institutions like the International Monetary Fund (IMF) and the World Bank spend a lot of time studying these lessons. Chinese and Indian economists travel far and wide trying to understand what has and has not worked in past efforts. (India, which has a lower per capita income than China, in theory has an easier pathway ahead than China and has room to grow substantially before it hits the middle-income trap. This is one reason that some economists are more bullish about India's near-term prospects than they are about China's.)

Still, even economists optimistic about the ability of China to navigate this shift acknowledge that it requires multiple and simultaneous transitions in the way China organizes its economy. It also requires political transitions: among other things, it requires a decisive shift toward the rule of law and the liberalization of state-owned enterprises, no minor challenge.[16] Among other things, this means tackling corruption in a serious way. Corruption is compatible with early stages of growth (despite the orthodoxy in development institutions), but it is a corrosive force for a country striving for the innovation and efficiency necessary to high-end industries. China watchers who are pessimistic about the prospects of winning the fight against corruption often point not just to the scale of corruption but also to the intrinsic relationship between corruption and the dynamics of the Communist Party—and dismiss recent anticorruption efforts as paper-thin and designed only for show.[17]

Third, despite these challenges, the big three have already reached an economic scale that makes them necessary actors in the management of the global economy. The Western economies no longer, by themselves, drive global economic and financial policy. This role is shared with China, India, and, to a lesser degree, Brazil, Turkey, Indonesia, Mexico, and others. Put crudely, it is a G-20, not a G-7, world. Even the president of the United States has acknowledged this most basic reality.[18]

This chapter focuses on the following essential question: Given their new position in the global economy, are the major emerging powers hoping to challenge the rules of the game of the international economic system in some fundamental way? Or do they simply want to gain more influence over the direction of the one that exists?

Unequal Treaties and "Free Trade"

In part 1, I argue that a legacy of "unequal" treaties has shaped the emerging powers' attitudes about engagement with an international system until recently dominated by the West. Nowhere has that been more true than in free trade. But as I also point out, the emerging powers are torn: as much as they resent some of the terms of the rules of the trading system, they grew precisely by participating in that system—and their continued growth is still reliant on it.

The notion that the emerging powers would resist further unequal treaties was made evident in some of the recent rounds of negotiations in the World Trade Organization (WTO). Since 2000 those negotiations have been organized around what is called the Doha round, negotiations over issues critical to the emerging economies: trade in agricultural goods, trade in services, government procurement, and intellectual property.[19] These are among the industries most closely protected by government restrictions, tariffs, and subsidies, and they are industries essential to the growth prospects of the big three, especially India and Brazil. Not for nothing was this known as the "development round"—its objective, in theory, was to improve the economic fortunes of what were still then referred to as the developing economies of Brazil, India, China, and others.

The evolving geography of power was reflected in the negotiating configuration within the Doha process. Traditionally, although there are more than a hundred members of the WTO, the key negotiations have been undertaken by a foursome of major trading partners, the so-called quad: the United States, the European Union, Australia, and Canada. In 2006 that grouping was reshaped to add Brazil, India, and Japan; and in 2008 China was added as well.

Several iterations of the Doha round failed to reach any significant agreements on tariff reductions or the removal of other industry protections. The European countries resisted liberalization in farm trade, in the form of both opening markets and reducing subsidies. Nor were the emerging economies willing to liberalize agricultural or dismantle remaining barriers in industrial goods and services. After repeated rounds of negotiations, the Doha talks produced a stalemate.[20]

A defining moment came in 2008. Seven years of frustrating negotiations were getting nowhere. There was a proposal on the table to clear the logjam. Brazil and the United States in particular had agreed to changes on agriculture, the most difficult issue. But Brazil could not rally the other BRICS, and the United States could not get enough movement out of the European Union. And for the first time in the history of postwar trade negotiations, it was a developing country that actually stood up and walked: faced with what he viewed as an unbalanced deal, Kamal Nath, the Indian trade minister, walked away from the negotiations.[21] The emerging powers were not united over strategy; Brazil had more to gain from the deal on the table and resisted the Indian decision to walk away.[22] Still, the fact that one of the big three had the weight and the confidence to halt the negotiations was one of the earliest markers of the emerging powers' new weight in the international system and of their willingness to block new rules that did not accommodate their concerns.

Significant developments in global trade since then have not come from the WTO; they have come from the United States. As the Doha round sputtered to a halt, U.S. trade negotiator Robert Zoellick announced that the United States would shift to pursuing bilateral and regional deals. It has pursued this path, notably with Colombia and Korea. And then, in 2011 and 2013 respectively, President Obama announced U.S. engagement on two more major trade initiatives—the Trans-Pacific Partnership (TPP) and the Transatlantic Trade and Investment Partnership (TTIP). Both initiatives have a double logic: driving economic growth and reinforcing core alliances.

There is a minority but compelling view that the TPP can be viewed as a tool for isolating and containing China.[23] The upside is that the United States reinforces its relationship with its Asian allies. But the risk is that if it reinforces a Chinese perception that the Western powers have no intention of accommodating its continued economic growth, then it will reinforce patterns of strategic distrust (see chapter 6).[24] Recently, though, China has begun to explore joining TPP.

Economists are also divided on the question of whether these two trade blocs will undermine or strengthen global free trade. Does the launch of these major new trade initiatives, outside the remit of the WTO, undermine that body and the concept of open trade?[25] Or will they rejuvenate global trade more generally and, by doing so, make it possible to advance the Doha round issues in the WTO?[26] This matters, because open trade among the powers has been the bedrock of the open international system and is a potential bulwark against rising tensions (see chapter 8).

What is notable is that despite these moves, several of the emerging powers remain committed to the Doha round, as do, rhetorically, some of the Western powers. Several of the emerging powers (Brazil, Mexico, and Indonesia) put up candidates for the position of managing director of the WTO in 2012–13, all pointing out that their primary purpose was to rejuvenate the Doha round. Brazil eventually won the campaign. They have not, for the most part, attempted to forge alternative trading blocs— although some would argue that China has been consolidating its trading relationships in East Asia and that a Chinese-dominated trading bloc is becoming evident. The tension between Chinese trade developments and the TPP might be an issue in the coming years.

Tools for Financial Crisis Prevention

Meanwhile, while trying to build their own bank for development financing, the emerging powers have continued their efforts to gain more seats and more say in the IMF—the most important of the international financial institutions, because it is the place where the rules of the game are interpreted and where rescue operations for crises are mounted. The fact that the emerging powers have placed so much emphasis on gaining more influence in the IMF is strong evidence in favor of the argument that they are looking to shape the system from within, not to challenge it from without. And whereas they have been divided over the question of candidates for the helm of the IMF and the World Bank, they have maintained closer unity where it matters most—in getting more voting weight on the IMF governing board.

IMF reform created strange bedfellows. The emerging powers' claim for increasing their voting share on the board necessarily translates into fewer seats for the West. Europe, while rhetorically recognizing the rising powers' claims to greater representation, has resisted losing voting share. So when negotiations over IMF reform came to a head in 2010, the United States played a firm role—backing the emerging powers. It was the United States that brokered a deal, through the G-20, that will eventually see a shift in voting weight away from Europe, which will lose two seats (according to the EU's own determining), and toward the rising powers, which will gain in voting weight. (A senior European diplomat told me that most EU officials were "humiliated" that they had had to lean on the United States to broker the deal.)

Negotiations have broken down since, essentially because Europe has not been able to choose which countries should give up their seats. In the interim, the emerging powers established a small fund ($100 billion) to help prevent financial crises in their own economies (traditionally, the IMF's job). This has been taken by some as a clear sign of the emerging powers starting to move outside the established international economic order, the first concrete manifestation of the post Western world. Not so fast. The Contingency Reserve Arrangement (CRA) is far too small to be an alternative to the IMF.[27] And when the BRICS investment tool actually came online in summer 2013, what was its first announcement? A policy decision that the fund would only act "in lockstep" with the IMF. And who drove the decision? China. Far from evidence of challenging the existing order, it is one more indication that the emerging powers intend to exert their influence *within* the economic order.

Dollar Power

The strength and credibility of the U.S. government over seventy years has resulted in the U.S. dollar being used as an international reserve currency. This role has come to be a powerful symbol of U.S. leadership. It is now being challenged—at least rhetorically—by China.

Being a reserve currency means simply that most governments use it when conducting trade. When British and Brazilian companies sell things to one another, they do not do so in pounds sterling or Brazilian reals but in dollars. So do Chinese and Australian companies, Russian and Venezuelan companies, and on and on. The reason is twofold: using one currency as the basic reference point for trade avoids having to manage the currency fluctuations and exchange transactions associated with multiple currencies. Also, everyone has confidence that the government behind the dollar, the United States, will maintain its value; there is no risk that the country will collapse or that the currency will fold. (When U.S. politicians debate the debt ceiling, they often invoke the phrase "the full faith and credit of the U.S. government"—language drawn from the U.S. Constitution but spun to refer to the U.S. government's standing with its creditors.)

The United States enjoys some important advantages from dollar supremacy. Basically, it means this: the United States can borrow more cheaply on international markets. This is especially so in times of crisis, because when there is uncertainty, investors around the globe rush to put their money into dollars. During the global financial crisis, this advantage was an enormous one, in that it allowed the United States, unlike other governments, to borrow huge sums of capital on international markets for stimulus and recovery—more than a trillion dollars a year—at extremely low rates.[28] And in so doing, it passed on quite a lot of these costs to China.[29]

This advantage has been referred to as America's "exorbitant privilege."[30] That phrase comes from the country that has most consistently railed against the U.S. dollar's privileged role, the same country that most recently tried to put the issue up for formal negotiations—yes, France.[31] The dollar's role has also been referred to as an exorbitant burden, because it does mean that the United States is the last one holding the bag when a crisis hits. When Mexico's currency hit the skids in 1994, for example, it was the United States that acted as the guarantor of last resort—that is, the country that will pay when no one else can. The Mexican bailout cost the United States roughly $40 billion.

It matters for the global economy that someone is prepared to play that role. In the Mexican case, the logic was simple: a deeper crisis would have spread to other currencies, and in the meantime Mexico would have been unable to operate economically, including as the purchaser of billions of dollars worth of U.S. goods every year ($198 billion in 2011). The United States can share these costs, and usually does, through the IMF. But it helps to have a country that is willing to go first and pay more.

But can this arrangement endure? Why are 85 percent of global trade transactions conducted in U.S. dollars when the United States now represents only about 20 percent of the global economy?

Moving away from reliance on the U.S. dollar has been a rhetorical priority of the BRICS. In repeated summits, the BRICS have committed themselves to moving toward a more distributed system. Some of this is theoretically easy to do: for example, there is nothing whatsoever stopping India and China from denominating their large trade—more than $70 billion in 2011—in Chinese renminbi or Indian rupees. They repeatedly pledge to do so and repeatedly fail to do so.[32] If the BRICS were genuinely interested in reducing the power of the United States in the international system, this would be happening at a fast pace; but it is not. The only countries that have genuinely expanded their nondollar trade are China and Brazil.

The debate over the future of the dollar is rife with misunderstanding, much of which depends on the same basic fallacy that plagues the broader debate about the rising powers' challenge to U.S. leadership—that the U.S. dollar is *the* international currency and that at some near point it is going to lose that role altogether and be replaced by some other currency, probably the renminbi or the euro. But the essential point is that there can be more than one international currency.

Already the euro is being used as a trading currency, although the eurozone crisis may well staunch that trend; and soon the renminbi might be used more frequently by actors who trade extensively with China. If the euro and the renminbi were used more for trade in their respective regions, does this mean that the United States would lose some portion of the advantages that it has from the dollar being the dominant reserve currency? Yes, it does. Whatever percentage of international trade is denominated in those other currencies is roughly the percentage by which the United States would lose its financial advantage in overseas investments. But does this mean that the United States would lose all of those advantages? Absolutely not. There is no foreseeable scenario in which the U.S. dollar is not far and away the largest reserve currency and in which the United States does not still profit from that advantage.

Understood this way, the issue of reserve currency is a good metaphor for U.S. leadership overall: over the next decade or two, the United States—although it will continue to slip from its extraordinary recent highs—will continue to be the leading provider of reserve currency, just as it will continue to be the leading power overall.

The one event that would complicate this scenario is a systemwide crisis. If the United States were not the only guarantor of last resort, would crises be more complicated to manage? On the plus side, the presence of other financial powerhouses would mean that the United States would share the cost. If China saw an interest in forestalling the collapse of the Mexican market, for example, would it be willing to participate in a rescue? Every piece of evidence is that it would: it did when a currency in their region (Indonesia) faced a crisis in 1997, it did in response to the global financial crisis, and it did in the bailout of the euro in 2010–11. What is to suggest that it would not act in future crises? This is an essential point: China has nothing to gain and a lot to lose from the collapse of the current system and also from major crises within it. And so while China might like to see important changes in the system, it is not prepared to risk collapsing the system to get them. The same is true for India, Brazil, Indonesia, Mexico, and Turkey. Only Russia occasionally flirts with more radical proposals, but when it does, it meets strong resistance from the other emerging powers, including China.

The unity of the BRICS matters especially in matters of international currency. China cannot unilaterally shift how international trade is denominated. Indeed, across the terrain of economic issues, China has been preoccupied with maintaining BRICS unity for one simple reason: China understands that it is not now, and for a long time will not be, powerful enough to go head-to-head with the United States and win. Even if or when

acquisition, its consumption, and its contribution to climate sustainability. The reason for this is straightforward. Remember that China, India, Brazil, and Indonesia, among them, have more than 3 billion citizens. As they grow economically, they are turning poor people into middle-class consumers at an astonishing rate—already there are 1 billion middle-class consumers outside the West, and by 2020 that number will rise to 1.7 billion. Here is the issue: while these countries' GDP is climbing somewhat linearly, their increases in consumption are not linear. Middle classes consume not only more than the poor but differently from the poor. And everything they consume uses energy. This means that, to sustain their growth, the rising powers will use more and more energy—massive quantities of it. It has been estimated that to continue its growth at 10 percent a year, China would have to import almost 30 percent of the world's new energy supply—an astonishing challenge.

Backdrop: Changing Patterns

Carbon-based fuels still account for the vast majority—80+ percent—of all energy consumption, with oil being the most important of these fuels followed by coal and natural gas.[34] Between 1990 and 2008, global energy use grew by 39 percent, with an average increase of 1.9 percent a year and a decline in only one year (1992). The steepest growth in demand is among the emerging powers, with the United States experiencing a more modest but still significant increase (figure 5-1). In 2008 the United States, the European Union, and China accounted for over half of all energy use.

For the emerging powers, the demand for energy is not just about their new wealth; it is also about their continued poverty. Despite growing energy use, energy poverty remains a pressing priority in many countries, including four members of the trillionaires' club (China, Brazil, India, Indonesia). China has 423 million people and India 855 million people who rely primarily on biomass (plants and trees) for cooking, nearly half of the global total, and this is likely to be responsible for around 690,000 premature deaths from air pollution each year.

The energy needs of the countries of the Organization for Economic Cooperation and Development (OECD) are still growing. Even with efficiencies, the International Energy Agency predicts that their fuel

Figure 5-1. *Global Energy Consumption, 1990–2010*

Total primary energy consumption in quadrillion Btu

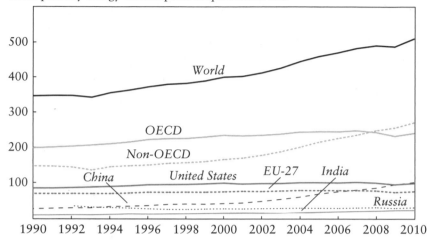

Source: U.S. Energy Information Administration, *International Energy Statistics, 2011* (www.eia.gov).

consumption will grow by roughly 3 percent by 2035.[35] But that will pale in comparison to energy consumption growth among the rising powers. There are uncertainties in the estimates, but taking modest assumptions of growth rates, projections are for a 65 percent increase in energy consumption by 2030.

The foremost consequence of this rapidly rising energy demand is that China and India will have to go out and find it. This search is already under way.[36] China's nationally owned energy companies as well as Indian companies and state enterprises have pursued a strategy of securing oil and other fuel contracts in virtually every corner of the world— from Angola to Venezuela to Kazakhstan. Indeed, by 2012, if we count oil production from assets in which China owns or holds majority stakes, China was producing 3 million barrels a day overseas, making it one of the largest oil producers in the world.

The problem with this overseas strategy is that it is vulnerable to two types of instability: political instability at the source and security risks during transport, especially through key chokepoints or where transport goes past insecure shores (like Somalia). Given energy trends, China will have more at stake in the free flow of trade through the Strait of Hormuz and the Strait of Malacca than the United States does, although it is still the U.S. Navy that safeguards seaborne trade (figure 5-2).

This vulnerability is based on China's and India's growth, which makes them hugely reliant on the import of oil from the Middle East. Oil that flows through the Strait of Hormuz is secured by America's Fifth Fleet. It cannot be easy for a rising power like China to be entirely dependent on a potential rival for the flow of its energy. India also relies quite heavily on Gulf imports, including from Iran, but it uses an overland pipeline to dedicated terminals—an issue that became sticky in the U.S.-India relationship when the United States sought to reduce other countries' imports of Iranian oil as part of U.S. sanctions on Iran (see next chapter).

So while China and India confront huge import vulnerabilities, the United States is moving toward a much more secure position and is increasingly in a position to use energy imports as a tool of foreign policy—rewarding allies, enticing new friends (like India), and holding back carrots that could be dangled in front of China. (To act, in short, like Russia.) But it is also in a position to help guarantee the flow of energy, including to the emerging powers.

Meanwhile, for the rest of the BRICS, Brazil is largely insulated from these trends, being mostly self-reliant on water-generated electricity and agrifuels. Brazil is also slated to start exporting energy when it develops a major oil find in what is known as its offshore presalt formation.

Russia is in a very different position altogether. Energy is a huge part of its economy and its export mix. Europe has been a major customer, and thus Russia has been a source of concern when it has cut off supplies to Ukraine and points beyond. Now, as Europe also looks to new sources—including American coal—Russia is also looking to diversify its exports, with the obvious market being China. There are some physical hurdles to overcome, but there will be a shift of Russian exports to China, especially as they prepare for a world in which the United States is a major exporter of natural gas.

Indeed, a growing China-Russia energy alliance is a real possibility—and one that worries me about the shape of the international order. China's managers are too clever, though, to become heavily reliant on Russia; and to balance their investments there, they have made substantial

Figure 5-2. *Chinese Oil Imports and Chokepoints*

Percent of Chinese imports from listed countries

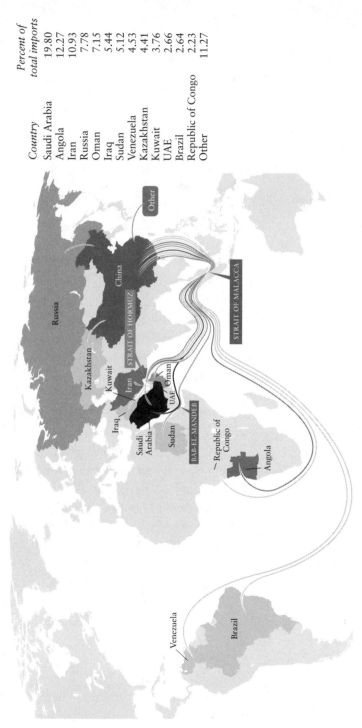

Country	Percent of total imports
Saudi Arabia	19.80
Angola	12.27
Iran	10.93
Russia	7.78
Oman	7.15
Iraq	5.44
Sudan	5.12
Venezuela	4.53
Kazakhstan	4.41
Kuwait	3.76
UAE	2.66
Brazil	2.64
Republic of Congo	2.23
Other	11.27

Source: Brookings.

investments in the United States. As the United States has unlocked new oil and gas fields, China has been investing heavily in the U.S. market. It is a point worth remembering when we turn to the U.S.-China relationship.

Energy Needs and Climate Change

The huge energy needs of the rising powers have another layer of implications: for climate change. First, China has already reached the lower end of OECD levels of energy consumption, which means huge carbon outputs, challenging efforts to mitigate the impacts of carbon on the climate; and India is set to generate the next huge set of increases in carbon production, as it grows in scale and energy intensity. Second, for China and India, it means that climate change negotiations are not just about dealing with planetary effects or water impacts or pollution, all of which matter to them but are broad concerns: it is about potentially choking off the primary ingredient needed both for growth and for poverty reduction.

No surprise, then, that climate change has been a source of clashes between the United States and the rising powers. It is an issue that has broadly united the emerging powers—for example, China, India, and Brazil hung together during the most intense phase of global climate negotiations, in the lead-up to a UN summit in Copenhagen in 2009. However, the divergence in Chinese and Indian per capita emissions are starting to strain even this tactical alliance.

There is a basic agreement in place that all countries have to reduce their emissions: the debate is about rate of reduction, how binding these commitments should be, and whether all countries will have the same target for cuts or whether the West should accept a greater share (because it contributed the lion's share of carbon emissions during its own economic rise).[37]

Negotiations on these issues have been like a road map to the new claimants to power. The summits have been held in Cancun, Mexico; Durban, South Africa; and Doha, Qatar. Each has made a microstep forward: in Cancun, a $100-billion-a-year Green Climate Fund to protect poor countries against climate change impacts and help them in low carbon development was established; in Durban, the United States reluctantly agreed to accept that the outcome of the negotiations would, eventually, be a legally binding agreement, as opposed to a looser formulation that the United States preferred (notably, it agreed under intense pressure from a joint coalition of Europeans plus the African states—another story of strange bedfellows in contemporary global politics). In Doha, some procedural obstacles were removed and "loss and damage" due to climate change was brought into the discussion, which could in principle make developed countries financially responsible for their failures to reduce emissions. But none of this has made any inroads on the core question of serious cuts, by the world's major economies, in their consumption of carbon-based fuels.

The failure to take serious steps toward climate mitigation through the UN-sponsored negotiating process is one of the major pieces of evidence used to argue that we now face a G-Zero world.[38] The failure of every summit is met with hair pulling by the world's climate community, along with denunciations of the moribund state of the United Nations. *Gridlock* is the title of one recent account of global governance institutions that uses climate negotiations as a central case study.[39]

But these arguments miss the mark. What goes by the meek term *climate mitigation* is quite simply the single most complicated economic and social transition ever attempted—the effort to shift the entire global economy away from carbon-based energy to other forms of energy, with implications for every sector, every industry, and every household in the industrialized and advanced developing world. The idea that a transition of this magnitude could be negotiated in a single global summit, or even a series of summits, is laughable.[40] The major tool for putting this idea forward and adopting it is an inclusive UN summit operated on the basis of the UN Framework Convention on Climate Change (UNFCCC). The inability of the UNFCCC process to provide a negotiated pathway to major shifts in energy and production is not evidence of a failure of global politics, but rather is evidence of the failure of imagination of the climate community to understand how to conceptualize a transition of this magnitude.[41]

Smaller, more focused bodies, like the Major Economies Forum on Energy and Climate (MEF), have had more success. The MEF is composed of the seventeen largest economies in the world and was formed by the Bush administration to tackle climate change negotiations. And while the world was lamenting the sorry state of U.S.-China relations and the general collapse of their ability, either bilaterally or collectively, to tackle major global problems, two important things were happening. In the bilateral relationship, steps have been undertaken to deepen the two economies' commitment to mitigation measures and a joint commitment to clean energy investment. And the United States used its market power to provide China with access to clean-energy technologies that only the United States (and a handful of other Western economies) can provide.

It is very rarely worth quoting the text of bilateral diplomatic statements; they are dry and dull and normally designed to paper over differences, not highlight action. So the text of the 2013 U.S.-China joint commitment on climate change is all the more striking. It starts with this: "The United States of America and the People's Republic of China recognize that the increasing dangers presented by climate change measured against the inadequacy of the global response requires a more focused and urgent initiative." Then, after some diplomatic verbiage about past efforts, the second paragraph contains the meat of the argument.

The two countries took special note of the overwhelming scientific consensus about anthropogenic climate change and its worsening impacts, including the sharp rise in global average temperatures over the past century, the alarming acidification of our oceans, the rapid loss of Arctic sea ice, and the striking incidence of extreme weather events occurring all over the world. Both sides recognize that, given the latest scientific understanding of accelerating climate change and the urgent need to intensify global efforts to reduce greenhouse gas emissions, forceful, nationally appropriate action by the United States and China—including large-scale cooperative action—is more critical than ever. Such action is crucial both to contain climate change and to set the kind of powerful example that can inspire the world.[42]

Nor were these just words. They were quickly followed by a detailed agreement (hammered out at a special U.S.-China summit in Sunnylands, California, on June 7–8, 2013) to joint efforts to cut one of the most corrosive forms of carbon emissions, HFCs (hydrofluorocarbons). At the same time, important commitments were reached in another of the trillionaires' major clubs, the Major Economies Forum (originally called the Major Emitters Forum). This body is designed to tackle climate change among the most important polluters, the top seventeen economies in the world, all of which are trillionaires.[43] Among the agreements is one on efficient buildings. This may sound like a detail, but it is far from it. In the industrialized West, buildings account for up to 40 percent of energy use. And in China and India, the issue is even more dramatic, because much of urban China and India is not yet built. As India and China grow, hundreds of millions of people are moving from rural areas to urban areas, generating massive new construction projects. If those buildings consume energy the way existing ones do, there will be very little mitigating of carbon outputs. If the buildings use new, cleaner technologies, carbon emissions will be mitigated.[44]

And how did this MEF agreement come about? Through the BRICS? Through the post-Western world? No, through U.S. leadership. In his February 2013 State of the Union speech, President Obama set a domestic goal: "I'm also issuing a new goal for America: let's cut in half the energy wasted by our homes and businesses over the next twenty years. The states with the best ideas to create jobs and lower energy bills by constructing more efficient buildings will receive federal support to help make it happen." And then U.S. climate negotiators turned the heavy diplomatic guns on MEF members, calling for two meetings in the spring of 2013, at which the details were negotiated. There is a lot still to be done in implementation, but on an issue that can make or break our energy future, there is genuine movement forward.[45]

The Strategic Consequences of Climate Negotiations

The essential issue under debate is whether the emerging powers will have the space to rise within established international economic rules or whether they will balk at the rules. For the past seventy years, one of the features of the international economic system (which the West benefited from) was continuous access to relatively cheap energy and an unlimited right to emit carbon into the atmosphere. Take away either or both of those features and the system changes significantly. So from the emerging powers' perspective, if the West is not serious about mitigating climate change or refuses to absorb the lions' share of the costs of a transition to clean energy, then it will be pulling up the ladder behind it.

For an American audience, it is perhaps easier to see this in the context of India rather than China. Put yourself in the shoes of a democratically elected Indian politician. There are still over 600 million poor people in your country—almost as many as in the rest of the world combined—and 400 million of them have no access to electricity.[46] Many of them have no access to modern energy sources at all, such as modern cooking fuels. But India has a lot of coal and can import oil and gas—all carbon-emitting fuels. Is any democratic Indian government going to consign its people to a future of poverty because global climate negotiations with the West dictate that India cannot burn carbon the way the West did during its economic rise? It is impossible. There is simply no way that any Indian politician can argue that India should curtail its own growth—or put more sympathetically, its effort at poverty reduction—to accommodate the West's belated concern for climate change. (In the United States, there is a parallel argument made about the need to continue to develop coal as a cheap energy source accessible to America's poor—though of course the United States has more options than India on this front.)

Here, though, India and China face a dilemma: carbon emissions affect them directly. In China, the continued burning of huge volumes of carbon is producing pollution on an epic scale, such that it poses a political challenge to the legitimacy of the regime. India is also terribly polluted and faces a different challenge as well: access to water. A major source of its drinkable water comes from Himalayan glaciers, and India fears that these could be threatened as climate change picks up pace.

Neither country can avoid the reality of a changing climate. If they want to grow, reduce poverty, and at the same time not face a barren climate future, they have no choice but to engage with the West on navigating a movement away from carbon-based fuels. This may seem unfair—no, actually, it is, grossly unfair; but it is a reality. How fast countries are expected to shift from carbon-intensive fuels, and who pays what share of the cost, will be hugely controversial issues and will shape each country's perception of the West. But there the simple fact that they cannot escape the consequences of climate change means that while the impulse to challenge unfair agreements and the impulse to rivalry may be strong in the realm of climate and energy, the core realities will necessitate some degree of restraint and cooperation.

There is a big bet that the United States could make, perhaps a surprising one, that would serve both to strengthen our strategic position and to improve the options for climate change. That bet is on clean energy in India. The math is simple and compelling. India has, as noted, 600 million poor people, with 400 million of them with no access to modern energy; and India's population is set to keep rising. In spite of these figures, politicians in India feel that they have no choice but to continue to pursue every source of energy, clean or not. India simply will continue to try to grow, and that inevitably means greater energy use in the near term. If India succeeds in doing what China did before, pulling 300 million people out of poverty, it means adding a population the size of Europe to the overall carbon emissions mix. They are certainly justified in doing this—what possible ethical or moral precepts could justify the West continuing to emit carbon while 600 million Indians languish in poverty. But this will crater any credible efforts to stabilize the climate.

That is, global climate mitigation will crater unless India develops on a green-energy pathway—or at least a less carbon-intensive pathway. To do this, India needs to invest between $50 billion and $100 billion over the next ten years in natural gas infrastructure, renewables, and clean building technologies. Even that sum does not capture the scale of resources necessary when considering what needs to be done at more local levels. As India's rural poor increasingly move to cities, its cities will require new infrastructure; 70 percent of its buildings of 2050 have yet to be built. If these are built with existing building technologies, massive carbon emissions will be built in. The new building can be done with green technology, but India by itself does not have the resources—financial, technological, or planning—to manage it.[47]

So India is going to need help if it is going to navigate the clean energy transition it now faces. Granted, it could reprioritize its spending and cut down drastically on its navy and other defense spending. But here is the thing: the United States does not want it to. As long as China increases its defense budget, the United States wants India to do so, too. As long as China is investing in its blue-water navy, the United States wants India to do so, too. It is profoundly in the U.S. interest that there be a strong and growing India, an India that is domestically stable and contributing to a stable Asia and Indian Ocean.

The United States can make a critical difference here. It could reapportion part of its international development budget toward India's effort and push for greater allocations by the World Bank and other international institutions. It could create a way for U.S. cities that have successfully used clean building techniques to work with Indian cities. It could invest in Indian education in urban development that uses the latest science.

This is the only way India can navigate the energy transition it faces—and also the only hope of stabilizing the climate. If the United States takes the lead on helping India navigate toward clean energy—not using climate negotiations to pull up the carbon ladder behind it but using bilateral ties and the MEF to offer to help build a clean energy ladder for India—it could be the kind of investment that cements ties between these two countries. From the perspective of a stable international order, that is a big deal: the United States and the international order are better off if India is strong, growing, and stable—and increasingly friendly to the United States.

Back in the Arctic

And back in the Arctic? Rather than a deepening of tensions, there has been the opposite: the emergence of new tools for deconfliction and cooperation; the morphing of rivalry into restraint.[48]

Some of the Arctic powers have solved bilateral disputes. Norway and Russia have signed the Barents Sea treaty, bringing to a close a nearly forty-year dispute. This not only settled a boundary dispute but also established an important precedent: a commitment that transboundary energy reserves will be exploited as a shared unit. (The basic reason for Russia's interest in resolving the dispute was that it needs access to Norwegian technology for northern energy exploration.) There was an agreement among the five major Arctic countries to resuscitate the Arctic Council as a forum for the management of different interests, and there was an agreement (the Nuuk Declaration) for joint and coordinated search and rescue efforts. Norway and Denmark played a major role in forging these cooperative documents. This is a pattern in international politics that gets little attention but that is important to a stable international system: when tensions between bigger powers rise, middle powers can step in to negotiate a pathway forward. Most important was the signing of the Ilulissat Declaration in May 2008, which, despite its brief seven paragraphs, codifies a decision by all of the leading Arctic players to peacefully resolve disputes over their continental claims. This is accomplished through the UN Convention on the Law of the Sea and its tribunal for dispute resolutions, which has already been invoked by Russia.

These agreements could be precedents for cooperation on similar issues in other contested seas: freedom of passage, the protection of indigenous rights, and minimum standards for oil and gas exploitation. Already China and other claimants have been granted observer status at the Arctic Council, bringing them into a cooperative framework for managing the Arctic (though I believe that U.S. diplomacy missed a trick by not making the arrangement contingent on progress toward a code of conduct for stable behavior in other contested seas).

In the Arctic, despite the potential for economic and energy interests to feed security tensions, an alternative approach prevailed: the forging of multinational agreements to lower tensions and reconcile interests.

Sustaining Globalization

Others have written extensively about what still needs to be done to return to genuine growth in the U.S. economy—both in terms of the domestic steps that the country has to take (balancing continued stimulus with a medium-term plan for debt reduction, continuing to tackle household debt, and investing in flexible education and smart infrastructure) and in terms of the global challenge. At the global level, two things stand out: the need for countries of the G-20 to coordinate their macroeconomic policies; and the need for multinational negotiations over the rules governing financial institutions.

Among the necessary measures is revisiting the Financial Stability Board (FSB), which was established in the wake of the global financial crisis. There is virtually no economist who believes that the FSB is equipped to prevent another crisis. Economists believe that an FSB 2.0 is going to be necessary, alongside continued efforts at IMF reform. In all of this the United States will have an essential role but should approach the issues with some humility: despite the talents available to the United States from Wall Street and the administration, it was Wall Street and the U.S. Treasury that brought us the biggest financial crisis since World War II. The United States should pay attention to and learn from countries that have done a better job of growing their economies while managing financial risk.

The economic realm is a microcosm as well as a critical element of the changing order: there are both an impulse to rivalry and an impulse to compete. There are also powerful incentives for restraint. But in navigating the balance between rivalry and restraint, attention must be paid to energy and to the way changing energy patterns affect relations among the United States, the allies, and the emerging powers. Where there are no tools to manage relations between the major players, they should be forged. One notable weakness is that the main international mechanism for dealing with energy, the International Energy Agency, has only Western members. In other words, several of the world's largest consumers—including China and India—are not among the members of the main body charged with helping the world's major energy consumers maintain price stability in global energy markets and organize emergency reserves. An "outreach" mechanism for China, India, Brazil, Mexico, Indonesia, and South Africa was recently agreed to by the IEA board, but it remains to be seen whether this light mechanism results in genuine coordination; a stronger tool may be needed. And given America's rising energy strength, it is in a strong position to forge it.

And then there is climate change. I cannot do justice here to the overwhelming challenge that climate change poses. Here, I only highlight two issues. First, that climate change ought to be understood as part of Washington's core strategic relationships with the emerging powers, rather than only an energy and economic issue. Second, rather than focusing on large, complex deals negotiated through the United Nations, the United States is going to have to focus on concrete, practical steps that can move it from the current unsustainable pathway to a more realistic pathway— probably blending natural gas, efficiency measures, and renewables. The United States will have to start at home and build outward. In this sense, the United States is a poor leader: its per capita energy emissions are triple those of the next country. But it also has the potential to be a leader in a genuine sense; as its per capita emissions have started to fall—and as they fall farther as new regulations come onstream—the country has begun to work with China on bilateral efforts. It can build on these efforts in concentric circles, outward, using flexible, multinational arrangements like the Major Economies Forum and the G-20 to drive concrete actions. And it can use its leading technology to help countries chart effective pathways to cleaner energy. That is the only way to bridge the need to stabilize the climate with the need to accommodate the growth of the rising powers. The lessons from the Arctic show that it is possible to take an issue that generates rivalry and forge the tools necessary for restraint—even cooperation.

CHAPTER SIX

MUDDLING THROUGH AND MISSED OPPORTUNITIES

Crises and Intervention

There is another instance of the emerging and established powers cooperating on the high seas, and it is off the coast of Lebanon. There, in the eastern Mediterranean, the Turkish, Indonesian, and Brazilian navies copatrol alongside those of France, Germany, Spain, and the Netherlands, monitoring the boundary between Israeli and Lebanese waters.[1] But in Lebanon, cooperation between these powers is not limited to the seas; it extends to land as well—troops from Brazil, China, Turkey, India, and Indonesia form part of a peacekeeping force alongside troops from France, Germany, and Spain, among others. These troops were deployed under an unusual arrangement put in place by the United Nations in August 2006 to help stabilize Lebanon after a thirty-four-day war between Israel and Hezbollah.

One of the sharpest claims of the "coming disorder" and the decline of the American-led world is that the emergence of new powers will erode the ability of the Western-led order to manage crises—or at least that signs of this phenomenon are becoming evident.[2] When crises raise the prospect that one or more of the major powers may intervene in the conflict, they pull on the most sensitive trip wires in international politics, the issues of sovereignty and the use of force. The further risk is a return to proxy wars that characterized the U.S.-Soviet entanglement in the Middle East, South Asia, and other parts of the developing world during the cold war. Proxy wars risk direct U.S.-Russian or perhaps U.S.-China confrontation, to say nothing of tremendous human suffering.

Russian and Chinese intransigence over potential UN action in Syria, and that country's descent into a hybrid internal, regional, and proxy war, is a case in point.[3] Indeed, Syria has become a kind of perverse poster child for deadlock in the international system and the collapse of American leadership.[4]

Consider the following. A ruthless government with a strong and effective army is attacking civilians, using every weapon in its arsenal. An opposition is fighting back, but the violence has already produced tens of thousands of deaths and the outflow of hundreds of thousands of refugees. The UN Security Council, deadlocked over forceful action, is limiting itself to expressions of "grave concern." It agrees only to deploy an unarmed civilian monitoring team, which will, later, have to retreat under fire. Russia is leading the opposition to the more forceful UN intervention. The United States is contemplating intervention through NATO but is hesitant. It continues to pursue diplomacy with Russia to see whether a peaceful resolution can be found. Is this Syria at the onset of American decline? No, it is Kosovo in the fall of 1998, at the peak of American power.

To point to past tragedies is not to downplay the significance of new ones, but the past does serve to remind us to use a reasonable yardstick in assessing the current landscape. And the fact is, in the contemporary moment, Syria is an exception, not the rule. There is little in this landscape to indicate a decisive shift to international deadlock and proxy war. Different crises elicit different behavior, and across the range of cases we see repeated instances of joint action and cooperation, as in Lebanon. Only one type of crisis—authoritarian crackdowns on a civilian population—divides the powers. And even then there are important divides among the emerging powers; some of them—notably Brazil and India—are on the fence about issues of intervention. The United States has missed important opportunities to pull these states into broader political coalitions in support of crisis action. Fixing that is essential to effective international crisis management. If deadlock between the Western and the authoritarian powers over the crisis in Syria were symptomatic of a broader breakdown, then we should already be seeing signs of a breakdown of efforts through the UN Security Council to respond to internal wars, both to protect the state and to protect citizens. But the opposite is true.

Internal Wars and Threats to the State

Coordinated international responses to internal wars have not always been a feature of the international system. Indeed, during the entire cold war, international engagement to contain or mitigate civil wars and humanitarian crises was rare.[5] Humanitarian assistance was confined to refugees—a status people could claim only after they crossed an international border. The phenomenon of international mediators trying to forge a peace agreement in internal wars, of international peacekeepers deployed to quell violence inside the borders of a state, of humanitarian workers deployed inside a country at war—these are all creations of the post–cold war era.

This first wave of increasing involvement in internal wars occurred before the emerging powers had experienced their growth spurt and before they had begun to assert themselves on the international stage; and it also happened at a moment of Russian internal disarray. China already had a permanent seat on the Security Council, though, and used it to vote in favor of no less than fifty instances of UN peacekeeping interventions, including operations that used force and overrode sovereignty.[6] India participated, too, as the largest troop contributor to UN peacekeeping operations. In the 1990s the state of the Indian economy was such that India still fell into a category of states that profited from participating in UN peacekeeping operations by virtue of having its soldiers reimbursed at a higher rate than they were paid domestically. Those days are long past, yet Indian troops continue to form the bulwark of UN operations.

The first decade of the new century, when the emerging powers were starting their ascent, saw a dramatic expansion of international involvement in internal wars, both through the UN and through NATO. Ironically, the George W. Bush administration oversaw the largest-ever expansion of NATO's engagements in internal wars (in training operations in Iraq and in combat operations in Afghanistan) and the largest-ever expansion of UN peacekeeping and of the powers and scope of the UN Security Council. When Bush entered office, there were just over 20,000 UN peacekeepers deployed internationally; when he left, there were just over 100,000.[7] Presiding over this expansion, Washington encountered no resistance from the rising powers and, in many cases, had their active agreement.

Not all of these conflicts mattered in any meaningful way to international security or to relations among the major powers, so the cooperation there may not signify much. That being said, it is easy to forget what actual deadlock in the Security Council looked like and how commonly small wars in what seemed like geopolitical backwaters became the site of proxy wars between the cold war rivals.

A reasonable measure of whether a conflict matters in geopolitical terms is the military engagement of the top powers. So we could, for example, look to those places where the United States (or one of its close Western allies) has deployed special operations forces. If the United States is deploying one of its most valuable fighting assets, there must be some salience to the conflict. If Russia and China, or other of the emerging powers, were unwilling to join forces with the West to quell internal conflicts, these would be natural places for this opposition to emerge. Yet in Yemen, Somalia, Mali, and Uganda, where Western special operations forces have been deployed, this is not evident. For each one a decision by the unified UN Security Council has been made, and a range of international actions has been designed to help contain the conflict, protect the state, or protect civilians from the worst abuses.

Have any of the rising powers—particularly China, India, Brazil, Turkey, Mexico, and Indonesia—sought to weaken this effort? No, they have not, and for two reasons. First, they have a strong disposition to protect sovereignty, since sovereignty is a bedrock principle of international order and essential to their claim to internal cohesion. Second, they have a growing network of interests in every region and subregion of the world, and for this reason have a stake in cooperation with these powers.

As members of the trillionaires' club, the rising powers increasingly participate in international conflict management. Notably, the United Nations authorized a forceful operation into Mali in 2013, after an al Qaeda affiliate attacked Western oil interests in neighboring Algeria. China actually contributed 500 troops to the force.[8] The UN action is a vivid illustration of two things: blockage in the UN Security Council over Syria is not spilling out into a wider stalemate; and (as pointed out in chapter 4) China is interested in stabilizing its far-flung sources of energy and resources. Because China does not have the military capacity to do that alone, working through the UN is its best option. And China is not alone in using the UN to help secure stability where its own power does not extend. Brazil led the UN operation in 2004 to stabilize Haiti and continues to lead it still. And in 2013 it agreed to provide the military leadership for one of the most complicated forces the UN has mounted in the post–cold war era—an "intervention brigade" in the eastern Congo, designed not merely to keep the peace but also to enforce it against rebel militias.[9] Turkey, as noted, has engaged in mediation and peace-building activities in Somalia and Somaliland. And Russia voted alongside the United States and China in favor of establishing each of these operations.

Much of this has been done by UN-commanded peacekeepers and some of it by regional organizations. Less common but not unheard of has been the deployment of what are known as UN-authorized multinational forces: a few member states joining forces under UN authority but not direct UN command. Such a force deployed to eastern Congo in 1995 to stop large-scale killings there, and a similar force stopped a slaughter by Indonesian forces in East Timor in 1999. And when Israel and Hezbollah clashed in southern Lebanon in 2006, a variant on this model was deployed; it combined the unifying mechanisms of UN command with the efficient logistics and command and control capacities of individual troop contributors.[10] I believe that this instrument—multinational peacekeeping—may prove quite valuable in the period ahead.

In short, the business of quelling internal crises has become the norm, not the exception; and the rising powers have only increased their engagement as their influence has risen.

Interventions: Crises of State Abuse

More controversial, of course, is the notion of intervening to protect citizens against the state itself—to intervene not with the consent of the state in question but precisely against it.

Another strong claim of the post-Western-world argument is that the rising powers will want to rewrite the rules of the game to their advantage. But the most important rewriting of the rules we have encountered is about the relationship between sovereignty and intervention—and it is the West that is doing the rewriting.

Few issues in international politics so easily roil and divide countries as the topic of humanitarian intervention—and for good reason. Sovereignty and the requirement of states not to interfere in each other's affairs are cardinal principles of the international order. They reduce interstate conflict and protect weak states against occupation and colonization. In practice, though, they are also principles that leave peoples unprotected when their state turns against them—and in those instances, they are in direct tension with other important principles of human rights and freedom.[11]

As newly influential actors enter the global diplomatic stage, issues of self-determination and human rights are becoming more controversial. This may seem odd: as formerly colonized states, countries like India and Brazil have long spoken out in defense of downtrodden states. But here we return to the psychology of the emerging powers, which view themselves as having suffered the consequences of Western domination of the international system. Western observers of India, Brazil, China, and other emerging players often neglect to acknowledge that, as recently as the 1980s, these countries were the subject of intrusive financial pressure from Western-led institutions and, for some of them, various forms of sanctions as well. They have watched neighbors and friends experience Western military intervention. And they are firmly opposed to the use of coercion that violates other countries' sovereignty (except, in the case of Russia, when it does it itself). The notion that what happens inside a country's borders is a matter of concern for more than that country's government sits uneasily in Brasília and Delhi, let alone Beijing.

It is not that the emerging powers have fully formed views on the issues; in fact, they exhibit a great deal of confusion on the point. Just as in their efforts to reform, but not break, the free trade and financial systems they long resisted, they are torn between the old and the new—an old impulse to resist intervention and new interests in the outcomes of events in far-flung places.

Libya and the Responsibility to Protect

The debate over these principles came together in a powerful fashion in early 2011. All of the major emerging powers—and the full membership of the BRICS—were present in the UN Security Council in 2011. It was their chance to show what they could do on the world stage. Unfortunately for them, the citizens of the Arab world stole their thunder, for January 2011 was also the start of the Arab Spring. This began with citizens' revolts in Tunisia and Egypt and led to the collapse of those two regimes and to a broader uprising across the Arab world.

The uprising also took root in Libya, which at the time was ruled by the idiosyncratic and brutal Muammar Qaddafi. The Libyan uprising quickly turned bloody, as Qaddafi sought to suppress it with force. The United States, after some dithering—and under pressure from other Arab states, the United Kingdom, and France—decided to join a coalition of states to stop Qaddafi's forces as they prepared to stop the opposition in Benghazi.

On March 13, 2011, the League of Arab States, in a highly unusual move, called for international intervention to halt the violence in Benghazi.[12] Traditionally, there has been no body in international politics more skeptical of outside intervention than the Arab League, so this was a striking and important shift—and evidence of the widespread loathing of Qaddafi in the Arab world. The United Kingdom and France had already offered a resolution in the UN Security Council calling for the establishment of a no-fly zone in Libya, but they had received little support for it—including from the United States, which was hesitant to get involved in yet another war in the Arab world.

On March 16, just three days after the call for intervention, I attended a dinner during which I was offered a glimpse into the White House decisionmaking process regarding Qaddafi's forces entering Benghazi. Also present at the dinner were Denmark's prime minister and its national security adviser. These men had just been to see President Obama and the U.S. national security adviser, Tom Donilon, to discuss Afghanistan and Syria. (Denmark's former prime minister, Anders Fogh Rasmussen, was then the secretary-general of NATO, so Denmark wielded a degree of influence in NATO circles.) Three other guests were at the dinner, one of whom was a senior figure from Human Rights Watch.

This advocate spent much of the dinner on his Blackberry, because Human Rights Watch contacts were receiving real-time reports about Qaddafi's troops massing outside of Benghazi, and he was relaying the messages to contacts inside the White House. The Danes spent a lot of time on their Blackberries, too, reinforcing a message they had given in their meetings with Obama: If you go in, NATO will be with you. Later, people would accuse the United States of having always intended to enter Libya for regime-change purposes. But watching the exchanges between my dinner companions and the White House that night, and through other contacts with American decisionmakers at the time, I am convinced that the critical piece of information that shifted Obama's decision was the human rights community's reporting—detailed, real-time, on-the-ground reporting—of the impending entry into Benghazi of Qaddafi's forces, an action that would likely have been accompanied by thousands of civilian casualties. That evening, President Obama made the decision in principle that the United States should try to stop the killings.

President Obama also set two important conditions: he wanted NATO to commit to leading the operation after a short initial phase; and he wanted UN Security Council backing. And so U.S. ambassador Susan Rice was sent to the Security Council to get it.

The atmosphere inside the Security Council chamber the next day was tense. The decision to call for a meeting on short notice on the Libya question suggested a major shift in the U.S. position. And yet for the first several minutes that Ambassador Rice spoke in the council, the U.K. and French ambassadors were deflated; they thought that she was again arguing against the no-fly zone. In effect, she was: a no-fly zone was going to be ineffective and insufficient, she argued. Rather, if Qaddafi's forces were going to be stopped from entering Benghazi, a far more substantial military action had to be authorized. It began to dawn on the council that Rice was not arguing against a no-fly zone so much as arguing for a far more ambitious military intervention.[13] Later some states would argue that they were misled about American intent—but certainly, no one in the Security Council that day could have been misled about the fact that major force was going to be deployed in the Libyan theater.

And thus the emerging powers were put to the test, sitting at the decisionmaking table as a critical test of international order was put to them. Their reaction was confused.

At first China, Russia, Brazil, India, and South Africa voted in favor of three actions by the Security Council—referring Qaddafi to the International Criminal Court; imposing sanctions (no minor step for China,

India, and Brazil, which historically oppose the use or threat of sanctions); and most impressive of all, invoking for the first time the concept of the "responsibility to protect" (R2P), which implicitly threatened coercive action should Qaddafi fail to stop the bloody crackdown. Then, when the situation worsened and the United States decided to push for military action, the emerging powers were more or less united, even though in a kind of odd fence-sitting way: Brazil, India, China, and Russia abstained on the UN vote.[14] Brazil and India both argued for more time, stating that they did not know what was happening on the ground and sought more information from an African Union mediator who had been dispatched to try to talk Qaddafi out of the attack. This was a rather hapless protest from two powers arguing for permanent seats on the Security Council. South Africa voted in favor of the resolution, while the West saw one defection, as Germany abstained. Still, most observers saw the emerging powers' votes in glass-half-full terms—the emerging powers may not have been full throated in support, but they did not vote against; and the Russian and Chinese decision to abstain, not veto, was clearly significant.

Anyone in any doubt that the United States is still the leading power in the world should go back to the days immediately before and after the decision to act in Benghazi. One allied diplomat described it as if someone had flipped a switch: "Before the U.S. decision, we were dithering in the dark. The day after, the massive machinery of the U.S. military and intelligence communities were in full gear, and we were surging to action under the floodlights."[15] Only two days later, France and the United Kingdom would begin flying sorties over Libya, and the next day, the United States began a massive aerial and sea-based bombardment of Libya's air defenses and Qaddafi's forward forces in Benghazi. After two weeks, Qaddafi's forces were seriously degraded, and the United States handed the baton back to NATO to complete the operation, which it did over the ensuing months. By then, however, a liberated opposition was in full-scale civil war against the remnants of the regime, and the West's judgment—correctly, I would argue—was that there was no way of avoiding a deterioration into sustained war without going the rest of the distance: overthrowing Qaddafi's regime. So NATO turned its efforts to the redoubt of Qaddafi's forces and loyalists, Tripoli and Qaddafi's home town of Sirte. It took another three months to complete the overthrow of Qaddafi.

In all of this, I believe, the Western coalition made three mistakes, and it missed opportunities with some of the emerging powers.

First, most important, having overthrown Qaddafi, the Western powers then shied away from mounting a short-term multinational stabilization operation. The rebels did not want one—but given that NATO had just removed Qaddafi for them, NATO was in a pretty strong bargaining position. In the absence of a stabilization operation, a series of problems arose in post-Qaddafi Libya: internal violence; threats against the nascent government, including from radical Islamist groups; and the outflow of both militias and weapons to neighboring Mali. Among other effects, these complications gave ammunition to those actors who saw the application of the R2P principle in Libya as a mistake.[16]

Second, earlier, as NATO was shifting strategy from protecting civilians in Benghazi to overthrowing the regime, no one had the foresight to talk to the emerging powers in the Security Council. A lot of effort had gone into securing their positive vote on the first resolution and their consenting abstentions on the second. But when the action shifted away from the United Nations and toward NATO, neither London nor Paris—nor Washington—thought to keep those powers in the loop. This should be Diplomacy 101—in fact, it is Human Relations 101: if you want support from someone later, you have to keep them in the loop when you are making your decisions. By excluding these emerging powers from the diplomacy on Libya after the second resolution, NATO reinforced their concerns that the West would merely maintain a façade of consultation with them and treat the resolution as a blank check. And, indeed, the emerging powers reacted furiously to the West's decision to extend the operation to the overthrow of Qaddafi. A senior aide to Hillary Clinton later acknowledged that U.S. actions could be seen as having inadvertently pulled a bait and switch.

Third, the Western powers missed an opportunity to repair the diplomatic damage and build a wider consensus on R2P issues. The opportunity came when Brazil rejoined the debate, after Libya, with the introduction of a proposal on what they termed "responsibility *while* protecting"—the notion that any body (like NATO) authorized by the Security Council to undertake an R2P operation should report to the council regarding their efforts to protect civilians.[17]

Brazil's proposal was poorly timed and went too far. Launched while temperatures from the diplomatic fallout on Libya were still high, it was received by many in Washington as a direct criticism of U.S./NATO actions. It asked for too much by way of Security Council oversight of operations, conditions that no troop contributors would ever consent to.[18] But in dismissing the concept out of hand, the West also missed an opportunity to generate deeper involvement by Brazil and thereby create a powerful non-Western voice in support of this principle.

Brazil is a country deeply rooted in traditions of nonintervention and deeply suspicious of the West's interventionist past (a pretty well-rooted suspicion in any Latin American country), so it is important to record where Brazil's position paper started: acknowledging the R2P principle by affirming that there are circumstances that warrant outside military intervention in defense of human rights.[19] That is a hugely important normative evolution for Brazil and one that could be captured and built on. (Brazil had earlier been heavily involved in promoting the more limited concept that peacekeeping operations should adopt "protection of civilians" mandates and not be limited to stopping fighting between state forces and rebels.) The Brazilians were aiming for rather too much in their proposal, in terms of the degree of oversight suggested over NATO or other coalition actions; but diplomatic negotiations could easily have produced a more workable compromise. If some formal reporting—with no impact on NATO operations—is what it takes to broaden the coalition in support of humanitarian intervention, it seems a pretty minor price to pay (and one that NATO has accepted before, in Bosnia).[20] Later, after temperatures had cooled, some officials in the U.S. National Security Council regretted their rejection of Brazil's proposal: "We were too hasty," one told me. "We should have grabbed the paper and worked with them to widen the R2P consensus beyond the West."

It is not the last time the United States failed to understand the domestic situation that influenced emerging powers' offers nor the last time opportunities will be missed to bring these powers into a coalition with the West. But as to the notion that these misunderstandings and missed opportunities are hardwired into relations between the powers, I doubt it. While the fallout over Libya was in full swing, there was another vote in the UN Security Council—this one, almost entirely ignored in the Western media.

It was a decision to mount a forceful operation in the Ivory Coast, where a recalcitrant government was refusing to stand down after losing closely fought elections. The French government sought a resolution in the UN Security Council to authorize, under the R2P principle, a military operation to compel the government's compliance. The vote was 15-0 in favor, with Russia, China, India, Brazil, and South Africa joining the majority. In other words, these emerging powers voted in favor of using force to compel a sitting government to stand down in the face of democratic elections.

The experience in Libya illuminates an important challenge for American foreign policy. In military terms, for some time to come, the West will be able, should it choose, to ignore the concerns of the emerging powers when issues of crisis management and intervention arise. But there will be costs. If countries like Brazil and India and Turkey believe that the West will continue to use its military muscle to dominate international debates, they will harbor resentment and anti-Western sentiment—hardly a positive for the United States in today's complex and shifting international terrain. This is not a question of the United States giving up on fundamental goals, like defense of freedom and human rights, in order to foster good relations with newly influential powers. At least it was not the case in Libya. Rather it was a question of tactical mistakes and old diplomatic habits that have yet to adapt to new realities. The good news is, these are (relatively) easily fixed.

Is it worth the effort? Does the issue of Security Council authorization matter? I believe the answer is yes, for the following reason. It goes to the debate over the concept of legitimacy—one of the most debated concepts in international politics but one that reduces to this: countries involved in forging the rules follow the rules with some degree of willingness, notwithstanding the fact that there is genuine power behind those rules, too. This is a complex issue, one that has not been resolved through years of political science debate.[1]

My own take on the phenomenon of legitimacy, from the experience of dealing with states interacting with one another in the Middle East peace process, at the Security Council, in the international financial institutions, is as follows. For starters, most state officials, most of the time, understand the realities of power: there is the United States, in a category of one; there are other major powers—the Soviet Union during the cold war and now constellations of European, Pacific, and non-Western powers; and there is everybody else. There are two categories of everybody else: the middle and regional powers (those with enough economic and political weight to protect their interests through bilateral ties to one of the bigger players) and the rest of the world (those that have to submit to outside pressure and influence from larger powers).

International outcomes on any issue that matters (as distinct from the hundreds of irrelevant resolutions, outcomes, and so on that are negotiated through international bodies) are mostly a result of negotiations among the major powers, although these outcomes leave some space for negotiations between the major powers and the middle powers—and often have some small degree of rhetorical accommodation of the concerns of the rest of the world. It helps state elites in the middle powers explain the outcomes to parliaments or populations at home if they can say that they were in the room when the decisions were made. (For the most part, of course, they were not: they were in the corridor outside the room where the decision was made—but close enough for public consumption.) This is the core of legitimacy—it is a sweetener that helps the middle and regional powers swallow the pill of great power politics. This definition of legitimacy should not be discounted. It is going to be more, not less, important in a world in which several non-Western powers want a seat at the decisionmaking table and have the economic and diplomatic capacity to complicate crisis management efforts.

The Tragedy of Syria

A much tougher problem than Libya is Syria. It has been argued that the fallout from Libya helped to scuttle the prospects for unified action in Syria, when the Syrian government began attacking its civilian opposition. In fact, there is scant evidence for this. Russian opposition to Western military action in Syria has deeper roots.[22]

Syria has been the subject of an intense game of diplomacy and tactical maneuvering between the Western powers, on the one hand, and Russia and China, on the other—with India and Brazil, sitting on the Security Council for some of this, caught in the middle. Mediation has been tried twice, once through the offices of Secretary-General Kofi Annan and then through the negotiator who two decades earlier had brokered the end to the Syrian invasion of Lebanon, Lakhdar Brahimi. Syria has become the site of what amounts to proxy war: the rearming and diplomatic protection of the government by Russia; the arming and training of some of the rebels by a combination of the United States (training and civilian assistance) and European allies (diplomatic recognition, coalition building among the rebels, governance support); the deployment and support of Hezbollah by Iran; and support to other rebels, including Islamists or rebels with ties to Islamist groups, by other powers (including Qatar). The prospects for anything other than an anarchic outcome have receded.

There is some truth to the claim that the Libya debate influenced attitudes toward Syria, but this had limited impact on outcomes. It is true in the case of Brazil, but that does not matter much, because by the time the crisis was in full swing, Brazil's two-year tenure on the Security Council had come to an end. And divisions over Libya influenced the first vote that India took on Syria, voting against the West. But broader realities soon intervened on Indian policy. After their first negative vote, the Saudis sent a clear message to India: Shift your vote or kiss goodbye your access to Saudi oil reserves in the event of a crisis with Iran.[23] Also, the consequences for the U.S.-India relationship were impressed upon Delhi, and this resulted in two things. One, in the second vote, India voted in favor of the West's resolution, which called for Assad's removal. Two, the Indian national security adviser, Shivshankar Menon, told the U.S. deputy secretary of state, William Burns, that India was prepared in principle to support intervention in Syria as long as the United States could explain the plan for what came afterward. That, the United States could not do.

Most important: there is very little evidence that Russian opposition to intervention in Syria has anything to do with Libya. Russia is typically suspicious of any interventions other than its own. More specifically, Russian opposition to the West's position in Syria had two strategic logics. First, Syria was one of Russia's few remaining allies in the world and the site of its only base outside former Soviet territory. Second, Russia had a genuine concern that the fallout from chaos in Syria would be the metastasis of a new strand of Islamic radicalism, made all the more worrying for Russia because of strong links to Islamic radicals in Chechnya.[24] The United States offered no compelling counter to this argument. There is no reason to believe that had the Libya operation not happened, Russia would have been quiescent about the prospects of Western military action in Syria. As for China, it is uncomfortable in general with humanitarian interventions, does not want to see an expansion of NATO's presence in the Middle East, and was unconvinced by U.S. explanations about its strategy—such as it was. And so China basically followed the Russian line—with some discomfort, given its oil interests in the Gulf.

As a result, Syria has descended into internal war and bloody government oppression and has become the site of a potential regional sectarian war.

Ultimately, U.S. forces may have to go into Syria, most likely in a scenario of Assad collapsing and the situation descending into even greater anarchy, with large-scale sectarian killings of minority groups. In such a context, U.S. marines who are forward deployed in Jordan to deal with the chemical contingency could move in to secure key facilities, including the airport; and a U.S.-led multinational force could be deployed.[25] The lore about multinational operations is that they are cumbersome. But the reality is, they can be fast: in 2006 the UN deployed a multinational force into Lebanon in just under a week. The presence of French, German, Italian, and Indian troops in southern Lebanon, as little as twenty-five miles from Damascus, would ease deployments into Syria.[26] Russia might well also choose to deploy its forces, especially into Alawite areas. This could result in clashes between U.S. and Russian forces, but just as feasibly it could result in deconflicted deployments of the kind that occurred in Kosovo in 1999.[27] Brazil has signaled that it would be willing to participate in a coalition of multinational forces if the UN Security Council authorizes it—which it would probably easily do, given that, in that scenario (after the fall of Assad), Russia would far rather see a UN-mandated force than a NATO one.

But here is the tragedy: given that the major powers may ultimately have to deploy a range of forces to stabilize a post-Assad Syria, they could have done so earlier, in the spring of 2012, to avoid the huge civilian death tolls since then.[28]

For this to have been a credible scenario the United States would have had to put less explicit emphasis on Assad's departure. That would have been tricky given the abuses he had already committed at that stage; but it is worth recognizing here that U.S. policy in Syria has turned on its head Theodore Roosevelt's injunction to great powers—to talk softly and carry a big stick. By insisting that Assad must go but not being willing to put the weapons or military skin into the game to make this happen, the United States narrowed the range of options dramatically. In Syria, the United States talks loudly and carries a twig.

Had the United States taken a different approach, one more narrowly focused on avoiding civilian casualties and a breakdown into anarchy, and had it been open to a transitional negotiating process with Assad, the same powers that will ultimately have to deploy into a chaotic Syria might have deployed a stabilizing force early on. If the United States had not made Assad's departure a precondition, Russia might have gone along with the deployment of a UN-mandated stabilization force.[29] In that scenario, more than a year later, it is hard to conceive of any credible scenario in which Assad would still be in power by 2013—a brokered transition process would have required the various Syrian political forces to maneuver for power, and if separated from the backing of his army, Assad's shallow political base would have left him in a very weak position. At the very least, the link between Assad and the army would have been weakened. There are unpredictable factors in this, and it might have failed. But there is at least a probability that some of the death toll and damage of a collapsing Syria would have been avoided.

The point here is less to relitigate the pros and cons of U.S. or Russian policy on Syria than it is to note that UN deadlock in Syria cannot be divorced from U.S. policy—a policy that set the goal of regime change but did not deploy resources to accomplish that goal.

In summer 2013 U.S. policy changed again—and again, and again— when Assad's forces reportedly used chemical weapons, including sarin gas, in an attack on August 21. I return to Syria in the conclusion of this chapter, for the episode, and President Obama's perceived bungling of it, came to symbolize much that is wrong with the contemporary management of American power.

Iran: The Acid Test

Of course, looming over the debate about Syria is the fraught question of Iran. There is a good reason that, for the past decade, Iran has loomed large in international politics. Tensions between Iran, its neighbors, and the West touch on virtually every major issue under negotiation in the changing international system. Every rising power, from Russia to China to Turkey to India, even Brazil, has stakes in the issues and the outcome—especially as it impacts the flow of oil from the Gulf and a stable Middle East and Central Asia. And the fact that the tensions hinge on nuclear weapons makes the Iran face-off a crisis of global significance, a test of whether the international system is still capable of restricting the world's most dangerous weapons.

Iran's precise end goal—whether it wants a nuclear bomb or just to be able to develop one extremely quickly when it may need to—is unclear.[30] Certainly its quest for a nuclear program, perhaps a weapon, has become deeply linked to the prestige of the regime. Polling consistently shows that the Iranian population is less hostile to the West than its government, but it also consistently shows that the population supports the government's argument that the West should not be allowed to curtail its claimed right to civilian nuclear power.[31]

Iran's nuclear program is particularly worrisome because of its potentially destabilizing influence on the region. Tensions between Israel and much of the Middle East, as well as many Middle Eastern states' distrust of Iran, make many concerned about a nuclear arms race. Most informed governments believe that were Iran to develop a nuclear weapon, or even reach the threshold of one, Saudi Arabia, Jordan, and perhaps Turkey would immediately feel the need to nuclearize as well. Thus the threat of an Iranian nuclear weapon is not just about its own weapon, it is about the nuclearization of the Middle East—and the consequent erosion of the nonproliferation and disarmament regime. There is of course the argument that nuclear-armed states would be less likely to go to war with one another.[32] But that scenario would necessitate regime stability, effective administration and decisionmaking, and state rationality trumping populist fervor and religious sentiment.[33]

In a sense, Iran is the perfect encapsulation of the modern game of great-power rivalry and restraint. Every modern economy depends on Gulf oil, which reaches global markets through the Strait of Hormuz—which Iran borders. This is perhaps the most critical of globalization's networks. The rising powers, especially India and China, are hungry for

Iran's oil—but so too are Japan and Korea and Europe. Two major international institutions, the International Atomic Energy Agency and the UN Security Council, play an important part in the relationship between the great powers and Iran. The way the Security Council works in Iran is also a perfect illustration of the relationship between the major powers and international institutions. It is not the case that the UN, through some mysterious agency, itself limits the great powers, nor is it the case that the great powers agree on strategy. Rather, what the Security Council provides to the United States and its Western allies is a tool to put collective pressure on Iran but to do so in a way that is negotiated with the non-Western powers, so that actions taken in Iran do not affect relations among the great powers themselves. It is a tool, in other words, for containing the fallout over differences in the great powers' interests in Iran—no minor thing.

The United States and the other powers have partially shared interests—none actually profit from a nuclear Iran, and none can afford a long disruption in the flow of oil through the Strait of Hormuz. But there the convergence ends, and the different players have sharply different assessments of the scale of risk, the timetable for playing it out, and the price they are willing to pay to prevent Iran from gaining the nuclear weapon.

China's and Russia's positions on Iran are complex. They have strong economic incentives to sustain their relationships with Tehran, for commercial and nuclear trade (Russia) and for oil (China). Neither has any interest in seeing a nuclear Iran. The threat is less immediate for China, but on the other hand, China has a deeper interest in ensuring that Iran does not try to choke off the Strait of Hormuz, and when Iran has threatened that possibility, the Chinese reaction has been firm and swift.[34] Both China and Russia have been brought on board with UN sanctions on Iran.[35] Moreover, in several variations of negotiated outcomes that have been mooted, an important part of the deals involved Russian guarantees to Iran of access to nuclear fuel processed outside its borders, perhaps in Russia itself.

India, which has a long historical relationship with Iran, also has reasons to be concerned with the U.S. Iran policy. India relies on Iranian oil imports, it fears a surge in domestic terrorism that might follow a U.S. attack on Iran, and it relies on Iranian supply routes into Afghanistan—the only routes that bypass its rival, Pakistan.

But despite Russian, Chinese, and Indian concerns—and despite a general hesitation on China's part to agree to wield the tool of sanctions—the UN Security Council voted on two occasions to impose sanctions on Iran in relation to its nuclear program. They were limited sanctions, though, and by early 2010 it was apparent that they were not working. So in June 2010 the United States went back to the Security Council to ask for tighter sanctions. Russia and China predictably opposed the move, and negotiations got under way.

At this point, Brazil and Turkey entered the game. Earlier that year, Brazil and Turkey had been elected to temporary seats on the UN Security Council. The rules of the Security Council are very clear: the permanent members lead the charge on any issue of substance, and the elected members do, well, nothing much. They can vote, obviously, and every now and again an issue divides the council in such a way as to make the votes of the elected members relevant; but this seldom happens. Elected members are expected to make the occasional statement, vote in favor of resolutions that the permanent five present, and otherwise stay out of the way.

Brazil and Turkey decided not to play by these rules. Together, they launched a diplomatic initiative to negotiate with Iran over its nuclear program, ultimately making a deal with Tehran.[36] President Lula of Brazil and President Abdullah Gül of Turkey announced the agreement on May 17, 2010, with the intention that the deal would head off a new round of UN sanctions.

It has been argued since that Brazil and Turkey were essentially rogue actors here and that is why the initiative eventually did not pass. But their involvement came as a result of a direct request from President Obama to use their relationships with Tehran to try to unlock the negotiations. The deal they struck with Tehran was based on a letter from President Obama to his Brazilian and Turkish counterparts. The agreement presented to, and eventually accepted by, Ahmadinejad was crafted using the precise wording of the letter. Because this was so, the Brazilian and Turkish teams were confident that they had American backing for their deal.

In staking out a new role for themselves in global politics, Brasilia and Ankara seem to have neglected the fact that the United States holds a strong hand in the global game: the ability through signals intelligence to eavesdrop on virtually any phone call that takes place between foreign nationals anywhere in the world. (As former NSA employee Edward Snowden would eventually reveal, to dramatic effect.) In the case of the Iran negotiations, what U.S. officials heard of the exchanges between Turkish and Brazilian officials during this process did little to reassure them about the efficacy and intentions of the two countries' diplomacy.[37]

Four other factors affected the outcome. First, there was a basic lack of confidence among senior U.S. officials in the Turkish-Brazilian process and a dearth of the kinds of relationships among top officials on all sides that could have managed a more constructive process. Second, a move toward new sanctions was under way, and making decisive progress, with Russian and Chinese support. Third, there were differences between the signals sent by the White House and the State Department, sometimes at the same time—creating confusion in Ankara and Brasilia. And fourth, time elapsed between when Obama had spelled out the terms of an acceptable deal and the signing of the Brazil Turkey deal; and during that period the Iranians had enriched more uranium—thereby moving the needle on what, from an American perspective, was an acceptable deal. Seen from Washington, the Iranian agreement to the Brazil-Turkey deal was simply a tactical maneuver to escape from what were set to be serious sanctions.[38] Thus when the agreement was reached in Tehran, the reaction of the United States was swift: it rejected the deal and, within hours, pressed ahead in the Security Council for the sanctions.

There were dangers in Brazil and Turkey's initiative. The issue of Iran's nuclear arsenal is in its own right extremely dangerous—dangerous if it is overestimated, and the West or Israel launch an unnecessary war; dangerous if it is underestimated, and Iran develops either a nuclear weapon or a threshold nuclear capacity. The near-certain result would be the introduction of nuclear weapons across the Middle East. It was dangerous, then, to introduce confusion into the negotiation process—and absent solid intelligence capacity and diplomatic ties to Washington, confusion was the inevitable result of the Brazil-Turkey gambit.

That being said, the way that Washington reacted was probably a mistake. The alternative option was to pocket the progress made by Brazil and Turkey in their negotiations and send them back for more. The Obama administration maintains the line, seemingly genuinely, that it prefers a negotiated outcome with Tehran to a new, inevitably dangerous, war in the Middle East. There is a huge gulf between Tehran and the Western powers; neither trusts the other. So actors that are more trusted by both sides could help to bridge this gulf.

One thing that was evident in this episode: Washington and the emerging powers do not have the kind of relationship that would allow for the tactical coordination necessary for a negotiating process to succeed. And that is a problem, because whether through the UN Security Council or not, the emerging powers are expanding their diplomatic reach and will be a factor in geopolitics whether the United States likes it or not. This is a reality that U.S. diplomacy will have to address, and sooner better than later. Brazil's foreign minister captured the essence of this some months later:

> Of course it is very important for the world that the economy of the United States continues to be vibrant, but it's obvious also that the United States should understand . . . that the world is a different world. And whatever you think about the Iranian—the Tehran—declaration or whatever you think about our efforts in climate, I think there is no way in which the United States can impose its will. But it's also [true], there is no way that you can change things without the participation of the United States.[39]

Finally, an important dynamic in the episode was revealed, not by Washington's or Brasilia's or Ankara's behavior, but by Moscow's and Beijing's. For when Brazil and Turkey made their deal and tried to bring it back to the Security Council, it was not the United States that was most vociferous in shutting them down—it was Russia and China. They slammed the door shut on Brazil and Turkey in no uncertain way. When the United States brought the question of a new round of sanctions to a vote—a mere two hours after Brazil and Turkey had presented their deal—either Russia or China could easily have asked for a delay, or have spoken in favor of the deal, or have used it as a platform for new bargaining. They did none of these. Instead, they voted in favor of the new round of sanctions, snubbing Brazil and Turkey. Here again we see that when one of the emerging powers already has a privileged position within existing international arrangements, it joins forces with the West to protect that position—instead of siding with the aspiring powers to shake things up.[40]

What has happened since is that the United States has used its energy diplomacy to alter the playing field. It has passed legislation imposing sanctions on any country buying Iranian oil, with waivers to exempt some states. Under U.S. pressure, but also as part of a quiet deal with Washington about exemptions to the sanctions, India has started to reduce its dependency on Iranian oil imports.[41] As did Turkey—partially because Turkish businessmen with financial holdings in the United States lobbied the government of Turkey to ensure that they avoided U.S. financial sanctions.[42] As Iranian oil sales to these countries has diminished, so the options for U.S. diplomacy and crisis management have increased.

Now, imagine a scenario in which Turkey and Brazil had made more of an effort to coordinate with Washington and Washington had unified its communications and messages for that coordination. Neither is beyond the scope of the imagination (though it is sobering to acknowledge that unified communications from Washington is the less realistic part). There would then have been one of two outcomes, both better than what happened: either Brazil and Turkey would have been able to pull Iran into a viable deal, avoiding a deeper crisis; or they would have failed, thereby recognizing that it was Iran that was being intransigent. If the Western powers had Brazil and Turkey in their camp in terms of dealing with Iran, it would strengthen the international isolation of Iran and ease the consequences of more coercive options if they become necessary.

At the time of this writing, the situation in Iran is fluid. Elections in 2013 produced a president known to be more moderate in his views about the West and the nuclear program; but it is unclear how much impact that will have as long as Supreme Ruler Khomeini is still in place. And in September 2013 the Iranian and American foreign ministers met, at the UN General Assembly, in the highest level meeting between the two sides since the fall of the shah. This was followed by a phone call between President Obama and President Rouhani and a formal relaunch of diplomatic talks, within the P5+1 framework.

In November 2013, following secret bilateral talks and two rounds of P5+1 negotiations in Geneva, the main elements of a short-term deal were reached, with Iran agreeing to limit several forms of nuclear enrichment activity in exchange for limited temporary sanctions relief. Should that deal hold, and a long-term deal to verifiably halt Iran's nuclear weapons program be achieved, it would be a significant and positive shift. There would be costs even to a deal: U.S.-Saudi relations will be deeply strained. But it would remove a significant thorn in the side of U.S. relations with the other major powers.

At the time of writing, we're a very long way away from a long-term deal, or from a peaceful resolution to Western tensions with Iran. What the short-term deal did reveal is that in this most complex of cases, Western and emerging power interests do substantially overlap. It will matter a great deal in the period ahead that there be close and constant diplomatic exchange with these powers, as well as U.S. allies. As in any complex deal, there's a high risk that it won't hold. If that is true, and coercive options are ultimately necessary, it will matter that the United States and other powers judge the extent of Iranian compliance or cheating similarly. The difficulties ahead are likely to be legion.

Looking Ahead: Avoiding Proxy Wars

From Kosovo at the peak of American power to Syria in 2013, the United States confronts a world in which some crises roil the sensitivities of other powers, which will seek to block American or Western approaches to grappling with them—especially when the proposed approach involves military intervention or regime change. That is not going to change. Tensions over crises and interventions are certain to be an enduring feature of international order. The question is, How serious will the fallout from individual cases be?

Individual failures do not tell the whole story. A wider look at the evidence and the patterns of behavior tell of the surprising persistence of cooperation and of a convergence of interests between the established and the rising powers. The rising powers share with the established powers a deep concern with terrorism in its various forms, especially Islamic radicalism. The rising powers also share with the established powers an orientation toward stability. Their economic interests give them one more reason to join with the established powers on stabilizing actions and interventions.

Where they part from the West is over regime change. Russia has always differed from the West on this, and China sympathizes with Russia on this issue—and has a deep concern, when it comes to intervention in the Middle East, about the stability of oil prices. Brazil, India, and Turkey remain to be won over case by case—they can accept in principle the case for intervention, but are leery of its effects—but not by missing opportunities to bring them into coalitions, to engage them on debates, and by failing to understand the domestic prism through which they are acting. These kinds of missed opportunities will add up and, over time, weaken the U.S. position in the "international electoral college."

Still, all in all, there is little in contemporary crisis management to suggest early signs of a coming disorder. Rather, the United States remains central, and myriad forms of cooperation endure. Some of what looked like muddling through when it happened, over time begins to look like success.

The United States will likely find it useful to devote more of its attention and energies to widening the use of multinational forces and to rethinking multilateral approaches to stabilization. Traditional UN peacekeeping forces have proved a valuable tool for stabilizing conflicts in weak states with small armies, and they should continue to be used this way. But as currently organized, the Blue Helmets are not adequate for stabilization or enforcement in more complex environments. Multinational forces provide a more credible option for tackling these situations. NATO's International Security Assistance Force in Afghanistan is one example of such a force. Another is a multinational force formed with UN Security Council authorization but managed separately.

The United States should also turn its attention to the international tools for postconflict stabilization. Coming out of Iraq and Afghanistan, the United States is at risk of learning the wrong lessons from those two interventions, of learning that postconflict nation building cannot succeed and should not be tried. In point of fact, there are many examples of successful or semisuccessful efforts at postconflict stabilization but, so far, only in cases of modest size and modest complexity. If the international tools are to be developed to do better, the United States will have to participate.

And if the United States does not take a leadership role in pushing for international tools for multinational crisis management and stabilization, it will be faced with two bad options: undertaking nation-building missions itself, which it is ill equipped to do; or letting countries deteriorate into long-running instability and turmoil. The risk is that currently underdeveloped, and frequently energy- or minerals-rich, countries will become the sites of new tensions, of a scramble for resources, and of race-to-the-bottom dynamics—even of proxy wars. Great-power relations can survive this, but there will be greater risks and a diminishment of the values that American leadership is supposed to stand for.

Even if the United States does take this leadership role on, there is no realistic scenario ahead without substantial security crises, and there simply will be cases that divide the interests of the powers. But every effort should be made to identify overlapping interests, to forge multinational approaches, particularly between emerging and established powers, and to reduce the number of cases in which the great powers are at odds. There will be many reasons for tensions between the established powers; simple misunderstandings and lack of relationships should not be among them.

Experiences in Libya and Iran point to a structural oddity in the current international situation, which I call the G-gap in international politics. Before the global financial crisis, the main emerging powers were brought into a dialogue with the G-8, a dialogue that covered everything from international finance to terrorism to security issues. This was known as the G-8+5 process, which brought India, China, Brazil, Mexico, and South Africa into G-8 deliberations. With the shift from the G-8 to the G-20 this was curtailed, as we saw also a narrowing of the focus to global finance and the economy. Russia is still in the G-8, oddly. And Russia and China are permanent members of the Security Council, so there is sustained interaction with them on crisis management and security issues. But there is no part of the international system in which the democratic emerging powers—India, Brazil, and Turkey in particular—participate in international decisionmaking on crises. This is not deliberate but is, like so much else in international life, the result of muddling through—and the steady accretion of small decisions. But it means that the relationships among senior officials that could minimize tactical problems and missed opportunities (of the sort that arose in Libya and over Iran) are not being forged. This G gap could be tackled by UN Security Council reform, or the creation of informal mechanisms—a national security advisers' meeting for G-20 countries, for example, or an allies and partners forum hosted by the United States. But whatever approach is taken, there's only one state that has the reach and clout to forge new arrangements—the United States. And new tools to manage crises—on land and at sea—are sure to be needed.

CHAPTER SEVEN

COMPETITORS, NOT COLD WARRIORS

U.S.-China Relations

In September 2010 a Japanese coast guard ship collided with a Chinese trawler that it was chasing from the waters surrounding an island chain known to the Japanese authorities as the Senkaku chain and to China by the name Diaoyu. Japan detained the Chinese trawler captain, and China retaliated by halting sales to Japan of rare earth materials, which are vital to high-tech industry.

In April 2012 the hard-line governor of Tokyo started negotiating to buy some of the Senkaku Islands from its private owners, the Kurihara family. To preempt the governor's move, the Japanese central government bought several of the islands. This infuriated China. Chinese and Taiwanese fishing convoys entered the waters at various points over the summer and fall, in each instance provoking Japanese reactions. In December a Chinese surveillance aircraft entered the airspace over the islands, and Japan scrambled eight F-15s in response. In January 2013 multiple Chinese aircraft entered the islands' airspace. And in February, according to Japan, a Chinese frigate locked its fire-control radar onto a Japanese Maritime Self-Defense Force ship—an allegation that China denies.

In the West, politicians and analysts alike reacted with alarm. There are two worries. First is a Japan-China clash, which could result from the dispute over the islands escalating, possibly through an accident. Second, and even worse because of America's treaty obligations to defend Japanese-administered territory, a Japan-China clash could pull the United

States into active conflict in Asia. A *Financial Times* editorial warned, "The shadow of 1914 falls over the Pacific"; several opinion pieces and essays warned of mounting risks; and in a widely read foreign policy blog a long essay was titled, "Eve of Disaster: Why 2013 Eerily Looks Like the World of 1913, on the Cusp of the Great War."[1]

And this is just one part of a rising chorus of concern about the situation with China. One prominent international relations professor calls the situation "The Gathering Storm," warning of a mounting Chinese challenge to U.S. power in Asia. The U.S. Department of Defense points with increasing concern to the pace of China's cyberpenetration of the United States, both for purposes of intellectual property theft and to position itself to weaken U.S. command and control systems in the event of war. The U.S. Navy is increasingly perturbed by Chinese military investments in sophisticated weapons systems designed for one purpose only: to deny the U.S. Navy access to the waters off of China's long coastline, waters long dominated by U.S. ships. Politicians on both sides are warning of a new cold war.[2]

Will the changing balance of power lead to war, perhaps a new cold war, between the United States and China? The relationship certainly has rapidly deteriorated. During the election that brought President Obama to office, there was a lot of discussion about the possibility of a new arrangement for global leadership, a U.S.-China condominium—in shorthand, a G-2.[3] But instead the United States is in an active arms race with China in the South China Sea and the East China Sea.

But there are important exaggerations here, as well—exaggerations about the likelihood of worst-case scenarios and about time lines. Automatic conflict between rising and falling powers is too readily assumed. China would confront many obstacles should it try to mount a strategic challenge to the United States or to U.S. leadership of the international system. Even if the size of the Chinese economy overtakes that of the United States, the huge remaining gap in per capita income will persist, as will other disparities in capacity (see chapter 1.)

And since a peak of harsh rhetoric in 2012, in the run-up to the U.S. elections and the transition of Chinese leadership, cooler heads have been in evidence. The two countries have started a genuine discussion about forging a "new type of great power relations."[4] But hanging over even that optimistic formulation is this basic question, posed by the troubled history of power shifts: Does the rise of a new power necessarily result in conflict with the established one?[5]

That the rise of China is a complicated issue and one that will impact virtually every aspect of international life is in no doubt. And it is fluid: just as there is a debate in the United States about how to handle China, there is a debate in China about how to position it vis-à-vis the United States—whether to cooperate, to compete, or to do both. Tensions are particularly evident in the East China Sea and the South China Sea. But the die is not cast yet. In the space of five short years since the global financial crises, expectations of a new G-2 arrangement between the United States and China changed to fears of a new cold war, then improved again. The U.S.-China relationship is intrinsically competitive, and the tensions and risks in Asia are real. But there are limits to China's challenge from within the region itself and from the mismatch between China's global interests and its still only partial power. Here, as in the rest of the international system, is an active balance between the impulse to rivalry and incentives for restraint.

What Are the Risks of a China-U.S. Conflict?

Contemporary assessments of the situation in Asia often trace a new Chinese assertiveness to the period immediately after the global financial crisis, in 2009–10 in particular, when widespread talk of American decline stoked Chinese confidence about its ability to stake its claim.[6] And while there is some truth to this notion, it overlooks the fact that some of China's assertive moves in Asia began earlier, after the Iraq war.

As noted in chapter 5, the Iraq war, combined with political turbulence in Venezuela, generated constraints on the supply of oil, constraints that coincided with new demand from China and India. The result was a steep price rise. In China, the combination of rising oil prices and the U.S. military move into Iraq stoked fears about China's vulnerabilities. China's economy is almost 60 percent dependent on trade, and 85 percent of that trade—including most of its oil imports—is carried by sea.[7] And yet China's naval capacity is inadequate to protect the sea-lanes through which that trade and that energy flow—what Hu Jintao reportedly calls

China's Malacca dilemma, referring to the narrow strait through which almost all sea-borne trade into China flows.[8]

By the mid-2000s China had already substantially upgraded its naval and marine capabilities. Incidents between China and its neighbors intensified in that same period. In January 2004 Japanese security forces fired a water cannon on Chinese fishermen near the Senkaku/Diaoyu island chain. In January 2005, in the South China Sea, Chinese ships fired on Vietnamese fishing boats, killing nine people. And in September 2005 Japan discovered Chinese patrol boats in Japanese waters near a disputed gas field in the East China Sea. Nor were incidents limited to Asian navies. In October 2005 a Chinese submarine reportedly pursued the U.S. aircraft carrier *Kitty Hawk* during one of its patrols in the East China Sea. And in 2009 the Pentagon reported that five Chinese vessels shadowed and harassed a U.S. surveillance ship, the USNS *Impeccable*.[9]

The year 2009 marked another uptick in assertive Chinese claims in the South China Sea. In what is certainly China's most assertive move to date on the international stage, Chinese authorities made an ambitious—some would say reckless—claim to economic sovereignty over a huge swath of ocean off its southern coast. The same international law that gives every country exclusive sovereign and territorial rights up to 12 miles off its coast also gives it exclusive economic rights—that is, exclusive rights to fishing and energy—within a band of 200 miles. China made a play for much more—not by ignoring the international law but by arguing within an additional provision of that law, a provision that says that a country can extend its rights if its continental shelf can be proven to extend past the 200-mile zone.

The timing was no doubt influenced by the fact that, under the UN Convention of the Law of the Sea, the deadline for states to make seabed hydrocarbon claims was May 2009. These kinds of claims are relatively routine—but China's are vast in scope, especially by contrast to their often thin merits.[10] China has asserted territorial claims to a series of island formations—really, scattered, unpopulated rocks—along the rim of the South China Sea. And by doing so it has staked a claim to 2.4 million square miles of ocean. This extensive claim is one it is trying to back up both diplomatically and financially, with major investments in the scale and sophistication of its marine forces.[11] The island chains that form the outer edge of its claim are also contested by the Philippines, Malaysia, Brunei, Vietnam, and Taiwan. And there are other stakeholders as well: India has warned that it would be prepared to use its navy to protect its oil exploration (jointly with Vietnam) in the region.[12]

China has three reasons to risk a confrontation with the United States over a territorial claim. First, there are nationalist reasons to assert a Chinese sphere of influence in its own backyard: historically, at the peak of its powers, the Chinese empire did try to assert a sphere of influence in Asia, just as the United States has done in Latin America and Russia has done in Eastern Europe. (And as with those other two ventures, previous Chinese efforts at a sphere of influence have been a decidedly mixed blessing for China's central rulers.) Second, there are huge natural resources in play. The World Bank reports that there are more than 10 billion barrels of proven oil reserves in the South China Sea, as well as estimated reserves of over 100 trillion cubic feet of natural gas.[13] On top of the energy reserves, there are fish—6 million tonnes of fish are pulled out of the South China Sea each year. (That is, 6 million tonnes that get reported; the real number is certainly higher.) The presence of a lot of fish does not sound like a good reason to pick a fight with the world's largest naval power, but feeding your population is a most basic function of a legitimate state, and fish (after pork, which also recently became a subject of bilateral tensions) is a major source of protein for China's population, 500 million of whom live within a hundred miles of the South China Sea.[14]

Third, and arguably most important, by beefing up its maritime capacity to back up its audacious claims, China is also testing its naval capacity to challenge the United States. The U.S. Navy undertakes intelligence collection in Chinese territorial waters (within the twelve-mile range). It is the only country in the world to maintain that this is a form of "innocent passage" in the law of the sea. Worries about this position are arguably the reason that the United States has not signed the UN Convention on the Law of the Sea.[15] Some naval officials suggest that the intelligence that the United States gathers from these exercises is not worth the trade-offs.[16] Whether or not that is true, it remains an important friction in the U.S.-China relationship.

Finally, annual trade on the South China Sea amounts to 9 billion tonnes of goods. The route is one of the largest and richest trading routes in the world and is the lifeblood of the Chinese economy.[17] Since World War II the U.S. navy has protected this trade against piracy and has maintained the security of what are known as the sea lines of communication—that is, the key passages into, across, and out of the South China Sea. The U.S. Navy is understandably anxious about China's more assertive presence. But here we find a paradox, for as a country whose economy is 60 percent dependent on international trade imported by sea, China is hardly likely to want to block that flow of trade. Rather, it is fear that the United States might choke off that trade that forms the core of China's strategic concerns.

There are also complicating factors. For example, the United States has an alliance within the South China Sea with Taiwan, whose sovereignty China disputes. In addition, there is evidence that the Chinese navy, in order to justify greater funding and resources, may promote tension with the United States in the East and South China Seas. There are strong nationalist overlays, especially in the China-Japan relationship. All this may complicate the search for stable solutions, even if there are strong economic interests that should drive some degree of restraint.

Chinese Strategic Thinking and Military Investments

There are myriad sources of Chinese strategic thinking, including the lessons of its own history.[18] Ironically, however, some of the strategic concepts that appear to form the foundation of China's assertive naval play in Asia come in part from a prominent American thinker, Alfred Thayer Mahan. In policy papers, symposiums, and strategy essays, scholars and strategists attest to the influence of Mahan's thinking and principles for conceptualizing naval power.[19]

Mahan's insight begins with the notion that control of key choke points is indispensible to sea power and trade. His core principles include the notion that the seas are a "wide common"—a precursor to the modern notion of the global commons. But the key to sea power lies in the ability to control the sea-lanes and the critical passageways (sea lines of communication) through which flow commercial and naval shipping.[20]

Mahan's logic was primarily commercial. He wrote about the dynamics of naval battle, but he stressed that peacetime commerce is the real path to national prosperity, arguing that military considerations are subordinate to other interests.[21] Naval competition is the inevitable by-product, not the purpose, of countries' efforts to generate wealth. This is so even during peacetime, as navies are necessary for creating and securing an environment for free trade. This leads to the second aspect in Mahan's sea-power theory, which stresses the importance of forward naval stations and fleets and competition among nations for control of key geographical points. To control commercial passage through the sea lines of communication, even if ultimately for wealth-generating purposes, states must ultimately be able to deny competitor states access.

As noted, China is heavily dependent upon East Asian waters, including both the Malacca Strait and the South China Sea. Perhaps the biggest driver of Chinese behavior is its preoccupation with U.S. naval power. China fears that should the United States wish to, it could blockade these East Asian waters. Such fears are not unfounded. Not only does the United States have the ability to institute such a measure, but it also engages in what many see as provocative activities in China's established economic zone.[22]

There is an important historical precedent. In 1940 American concerns about an increasingly aggressive Japan led it to impose an embargo on Japanese imports of oil, to slow the development of Japan's military machine. Some historians argue that the need to circumvent America's embargo is part of what drove Japan to join the war against the United States on December 7, 1941, with the attack on the U.S. naval installation at Pearl Harbor. (Japan had already attacked allied bases in Singapore.)[23] This precedent is not forgotten in Chinese thinking—nor in American. It perhaps does not help matters much that the U.S. naval community writes in publicly available journals about the United States implementing exactly such an oil embargo again. Some part of China's strategic thinking is a reaction to this U.S. posture. But even if the United States foreswore this option, China would have to prepare for the contingency.

Because offensive and defensive naval capabilities are often hard to differentiate, it is impossible to discern China's intentions. Concern has grown that these intentions may be more aggressive than defensive. Such uncertainty has caused U.S. naval planners to hedge against a worst-case scenario.

Chinese military upgrades reflect the dual purpose of offense and defense. Some of this has been exaggerated. For example, there was a flurry of commentary about the launch of China's first aircraft carrier in 2012—a third-hand aircraft carrier that will be inoperable for several years. For now, China still only has the same number of aircraft carriers as Thailand and Italy. But other technologies are more concerning. Chinese weapons systems designed for so-called anti-access/area-denial (A2/AD) capacity are a powerful, asymmetric arsenal and could undermine America's naval edge in the region. American defense planners recognize that China is now clearly the number-two actor in the world in terms of defense budgets and that over time it will become a force to be reckoned with.

One type of military hardware that is being developed by the Chinese armed forces for A2/AD is the antiship cruise missile—a weapon that would also be instrumental were China to launch a military effort to retake Taiwan.[24] These missiles can be fired from ships, aircraft, and surface batteries and can reach U.S. forces stationed beyond China's immediate offshore waters. China can place these weapons away from shorelines in order to make a U.S. counterattack difficult.[25] Another type of hardware is the antiship ballistic missile; such a weapon would allow China to strike at advancing carrier or marine forces from especially long ranges (over 1,500 miles for some of these missiles), presenting the U.S. military with a major new challenge. There is, however, some question about the viability of this technology, which has not yet been tested in wartime conditions or even against moving targets.[26]

It is anticipated by the U.S. military that China would utilize these weapons in tandem with other weapons systems. One of these is the anti-radiation system that jams or incapacitates enemy sensors; in a worst-case scenario, this system could paralyze U.S. ability to win the information war that its technological edge has historically afforded it. Additionally, China is augmenting its capacity to strike from below via undersea mines and first-class submarines. The latter have recently caused much consternation for U.S. military planners because they enable China to convey information to military commanders about the imminence of an attack or counterattack.[27]

The key point to recognize is that China's growing A2/AD capacity could slowly be creating a military dynamic in which no state dominates the region's sea lines of communication and choke points (as the United States essentially does now) and in which commercial access and free passage can be denied to all and ensured by none. A major worry is thus of a particularly nasty security dilemma. Because of uncertainties regarding intentions, incentives to take unilateral measures to ensure passage will only grow stronger. And any such efforts, even if meant to be defensive, will almost inevitably reduce the security of other regional actors, threatening negative spirals and increasing the chances for confrontation and crisis. What is more, unlike the Arctic, where energy resources serve as a stabilizing factor, in the South China Sea competition over energy and fishing rights complicate the strategic challenge.

The worst fear is a China that feels confident enough, or sees the opportunity, to initiate a strike for the retaking of Taiwan. The assumed operational plan is that the Chinese offensive would be a lightning strike that would take others by surprise and impose heavy costs for intervention by outsiders. If the United States did not respond immediately, or did not see immediate operational success in its counterstrike, China could reclaim Taiwan and essentially force the region to accept it as a fait accompli. Beyond the political or national importance China places on the eventual reclaiming of Taiwan is the island's importance as a springboard for Chinese expansion.

The U.S. military has not sat idly by as China's maritime force has grown. U.S. planners have begun actively searching for ways to counter China's growing ability to deny access to waters on its periphery. What has emerged from the effort, formalized in a memorandum between the air force chief of staff and the navy's chief of operations, is the operational concept of air-sea battle.[28] Implementation of the concept would occur in two stages. The first has four components: withstand the initial attack and limit damage; execute a blinding response campaign against opposition battle networks; execute a suppression campaign against opposition long-range strike systems; and seize and sustain the initiative in the air, sea, space, and cyberwar domains. The second stage is made up of a series of longer-term actions meant to support U.S. strategy, including executing a protracted campaign against Chinese capacities, conducting "distant blockade" operations, and ramping up industrial production.

All of this produces a classic security dilemma: China sees the U.S. naval presence in the waters surrounding it as a threat to its interests and as a sign that the United States could execute an oil embargo like the one that hobbled Japan. China then makes what it sees as a defensive move.

The United States responds by beefing up its capacity—which reinforces Chinese fears about its intent. And off we go to the races.

And there is another dimension to the competition, namely cyber. Both the United States and China have invested substantial capabilities in using cybertechnology as a tool against the other. In the U.S. case, there are two purposes: preparing to cripple Chinese command and control networks in the case of potential hostilities; and spying. China does these two things and a third as well: it uses cybertechnology to steal U.S. intellectual property—in vast quantities.

Countries spy on each other; that is just a reality. And the United States and China spying each on the other is neither surprising nor a particular challenge for the relationship. Preparing for the possibility of cyberwarfare is more complicated, because, as with other weapons systems, what may actually be defense can look like offense (though no serious commentator is suggesting that China is planning to trigger large-scale hostilities with the United States, and vice versa). Still, preparations for cyberwarfare are going to have to become part of the evolving dialogue between the United States and China about bilateral military and defense issues, along with myriad other aspects of the two countries' military defenses. But what really risks driving a deep wedge between the United States and China is economic cybertheft.

In 2012 the United States increased the pressure on China over this issue, stressing to the Chinese leadership both publicly and privately that cybertheft is more than a problem for the government-to-government relationship: it also threatens to poison public attitudes about China, undermining the prospects for stable relationships. One close China watcher saw some impact of this, both among China's governing elites and among the economic elites, who now travel widely and are increasingly encountering anti-China sentiment.[29] One result of this was the launch of a U.S.-China working group on cyber issues—a good step, but one for which it is too early to predict results.

Asian Nationalism

It is not only with the United States that China's movements in Asia and its assertive international stance are creating risks. Japan, China, Russia, and the two Koreas all sit uneasily beside one another, nursing historical and territorial grievances left unresolved at the end of World War II, and still riven by strong nationalism and perceptions of threat posed by the others. Japan, India, Russia, and the Koreas are important military actors in their own right. Each has reacted to the uptick in China's assertiveness. South Korea and Japan have reinvigorated their alliance with the United States and enhanced their military preparedness. Japan has even increased its defense spending—something it was for many years reluctant to do, despite American urging.

India, too, has begun to think more seriously about its security relationship with the United States, as a counterweight to China's growing influence in the region. While there are historical reasons for India to be leery of the United States, the more proximate China is arguably more of a threat. Some of China's behavior has reinforced these worries. In April 2013, in a move that baffled even veteran and sympathetic China watchers, China deployed a small contingent of its army into the Depsang Valley in the disputed Ladakh region of the Himalayas. The Chinese pushed nineteen miles into territory that falls under Indian control, according to the 1993 agreement, the Line of Actual Control. The troops pitched tents in the valley, and India responded by deploying its forces and unmanned air vehicles. The result was a standoff, with Chinese and Indian troops facing each other from a distance of between 100 to 300 meters. Three army-to-army meetings (so-called flag meetings) failed to resolve the deadlock, and high-level political contacts were needed to resolve the crisis. China's actions hit the major fault line in Indian strategic thinking, strengthening the hand of those who see closer ties with the United States as serving India's best interests. (And if there were any illusions about how shallow is the unity of the BRICS, China's brief border incursion into Ladakh reveals the deeper tensions. Substitute the word *United States* for *China* and *United Kingdom* for *India* and think about the difference between relations among the G-7—genuine allies—and these two largest members of the BRICS.)

It is worth highlighting that all of these tensions take place in a region with nuclear weapons. China's nuclear weapons program is a double concern. China has provided nuclear technology to North Korea and Pakistan, it has become a major exporter of civilian nuclear power, and

Western governments fear that its lax security requirements may allow for a diversion of civilian materials for potential military purposes. China's nuclear program is also worrisome because of uncertainty about Chinese ambitions. Its nuclear weapons program is opaque, and little is known about the size of its arsenal, though it is significantly smaller than that of the United States or Russia. The Federation of American Scientists believes it to have an arsenal of just shy of 180 nuclear weapons.[30] However, even as the United States and Russia decrease their arsenal, China is believed to be building up its arsenal in part because it sees the nuclear option as a means to counter American conventional superiority. Some in China believe that the United States plans "to use its conventional superiority to 'blackmail' other nations."[31] China's rising nuclear capability is particularly worrisome in light of India's parallel rise. India and China have long-standing hostilities that raise the potential for a new regional nuclear arms race—with the same fears of accidental use, miscommunication, or preemption that defined the cold war.

At the same time that the region's reaction to China's increasing assertiveness bolsters America's strategic position, there are also serious countervailing risks. If scholars or politicians are ever tempted to believe that strategic logic outweighs emotion, they need only review the way in which Japanese politicians have exacerbated historical tensions with Korea with ill-advised and nationalistic references to World War II or other grievances—and the way in which Korea has met these moves in kind (with high-profile visits to disputed islands in the seas between the two countries). The two Western allies that would logically be allied in an effort to dull China's assertiveness seem to be finding every possible way to complicate their cooperation.[32] From a U.S. perspective, this is a major headache.

What Does China Want?

In 2010 I convened a meeting in Abu Dhabi of senior military figures, diplomats, and scholars from Brazil, India, China, Turkey, the United Kingdom, Germany, and the United States. The Chinese delegation comprised a senior army general, a senior official from the Chinese foreign ministry, and two scholars working for think tanks closely associated with Chinese intelligence. I think that the State Department and Indian officials in the room were as gripped as I was over the course of two days as these four Chinese delegates went at each other hammer and tongs, bitterly debating the question of what constituted China's core interests, and whether China should adopt a more assertive or more accommodating international posture. For a country with a reputation for keeping its dirty laundry hidden, it was a striking display of almost American-style internal debate.

I am not an expert on China's internal workings, but repeated exposure to Chinese officials and scholars and to expert China watchers in the United States, India, and Southeast Asia (and I do believe it is important to hear from China experts outside of the United States) leads me to one conclusion: anyone who tells you that he or she knows what China wants, or what China's goals are, is simplifying. Policymaking in Beijing is at least as complex, contentious, and turf ridden as policymaking in Washington, with the added complications of secrecy.

Genuine experts on China see a spectrum of opinions. Perhaps the most comprehensive account of these opinions comes from David Shambaugh, one of the world's leading experts on China and its foreign policy.[33] Shambaugh divides the spectrum into several categories. The "nativists" distrust the international community and international engagement and toe a line somewhat similar to American xenophobes and American isolationists. Those who focus on "Asia first" believe that China should focus on its immediate neighborhood, both to tackle insecurities on its borders and to consolidate its alliances, such as they are, and regional strengths. Still others see China's interests as located with the global south—that is, with the developing countries that have been China's natural allies (China still rallies these countries in multilateral settings like the UN General Assembly and global climate talks). Then there are the "selective multilateralists" and the "globalists," who occupy points along the spectrum similar to those in the United States who believe that interdependence, economic ties, and multilateral institutions allow countries to reconcile their differences and forge cooperative strategies.

But Shambaugh aligns with the prevailing consensus among China analysts by giving pride of place to the "realists" and to a variant of the realists, those who belong to the "major-powers school." Like their American counterparts, Chinese realists focus on national interests, sovereignty, and interstate relations—above all, those between the major powers. There are both "offensive" and "defensive" realists, the former believing that China must assert and use its growing power and the latter believing that husbanding its capacity is the better play for China. Among the major-powers school, Shambaugh and others identify a schism between those who believe that China's relationship with the United States is the key to a stable international order in which China can grow. Following this logic, China must seek to avoid hostilities with the United States.[34] A smaller but still important position argues that there is no real prospect of a collaborative relationship with the United States and that China should instead solidify its relationship with Russia, with which it has common interests in resisting Western hegemony, common interests on energy, and similar worldviews.[35] (As noted earlier, global energy dynamics do seem to be reinforcing a sense in China and Russia of a shared defensive interest—a dynamic also reflected in Chinese support for Russian positions on Syria. This potentially growing Russia-China relationship is one of the more worrying features of contemporary international politics.) But both nations are hedging their bets—Russia has even explored closer cooperation with Japan, to counter China's growing weight.

There are also generational issues in play. On a trip to Beijing in 2010 I had two back-to-back dinners with Chinese friends of different generations. The older group—people in their forties and fifties, most of whom worked in government or government-funded entities—spoke eloquently about their experience as the first generation to be educated and trained in China after the horrors of the cultural revolution and how this has focused their attention on education, productivity, and stability—especially on sustaining good relations with the United States.[36] The second group consisted of people in their late thirties, most of whom worked in the private sector. They had none of the humility of the older group. They were self-confident and sure of China's future—which, by the way, they were certain would be democratic. On the question of the United States, they were pragmatic: if the United States would cooperate with China, they would reciprocate. This was about business, after all. But if the United States would not cooperate, China would compete on its own terms.[37] This is anecdote, not evidence; but there is little doubt that as China's economy grows, so does its confidence.

Still, just as in Washington, certain core goals endure. Perhaps the crispest articulation of China's core goals comes from the long-time China watcher Andrew Nathan.[38] He argues, first, that these goals are rooted in the humiliation of the collapse of China's might in the 1840s and the humiliation that China endured during the period of postwar Western hegemony. Second, Chinese strategy is deeply shaped by its perceived danger from having many insecure borders and a long seacoast. These two sources of insecurity generate four core goals. The first is to seek to restore territorial integrity to China, especially with regard to Taiwan; and this concept can be extended into China's claims regarding the "nine-segment line" in the South China Sea. The second is to restrain—or to crush—Tibetan nationalism, both for reasons of China's own nationalism and for its use as a lesson to subnational or irredentist challenges to Chinese territory. The third is to thwart any other country that seeks to dominate Asia—including the United States. And the fourth is to arrange the international order such that China's policies and interests are given due weight.

The upshot is that China's objective is not to collapse the international order but to shape it in order to protect and advance its own interests. This would reconcile the core dilemma identified in chapter 3—that attitudes in China (and India and Brazil and Turkey) reflect the humiliation of "unequal treaties" and the subjugation of these countries to Western hegemony, while also recognizing that their very rise is contingent on the existing international system. That is, they seek simultaneously—and at times, irreconcilably—to reshape the existing order and also to defend it. There are also those—both inside China and beyond—who articulate a broader, more ambitious goal for China: to displace the United States as the top power in the international system. But if that is part of China's strategy, it is a long-term, aspirational one at most. Even the China analysts most skeptical of its leaders' intentions acknowledge that China has no capacity to displace the United States now or in the near-to-medium term.[39] Indeed, there is an important strand of Chinese thinking that suggests that China has already erred in overestimating the extent of American decline and China's gain.

The debate about Chinese foreign policy is echoed in the United States. But what I find striking is that even those who are deeply skeptical about

China's intentions do ultimately acknowledge that there is little or no evidence that China seeks a confrontation with the United States, now or in the near term. Nor should it: there is simply no credible argument that China would win a contest with the United States nor that it would profit from one.

And indeed, since coming to power in early 2013, the new Chinese leadership under Xi Jinping appears acutely alive to that concern. Xi's leadership has been described as refocusing on domestic consolidation and, therefore, adopting a more cautious stance with the United States. Initially, Xi signaled to the White House that he was looking for "off-ramps" from the rising tensions with Japan, in order to concentrate on reforms at home.[40] Xi wanted to focus on the economic transition ahead of him—and that is wise, because it is extraordinarily complex. However, there's a difference in Chinese thinking between pursuing stable relations with the United States and attempting to expand China's influence in Asia. Most U.S. officials don't see this in quite the same way, and this will likely produce tensions in the relationship—and perhaps crises.

These changes have created an opportunity, which both sides were quick to take advantage of, for deeper dialogue between the two countries, within a new framework of great-power relations. In June 2013 Premier Xi and President Obama met at Sunnylands, California, for a two-day-long meeting, mostly in informal settings. The subjects ranged across a gamut of issues. The meetings did not resolve the thorniest issues: on cyber matters and on the South China Sea, talks were tense. But on myriad other issues the two countries launched processes to resolve differences. And they did make an important deal on carbon emissions, as noted in chapter 5.

There is a reason for these positive steps. China's managers are very aware that for all of China's rise and assertiveness in Asia, it confronts tough challenges in the next phase of its rise.

Obstacles to China's Strategic Challenge

China confronts three distinct but overlapping and reinforcing challenges.

The first challenge is regional. The more assertively China behaves, the more it stokes anti-China sentiment and reinforces its neighbors' interest in alliances with the United States.

The second challenge is domestic. China (and to a lesser degree the other rising powers) confronts a middle-income trap—or at least a complicated middle-income transition. This transition entails a major shift in the basis of industrial production, from low-tech industries like agriculture to medium-tech industries. This is complicated enough.[41] But far more complicated still is the political shift. Even those observers sympathetic to China and bullish on China's prospects for navigating the middle-income transition acknowledge that a vital part of the transition is the move away from autocratic procedures and toward the rule of law.[42] This is no easy transition at the best of times, and states have frequently failed to make it. For China, with corruption so high at the top levels of leadership, it may be a very difficult transition.

And the domestic challenge is not just an economic one. Careful China watchers, some of whom are reasonably sympathetic to China's situation, note that China faces a growing restiveness among its population. For a country that closely controls the flow of its information, especially on any matter related to criticism of the Communist Party, it is striking that there are known to be roughly 80,000 antigovernment demonstrations a year; the real number is doubtless higher. China's clampdown on civil society in the wake of the Arab Spring is evidence of a state nervous about its own population.[43]

The third challenge is global and has several aspects.

When China looks beyond its immediate neighborhood, it sees few genuine allies. Yes, there are countries that are interested in deepening their economic ties with China—even the United States is deepening its economic ties with China. But its strategic allies are few and far between. There are recurrent references to China's arms sales abroad, which are growing. But look at the list of countries to which China sells weapons: Algeria, Argentina, Bangladesh, Benin, Bolivia, Cambodia, Chad, Colombia, Congo, Ecuador, Egypt, Gabon, Ghana, Indonesia, Iran, Kenya, Laos, Malaysia, Mexico, Myanmar, Namibia, Nepal, Niger, Nigeria, Pakistan, Peru, Rwanda, Saudi Arabia, Sierra Leone, Sri Lanka, Sudan, Tanzania, Thailand, Timor Leste, Turkey, Uganda, Venezuela, Zambia, and Zimbabwe.[44] Many of these are weak or failing or rogue states, with little or no capacity to support China in their own region, let alone beyond.[45] And even if we single out the stronger countries on this list, there is still no comparison to the suite of powerful allies in the U.S. corner. The "electoral college" of international politics is still stacked heavily in America's favor.

Another aspect of China's global challenge is that now and for the foreseeable future China is dependent on trade with high-income countries. Even if it successfully navigates the middle-income transition, it will need two things from the high-income West: imports of high-tech machinery and equipment necessary for it to develop new industries; and continued exports of low-to-medium-cost goods to finance the transition.[46] This relationship would be complicated by a substantial deterioration in U.S.-China relations or a further deterioration of China's relations in the region. (China's trade with Japan has already suffered because of their competing maritime claims.) According to a former U.S. assistant secretary of state for East Asian and Pacific affairs, Kurt Campbell, China's assertive behavior on cyber issues has made China's business elite uncomfortable, since these people are in constant contact with their Western counterparts and, Campbell argues, are increasingly internationalist in outlook.[47]

A further aspect of China's global challenge is its need to import both energy and food.[48] A particular problem is its energy dependence on the Persian Gulf along with its reliance on other countries to stabilize Persian Gulf countries and to secure the chokepoints through which that energy flows—especially the Strait of Hormuz. And although China's naval investments could, within a decade or so, give it the capacity to challenge America's capacity to close the Strait of Malacca, it will be much longer before it has the naval capacity to stop the United States from stopping the flow of oil through the Strait of Hormuz. (China's own estimate is that not until 2040–50 will it have a fully operational blue-water navy.)[49]

This dependence is not simple. It would be extremely complicated and extremely costly for the United States to execute a blockade of Chinese imports. Some analysts estimate that the United States could mount a blockade only in wartime.[50] But that is exactly the scenario that China needs to account for. Even if China chose to exacerbate the situation in the South China Sea, and even if the United States were met equally in that challenge, the United States has innumerable ways to complicate

China's life at a global level. Indeed, this vulnerability has led some Chinese officials and scholars to warn that China has overplayed its hand in Asia, has overestimated American decline, and is putting Chinese interests at risk.

There is an alternative, in that the United States and China have broadly similar interests (or at least overlapping ones) in the stability and the flow of oil from Central Asia and the Persian Gulf. China should, according to this argument, find common ground with the United States on China's western flank.[51] According to some Chinese strategists, rather than confronting the United States in the east, China should "march west"—that is, focus on cooperation with the United States in western Asia, where U.S. and Chinese interests overlap. As of yet there is no strong evidence that this strategy has taken hold, or even begun to take hold, in Beijing. But I am struck by the coincidence of its timing with steps taken by Beijing to reach out to Washington regarding Pakistan (see chapter 4). And the period since the Chinese leadership transition in early 2013, while still mixed, does seem to show some signs of China wanting to ease tensions with the United States.

A critical example is North Korea, long one of the major difficulties in U.S.-China relations. This is a difficult issue because the two sides have different perceptions and different interests. American concerns are the fact that North Korea's nuclear program is being run by a highly unstable regime. China shares this sense of North Korea's instability, but it has a different concern, namely that collapse of the regime would result in a huge outflow of refugees into China, provoke a crisis with the Republic of Korea, and perhaps result in the unification of Korea, with both South Korean and American troops right on China's border.

The situation in North Korea has fluctuated between crisis and negotiations since 2004, when North Korea first tested nuclear weapons and withdrew from the Nuclear Non-Proliferation Treaty. There have been on-again, off-again negotiations with the North Koreans ever since, mostly through the Six-Party talks involving the United States, Japan, South Korea, China, Russia, and North Korea. The latest crisis was in 2012, when the young and untested Kim Jong Un began to ratchet up North Korean rhetoric against South Korea and the United States and then tested a third atomic device. North Korea also tested long-range missiles.

The way China and the United States engaged in this crisis is instructive. In New York in January 2013 China's ambassador to the UN, Li Baodong, huddled with America's ambassador, Susan Rice. Over the course of three weeks, through intensive, sustained discussions, the two produced a joint U.S.-China draft resolution on a new round of sanctions against North Korea. These sanctions were voted on in the Security Council on January 22. To drive implementation of these sanctions, China's North Korea envoy, Wu Dawei, traveled to Washington for intensive talks with America's North Korea team.[52] Each side took bilateral steps and reached out to Korea and Japan. China not only took a tougher line with North Korea than it had in the past, but it also cut off ties to North Korea's major bank, placing major new financial pressures on North Korea.[53] Later, China also imposed restrictions on the sale to North Korea of chemical substances and equipment that could be used in the construction of long-range missiles.[54] This is hardly the behavior of two states locked into a new cold war.

Moving Forward

China confronts several obstacles to strategic competition with the United States. It faces substantial domestic challenges, both economic and political. It has also triggered a regional backlash to its assertive stance, has overplayed its hand, and has overestimated U.S. decline, all of which has strengthened America's alliances and its strategic position in Asia. Economically, China is dependent on trade with the West and will be for some time to come. And China now has global economic and energy interests that it has no means of securing if there is hostility between the United States and China.

None of this means that China won't use every opportunity to push for advantage. But these circumstances give the United States leverage. Moreover, there are important issues in which the United States and China have shared interests. And while relations deteriorated during the 2010–12 period, especially during China's leadership transition, other aspects of Chinese behavior, including U.S.-China cooperation on climate, suggest that the two countries are not locked in outright hostility. It is a difficult, competitive relationship, to be sure; but fears of a new cold war are not as yet warranted.

How do the two countries move forward?

First, they must make a sober assessment of their strategic relationship: that they are not now, or imminently, facing a new cold war. Economic ties create strong bilateral relations, and we've seen improved U.S.-China relations regarding North Korea and climate. High-level talks on cyber issues, which are on their agenda, could provide a channel to ease, if not fully resolve, one of the most difficult issues in the relationship.

Second, the two countries must anticipate competition. The idea of a U.S.-China G-2, where bilateral agreements between the two states set the stage for international cooperation, is going to play a limited role at best, perhaps most feasible on climate and energy issues. China is going to pursue its interests, as is the United States. China will try, while seeking to avoid a breakdown, to limit the extent to which U.S. leadership constrains its rise. The United States will try to contain the extent to which China's rise circumscribes U.S. leadership. Their interests overlap, but they are not aligned. Substantial tensions are an inevitable feature of the relationship, which will require constant, high-level management. That includes investment in new forms of arms control. These forms will involve both existing arms control processes (especially in the nuclear area, to incorporate China's growing capabilities) and new kinds of weapons systems (like drones and cyberwar).

Third, the United States must recognize China's insecurity and how that plays into Chinese strategic thinking—but also the ways in which it will attempt to use this "power of the weak" to negotiate for advantage.[55]

And fourth, the two countries must continue to deepen their economic relationship as a bulwark against tension. The single most important thing that can happen here is for China to join the Trans-Pacific Partnership (TPP). Given the initial Chinese reaction to the proposal, it is intriguing that, in late May 2013, China's chamber of commerce issued a statement noting that China was studying the option of joining the TPP. And at several meetings I've attended, Chinese officials signaled confidence that they could join the TPP.

From these four starting points, the United States can invest both in managing the inevitable tensions in the relations and in trying to forge what has been referred to as a new type of great power relations.[56] Despite some arguments to the contrary, there is nothing automatic about conflict between powers during periods of transition: policy choices matter, fundamentally. But it is also clear that there are risks of conflict and that if the countries ignore them, they may inadvertently unleash hostilities. So investments in U.S. alliances in Asia and in tools to manage the escalation of potential crises are both necessary.

In all of this, the United States should also keep a wider field of vision. It is often claimed that the U.S.-China relationship is the most important bilateral relationship in the world. That may well be true, but it would be unwise for the United States to focus on the bilateral relationship to the exclusion of working with other important powers in a variety of settings. China may be in a category by itself among the emerging powers, but the Japanese economy is almost the same size as China's; India is an important player in the Indian Ocean and is likely to scale up its naval presence there as fast or almost as fast as China; Europe and Korea and others all matter to significant degrees in a range of regional and international negotiations and tensions. The United States should of course have an eye on its allies' interests (and on the phenomenon of "torn allies"), but it actually serves both the U.S. interest and interests in a stable order for there to be more, not fewer, times when these various powers work together to deconflict their interests or solve problems.

Only the United States has the option of being the locus of this kind of diplomacy—it is a major arrow in its quiver, one not to be neglected or underutilized. Of course, the United States will have to have a strong bilateral relationship with China, and many issues will be tackled one to one. But wherever feasible, the United States should strive to pull other powers in, both ensuring inclusion and strengthening the U.S. strategic position.

Can We Avoid a War?

No less an observer of China's modern history than Henry Kissinger highlights the fact that interpretations of the history of war in great-power transitions form the subtext to much contemporary thinking about U.S.-China relations.[57] In his expansive account of China's international relations, *On China*, he ends with a long disquisition on this topic, focused on a discussion on the famous Crowe Memorandum of 1907. Eyre Crowe, a Germany expert in the Foreign and Commonwealth Office in London, wrote a long memo examining German capacity and intention and assessing the implications for British strategy. The essential point that the Crowe Memorandum conveys is this: Not only can we not know for sure what German intentions are, these intentions can change. And thus Britain has no choice but to judge Germany by its capacity, rather than its intent, and match capacity for capacity, to deny Germany the option of dominating Britain. Thus was a spiral of distrust and arms acquisitions begun, which was spent out in the devastating war of 1914–18.[58]

The prewar period of World War I is one of the most important points where evidence exists for the argument that conflict follows a period of redistribution in the balance of power.[59] That argument is taken as a given in much of the contemporary foreign policy debate. In point of fact, the evidence in support of this argument is contested. For example, a recent empirical study, now frequently cited in scholarly debates on this topic, measures the degree of power held by major states from 1642 to the contemporary period and depicts the change of this distribution over time.[60] The study identifies episodes in which one power has surpassed another and shows that only a portion of these has resulted in a war between these powers. For example, sometime in the late nineteenth century the United States surpassed Russia as the state with the greatest economic and military power in the international system, and yet no conflict ensued.

In other words, wars during power transitions, while a possibility, are not a certainty. Dominant powers can collapse internally, rather than through a challenge by a rising power, and dominant powers can accommodate the rising power.

Across the debate on this question, three risks stand out. First, war is most likely in the case of a rapidly declining power. Second, war is more likely when the rising and declining power reach some degree of parity *and* the rising power experiences dissatisfaction with its stake or position in the order.[61] Third, there is evidence that wars between second-tier powers are more frequent than wars between the rising and the dominant power.

The present reality conforms to neither of the first two points. Part 1 of this book arrays considerable evidence not of decline but of the continued strengths of the United States. Even though it is true that there has been a rapid shrinking of the economic gap between the United States and China, as well as India, Brazil, and others, the gap is still substantial, and there are significant other challenges that confront the rising powers.

In military terms, even China is not approaching parity with the United States, let alone the United States combined with its allies. And the United States not only enjoys current advantages in the intelligence, diplomatic, and institutional features of power, but it has significant advantages in demography, geography, and resource endowment—all sources of enduring strength (see chapter 1). China will confront multiple obstacles as it grows and attempts to flex its muscles both in Asia and on the global stage (see chapter 1). The fact is, the majority of the world's top powers are American allies.

And there is disunity among the rising powers (see chapter 3). There is no bloc of rising states: important fissures and divergent interests between any two among India, China, Russia, and Brazil impede more than rhetorical cooperation, except in one area (gaining influence within the international financial institutions). There is not much mortar in the BRICS. There are divisions in the West too, to be sure, but there is no comparison between the degree of political, values, and security alignment among the Western powers and the much narrower economic alignment among the emerging powers.

In the near term, there is perhaps more reason for worry about the third risk—of conflict between the second- and third-level powers. Tensions over security between China and Japan and between China and India could lead to conflict. How this would play out is uncertain. In public debate and foreign policy commentary on this, there is an assumption that even a limited clash, once started, would be unchecked and lead to more dramatic scenarios. That is a possibility. But in the case of China and India, there is evidence that the two powers can experience limited clashes, move on from them relatively quickly, and continue to maintain economic ties. The question will remain central to U.S. alliance politics. And the Chinese leadership has taken steps to reduce the risk of accidental conflict.

Over time, the gap between the United States and China will narrow. Whether this happens slowly or continues at its present rate will have an effect on the tensions and reactions each has to the other. But then there is another factor: China's economic rise continues to be deeply tied to that of the United States.

Kissinger, in invoking the Crowe Memorandum—about the logic of acting on the basis of estimates of capacity, not intent—does not argue that the two countries are now locked into this dynamic, much less that they stand on the brink of the abyss. He points to two substantial differences between the pre–World War I period and the contemporary U.S.-China relationship, differences that distinguish their potential rivalry from that between England and Germany. The first, he argues, is acute awareness by decisionmakers in both capitals of the risks inherent in the parallel. The second, he argues, are strong economic ties.

Do economic ties really help forestall the impulse to war, as Kissinger argues? That argument was famously made by Norman Angell, who asserted that economic integration would stop the great powers from going to war—and made that argument in 1909.[62] He has been ridiculed ever since—and with him so has the notion that economic integration is a bulwark against war. But here is the thing: Angell's analysis of globalization in the post-war period was flawed. His argument was posited on the notion that in 1912 the powers were still deeply embedded in an integrated global economy. The reality was more complex. While there was substantial financial integration between the European powers in the late nineteenth and early twentieth centuries, there were also reversals. Following the conflicts of the 1870s, there was a move to reimpose tariffs, to renationalize production, and to shift the direction of trade. Seen from a trade perspective, rather than a financial perspective, the powers went to war during a period of *deglobalization*.[63]

Still, disproving a negative is not the same as proving a positive; the fact that Angell had his facts wrong does not necessarily mean that current economic incentives are a sufficient bulwark against the dynamics of war. But the evidence from part 1 about the current distribution of power and the evidence arrayed in part 2 about patterns of interaction in the economic, security, and energy spheres, suggest that something less dramatic than a challenge to the current system is emerging, though that something is less benign than smooth integration into it or cooperation within it.

Here, I would emphasize a further, crucial conclusion of the study of great-power transitions, namely, that choices made by the top power are a critical variable in whether war is or is not a feature of transitions.[64] There is surely no question at the current juncture that the United States could speed events toward war, or at least cold war, by its actions, just as China can. But equally, the United States, by its choices, can shape the pathway faced by China and the other rising powers and thus can affect the calculus that shapes the odds of conflict or cooperation. In sum, America can still affect the transitions that lie ahead. In this most fundamental sense, it is still ours to shape, still ours to lead.

A Postscript. As this book was going to press, the situation in the South China Sea had escalated. In December 2013 China announced that it was establishing an Air Defense Identification Zone (ADIZ), with boundaries that overlapped waters claimed by Japan and the Republic of Korea. The move seemed likely, even designed, to generate a crisis with Japan. Some China watchers believed it reflected a Chinese military that actively sought conflict with Japan to settle historical scores.

Events are playing out as I write, so I can do little more than note that this will be a major test of U.S. leadership. The events did seem to reinforce a conclusion in this chapter, that the greatest risks in the coming period lie not in U.S.-China conflict but in tensions between the second-tier powers. And, indeed, that U.S. leadership will be central to managing that problem. Shortly after China's announcement, Secretary of Defense Hagel issued a strongly worded statement asserting that the Japanese portion of the disputed territories fell under the purview of the U.S.-Japan alliance; and the United States sent unarmed B-52 airplanes through the Chinese ADIZ to test China. The Chinese did not counter these flights. Whatever China's aims in Asia in asserting the ADIZ, no evidence indicates the country actively sought a conflict with the United States.

This is unlikely to be the last episode. High-level crisis management in Asia is likely to become a major feature of future U.S. diplomacy. American foreign policy will need to prepare for this, while retaining a focus on other regions such as the Middle East. Simultaneously coping with crises in these two theatres is quite simply the necessary challenge of leadership in the coming period.

PART III

HOW AMERICA CAN
STILL WIN FRIENDS
AND INFLUENCE HISTORY

CHAPTER EIGHT

WHAT LIES AHEAD?
Of Scenarios and Shadows

At the most basic level, at this juncture in history, America can make two fundamental mistakes about the world it confronts and thereby lose its indispensable role in international leadership. First, it can underestimate the importance of the rising powers—or their impulse to rivalry, at the risk of unleashing it. Second, it can overestimate the threat or challenge that they pose—as does, in my judgment, much of the narrative and analysis around a "coming disorder" and around the U.S.-China relationship. If the country overestimates risks, then it amplifies their salience, misuses resources to meet them, and misses opportunities for leadership and coalition building.

There are different scenarios about how the international terrain might evolve; and there are shadows that lie over America's present and future options.

Of Scenarios

What are the scenarios for what lies ahead? In estimating them, there are critical ingredients we should contend with: the rates of economic growth of the various powers, the evolution of the internal political character of the key countries, and relations between the principal powers.

When it comes to economic growth, much of the debate on this relies on steady trajectories. But as discussed elsewhere, the growth trajectories of the major powers are uncertain. Few countries have ever sustained for more than one decade the explosive growth that characterized the BRICs in the 2000s.[1] And already the BRICs are finding it hard to sustain their growth. This does not mean that they are no longer a force in global economics and politics, but their allure is likely to dim in the short term. Moreover, in all of this, one near certainty is that of reversals. Economic forecasts often treat the likely scenario as linear growth, and they estimate that growth from a combination of fundamentals and recent performance.[2] But few if any OECD countries have escaped recession for more than ten years straight in any period since the end of World War II. The idea that there would be no significant setbacks in the economic trajectory of the emerging powers is hopeful at best. The greater likelihood is recessions and intermittent financial crises.

And all of this is to say nothing of the genuine political crises that could engross China in particular. China could well move from a course of steady and sustained growth to one of political turbulence and economic underperformance. The dynamic is not hard to envision.

As it is, China has forged an elite economic class that is profiting massively from its country's growth. This creates two tensions. First, there is tension with the still huge numbers of people who do not yet profit from China's economic growth and who nevertheless are confronted by some of its effects, such as extraordinary pollution. China watchers estimate that there are now up to 50,000 episodes of rioting or public unrest in China annually, with pollution a top complaint.[3]

The second tension is probably more challenging: the younger generation of the affluent class—private sector movers and shakers in their late thirties and early forties, people who came to adulthood in an era when Chinese economic reforms were already under way—look to their closed political system and seek change, specifically democratic change. China's political bosses are aware of these pressures and are making moves to accommodate them—but it would be easy to predict a scenario in which those changes move too gradually, and are too limited, to accommodate the rising demand for political opportunity among this powerful generation.[4] Many in China accept that they need to make a transition away from their current hybrid mix of market economics (with more than just a hint of robber baron capitalism) and crony authoritarianism.[5] But corruption, embedded elites, and sheer scale will complicate that transition.[6]

A tactical alliance among the young elites, some portions of the middle classes, and some of those who have not yet profited from the system could challenge China's current regime.

In debates about China, there is often an implicit—and occasionally an explicit—assumption that a democratic China will be easier for the United States to handle than the current China.[7] Perhaps. But young, aspiring democrats in China are also strongly nationalist, and transitions from authoritarian rule to democracy (including navigating first through blended authoritarian/market systems) are historically mixed: there have been successes, and there have been spectacular failures. The United States and other states' foreign and economic policies have to prepare for the possibility of a very turbulent period in China. The United States might find that internal crises in a democratic—or especially a democratizing—China could be just as complicating for the United States as growth, if not far more so.

India, too, could face, if not the same scenario, then a variation: political stalemate, elite dysfunction, popular dissatisfaction, an inability to resolve its internal disputes, an inability to control corruption, and sustained economic underperformance. Take its energy sector. No sector is more fundamental for India's next phase of growth than energy; yet its vital coal markets are controlled by competing mafias. I do not use that term loosely, to mean some sort of elite clubs; I mean literal organized criminal groups that use bribery and coercion to game the system and receive awards of massively subsidized coal concessions that they then develop at huge profits—and at great cost to India's treasury and to its ability to shape a credible energy policy.[8] The dysfunction of its energy markets is mounting, not receding; in the summer of 2012 a single blackout took out power to more than half of India—the largest power outage in contemporary history. If India's political system cannot muster the cohesion, the credibility, and the will to tackle that scale of corruption—and chart a credible pathway for economic and energy growth—India's prospects may well be stunted. A resumption of India-Pakistan tensions, or a return to violence in Afghanistan (where India has invested heavily), or inflation of the rupee would further drain India's resources.

Of the other members of the trillionaires' club, Brazil has seemed relatively stable, but it is of course possible that some of its past illnesses, now somewhat in abeyance, return to haunt them. Inner-city crime linked to a transnational drug trade, inflation, and political dysfunction among elites—these have sapped Brazil's energies in the past and could do so again. Turkey, similarly, could fall back into some of its older ills: regional tensions, or tensions between democratic forces and the army, could curtail its energies. During the summer of 2013 both states experienced large-scale middle-class protests against the government's entrenched power and privilege and the inequality exacerbated by rapid growth.

Darker still are the Russian scenarios. Indeed, watching Russia after Vladimir Putin returned himself to the presidency in 2012 (after four years of ruling from behind the scenes as prime minister), one fears that Russia has already entered a dangerous period. The present Russia exhibits a dystopian combination of highly centralized and personalized security and political power, with vast wealth (much of it "privatized" from the national treasury) held in the hands of a privileged few with close access to the center of power; far less prosperity beyond that immediate core; tight control over the media; and firm, sometimes brutal, suppression of dissent.[9] Russia is probably a receding, not a growing, power, but it retains nuclear weapons and a Security Council veto, which give it influence beyond its real strength.

The European and American versions of this scenario might not be as dramatic as those of the rising powers, but they could nevertheless sap the vitality of these two centers of power. Political gridlock in Washington and Brussels could impede efforts to move past current economic troubles. Both the European and American economies could potentially languish in slow growth or move in and out of recession for a long period. For a model, one need only look to the other former center of economic gravity, Japan, which spent two decades, between 1990 and 2010, in what became known too optimistically as the lost decade after the collapse of the Nikkei index in 1990. This collapse sparked a process of debt accumulation, failed reforms, and political gridlock superficially similar to that which occurred in the United States in the wake of the global financial crisis—and that is occurring in Europe now. In the United States, inequality is a growing, not a receding, challenge—one that helps explain how it is that Wall Street can have done so well since the global financial crisis while Main Street is only slowly recovering in what is, so far, largely a jobless recovery. This is a long-term threat both to the U.S. economic competitiveness and growth and, I would argue, to American democracy. (It is not, though, in the short term, a deep threat to American influence abroad.)

Japan may or may not succeed in its current effort to escape from its "lost decades" through a combination of strong stimulus and a move to reinvigorate its military. If it succeeds, it could produce a strong, confident Japan that is a powerful ally to the United States in Asia; but if too much of its drive for renewal comes from a desire to compete with China to regain the number-two slot in international affairs, the risks will rise. If it fails, we could see a Japan driven to emotional excesses of nationalism and competition.

A third and critical variable is relations between the major powers. America's European alliances look strongest. Various Europeans may pander to the Chinese over economic issues, but that is largely to the good if it increases the number of economic ties between China and the West; and in strategic terms, there is no indication of erosion in the core orientation of the Western powers. Asia could be more in flux. The U.S. position in Asia and globally would be weakened if there were a substantial shift in the relations between one of its core Asian allies and China—say, between Korea and China or between India and China. This is not particularly likely—there are deep nationalist and historical tensions pushing in the opposite direction. But relations could shift. If the United States misplays its hand with India, for example—perhaps by pulling back too far from its security commitments in the region, or taking a stance in global climate and energy negotiations that wreaks havoc on Indian growth—it could awaken older, semisocialist, and nonaligned sentiments that have not yet been put fully to rest in India. If India were to genuinely shift toward China, it would alter the overall calculus of the United States in Asia, in particular, but also in broader global dynamics. This is true to a lesser degree of Brazil and of Turkey—where U.S. missteps in the Arab world could cast doubt among Turkish elites of the wisdom of continuing to tie its own foreign policy fate to NATO, moving Turkey into the ranks of a "swing state."

This book argues that the fundamentals for the most part position the United States very well in terms of the potential shifting relations in geopolitics. But we should not ignore the fact that there are fundamentals and then there are perceptions—what we might call shadows.

Of Shadows

The most influential shadow is that of the future, and I turn to it in a moment. But in 2013 the odds that one of the major non-Western emerging powers would tilt decisively toward China, or in an anti-American direction, increased, marginally perhaps, as a result of a different kind of shadow. When Edward Snowden revealed, in the summer of 2013, the full extent of the U.S. National Security Agency's spying activities, both on U.S. citizens and internationally, it cast a pall on U.S. leadership abroad. The fact of the NSA's enormous scale of spying—not just against governments, not just against security suspects, but against businesses and friendly elites in friendly countries—caused enormous consternation in the media and among elites. Of course, no serious international relations professional or diplomat is unaware that governments routinely tap emails and phone calls to spy or search for suspected criminal or terrorist activity. But the sheer scale of the NSA's intelligence sweep, and the fact of individuals and friendly countries targeted for intelligence collection, did cause not only a chill among many of America's friends but also domestic debate.

Some of this was doubtlessly crocodile tears and tactical positioning. This may be particularly true of Brazil's president, Dilma Rousseff, who reacted most stridently against the revelations of the scale of NSA spying. The Brazilian government was in a difficult position, as the Snowden leaks revealed that Brasilia was the site of an NSA listening station. There is no credible way that the NSA would have an actual, physical listening station in Brasilia with no awareness of that fact by the Brazilian government. The Brazilian government was thus in the awkward position of appearing to be complicit with NSA's spying activities on Brazilian citizens, and there was a domestic uproar. Behind closed doors, President Rousseff instructed her senior foreign policy officials to tell the Brazilian Senate to "grow up—this is what governments do."[10] But in public, Rousseff—facing a reelection campaign, and having come through a period in which her government was marred by substantial scandals and domestic opposition—used the NSA scandal to position herself in populist terms, striking a strident anti-American note, which is still popular in many quarters in Latin America. Rousseff even used her speech at the UN General Assembly to call for new international regulations to limit the extent of government spying as well as for UN control of the Internet, the international equivalent of populism. The shallow character of Rousseff's outrage was cast in sharp relief by the reaction to the NSA revelations of the Mexican president, Pēna Nieto. When asked by the Mexican media about the NSA revelations, Nieto dismissed the issue. And in contrast to Rousseff, who cancelled a scheduled trip to Washington, he kept a scheduled visit from U.S. Vice President Biden.[11]

More worrying than Brazil's play was the reaction of elites in countries friendly to the United States, such as India, Turkey, and Germany. Again, no serious diplomatic or international relations professional is unaware that much of what is said by telephone or email might be subject to spying by numerous parties, in addition to the United States. But even then, the extent of detailed collection against individuals and the extent of penetration of friendly countries' governments and policy apparatus did come as something of a surprise to some and a source of concern to others. Moreover, for those elites who had been advocating a pro-U.S. stance within their domestic debate, it put them in an awkward position. From my own contacts with many of these individuals, I can attest that many were genuinely upset at the extent to which their privacy was violated by the NSA, as are many Americans.

Of course, some of this is a misunderstanding about the nature of NSA collection. In essence, the NSA sweeps huge volumes of data, literally tens of millions of conversations, into large data banks that can store material for a considerable period of time.[12] Then, only when there is a reason to examine an individual for tactical intelligence are those records examined in more detail, so it is very likely that the vast majority of those people caught up in the NSA sweep were in no way actually monitored in any meaningful sense of that word. Nevertheless, the revelations did cause many to be concerned about violations of their privacy, as well as putting them in an awkward position when asked for their reaction. And a number of those individuals have been moved, at least temporarily, to critique the United States about these activities in order to distance themselves.

Still, it is hard to imagine that anybody beyond perhaps the first flush of anger would think to themselves, "Surely China would never engage in this kind of activity." This is a recurrent theme in the book: even where America loses ground on an issue, China does not stand as a credible alternative. So while the NSA revelations have certainly dented America's reputation on civil liberties, it is hard to believe that it accrues to China's or any other state's benefit. And it is revealing, in the case of Germany, that the Snowden scandal did not halt or disrupt the TTIP negotiations, and that Germany's main demand was to join what's known as the "Five Eyes"—a small alliance of intelligence services that share product and offer each other certain protections. Thus, Germany's reaction was to seek closer ties to the United States.

Of other shadows there have been similar exaggerations. That was certainly the dynamic when the U.S. Congress in September 2013 failed to provide a budget or a continuing resolution on the budget, causing a government shutdown; some of the media gleefully crowed that the shutdown was symptomatic of U.S. decline. There were innumerable stories in social media and traditional media about how only a country in decline could allow this kind of shutdown of its essential government services, and both domestically and internationally people made hay of it.[13] But there have been shutdowns at many points in U.S. history, and they bear no correlation whatsoever to the trajectory of American power. That point is made evident by noticing that the last government shutdown took place under President Clinton in 1995, that is, at the onset of the highest peak of American power ever. There is no correlation whatsoever between American government shutdowns and the projection of power on the international stage.

But media reports are not all exaggerations. It was hardly absurd to be worried about the fact that for several days the shutdown seemed to threaten the ability of the United States to meet its international debt obligations. Governments from Tokyo to Beijing and leaders at the IMF and the G-20 reacted with concern. At one level, it reminds us of how central the United States still is. A U.S. default on its debt obligations would literally see the drying up of international financial systems within a matter of days. So central is the American financial system in the global economy that the global economy simply could not sustain a U.S. default. So on one level, the global concern about a U.S. government shutdown reinforces the centrality of the United States in the global economy.

But a possible default also surely did damage to America's reputation for financial soundness, just as the global financial crisis did. Over time, if the United States does not rectify a perception that it is becoming incapable of managing its global financial role, the willingness to participate in a system still overwhelmingly managed by the United States will be undermined. Chinese state-run media used the occasion to issue a call for the "de-Americanization" of the international financial system. For the short term, and for the medium tern, as argued earlier, this is not a credible alternative: it is simply not feasible for any of the emerging powers to develop an alternative financial system that does not have the United States at its core. Still, over the next decade or so, if the United States does not reverse its growing reputation for lack of political credibility, even for political incompetence, the emerging powers may well seek to try to develop alternative mechanisms. For the present, they do not have that choice, but over time, the United States is going to have to address genuine international concerns about the stability of its financial management; just as, in the face of the Snowden revelations, it is going to have to address the concerns of those emerging powers that wonder whether close ties to the United States come with more costs than rewards.

As noted above, perhaps the most important shadow upon the relation between the United States and the emerging powers is the shadow of the future. Countries make their decisions about economic ties and about strategic ties partly on the opportunities that present themselves at present and partly on a calculation about the future. The conventional wisdom has it, as noted earlier, that this favors China: if you believe that the United States is in terminal decline and that China is becoming a dominant power, there is logic in positioning yourself to take advantage of that shift—or at least to not be caught out by it. International elites' perception of the scale (and the reality of that scale) of Chinese growth led many countries to take advantage of China's economic opportunities This particular shadow of the future has been a pervasive part of the international narrative since the global financial crisis.

That being said, there are two counterpoints. One, as China rises it also casts another shadow of the future, and that is its growing military power and the uses to which that power will be put. These concerns drive some governments to hew more, not less, closely to the United States and to bolster other alliances. Two, perceptions of the future will shift as they catch up to the fundamentals: the continued phenomenon of America's enduring power, its energy renaissance, the fact that it continues to grow after the financial crisis, and the continued role of the dollar. As all of this becomes more widely appreciated, and as the slowing growth in the rising powers becomes more evident, the shadow of the future may change.

And the fundamentals, as I hope this book shows, are that the United States will continue to be an enduring power and that China, Brazil, India, and others will be significant players in the international system for some time to come. These rising powers will not, in the near to medium term, be genuine rivals to the United States. Most realistically, any elite or any government looking to the future is making decisions based on two realities: one, the continuing and enduring influence and weight of the United States; and two, the now present and potentially growing influence of the emerging powers. To date, and for the foreseeable future, no credible decisionmaker will be able to discount the weight of the United States. The shadow of the future should not blind us to the realities of the present.

Indeed, in my view, the most worrisome shadow of the future will not be cast by new great powers. This shadow, instead, will be cast by the evolution of technology and the devolution of the capacity to wield deadly technology from the great powers to smaller states; from smaller states to sophisticated terrorist organizations; from sophisticated terrorist organizations to unsophisticated ones; and ultimately to small groups of individuals and even lone actors.

With 9/11 we saw the capacity of a well-organized, global terrorist organization to challenge the basic structures of international order and the security of the world's superpower. The ability of terrorist organizations to disrupt international networks and flows continues to be a serious threat to the global economy and to various states' security. But what most worries me is the growing capacity of individuals, individual scientists, and even the lone terrorist to manipulate—with increasing sophistication and increasing access to technology—our biological future. As the scientific capacity to manipulate DNA shifts from being the terrain of highly specialized government programs to being the terrain of common university-level research, so the risks of accidental release of deadly biological material will grow, as will the prospects for terrorist use of biological material.[14]

I raise this point to suggest that those who worry about a change in the international order due to the rise of new powers may be missing a salient dynamic. Given the capacity of a small state, a terrorist cell, or an individual to challenge international order and international security, the rise of new powers is at worst a mixed blessing. Mixed because faced with a biological threat, the other great powers would have shared interests with the United States and reasonable capacities to help forestall, prevent, and contain such a threat. Their rise will add to not detract from net global capacity. It is true that in the short term the new powers, as noted in chapter 4, are sensitive about a strong international regime to deal with biological terror (because it invokes issues of sovereign capacity around the national health infrastructure); still, I think that that sensitivity will wane as their interests in stable globalization rise. However, if we want to worry about nightmare scenarios, it is not the shadow of 1914 that is most haunting, nor is it the specter of a U.S.-China conflict that should be keeping us up at night. No: it is the specter of a lone scientist with a DNA lab in his basement. Think of a more malign Edward Snowden with smallpox samples.

When we shift to discussions of strategy, we have to keep this in mind. This is a book about the shifting relationship among great powers, and the final chapter addresses that specific issue. But while in the coming period U.S. strategy will necessarily focus on the issue of the rising powers—of shaping China's rise, of creating the kinds of relationships that can pull U.S.-India and U.S.-Brazil relations into a more constructive pattern—it should not do so to the exclusion of transnational threats (or of human security). Just as it was a mistake in the 9/11 era to neglect the early rise of the new powers, so it would be a mistake in the coming period to neglect the worrying devolution of deadly technologies to the level of a terrorist organization or an individual. The good news is that the terrain of transnational threats creates opportunities for cooperation around overlapping interests.

Conclusion

Playing out the interactions between the variables discussed above, I see three broad scenarios that the United States should contemplate—one of which is more realistic than the others.

The first is a genuine rise-of-the-rest scenario, one that requires both the continued economic rise of India, China, Brazil, Turkey, and others and a higher degree of strategic unity among them. I believe that this scenario is unlikely, however, because of deep underlying tensions between the emerging powers. But if the West is recalcitrant about opening up the International Monetary Fund (IMF) and moving forward on the Doha round of free trade; if it is weak in the face of China's effort to stoke Asian nationalism, thereby eroding the Asian allies' confidence in American security guarantees; if China and India resolve their bilateral tensions; and if a long list of additional things happen to smooth the differences in interests among the emerging powers, the BRICs group might consolidate into a genuine political bloc. For this scenario to unfold requires, simultaneously, that the West remains in the economic doldrums, that the character of the alliance continues to soften, and that the United States fails to deepen its bilateral ties to India, Brazil, Turkey, Indonesia, and so forth. None of this is impossible, but current patterns make it seem unlikely.

The opposite, second, scenario could also occur. It is well within the realm of possibility that China could enter, a few years from now, a long period of strained and contentious political transition that undermines its economic trajectory—and the two phenomena could become mutually reinforcing.[15] China has a long tradition of discovering that overseas ambition quickly loses steam in the face of the extraordinarily complex job of maintaining stability in the Middle Kingdom.[16] India, simultaneously, could fail to make the next wave of policy changes required to stimulate a next wave of growth (or make them and then shift decisively to the West). Tensions between China or India and other emerging powers could mount. Meanwhile, after a few years, the eurozone could come back to life, and the United States could find just enough political unity to find a solid path to growth and deal responsibly with its debt. The current moment of concern about a rising China could have proved enough to shake Europe out of its doldrums and thus to reinvigorate the transatlantic alliance; and at the same time, China's moment of aggression may well have proved sufficient to consolidate the Asian alliances: not for nothing has China been called a self-containing power.[17] Thus the United States could face weakened and divided emerging powers and a rising and consolidated West. This has been referred to as the Atlantic scenario, though that is a misnomer, because the Pacific allies play a crucial part in it.[18] It is a possible scenario—but an awful lot of things have to break in one direction for it to come to pass.

The third scenario is far less simple and falls between these two poles. This scenario assumes that the various powers, both Western and emerging, rise and dip over time economically. The political character of each may evolve, but each may also for a considerable period of time stay essentially as it is now, including with its contradictions. And relations between the major powers will be in some degree of flux—largely hewing to existing patterns but episodically flirting with other arrangements or other ties. In my judgment, this is by far and away the most realistic scenario in front of us.

Pointing to uncertainty in the trajectories of the rising powers is not to deny this important fact: the rising powers are now shaping and will shape what is possible in international economics and international security—to say nothing of energy and climate. Only an acute crisis in Russia or China would change that—and probably only temporarily. For the foreseeable future, the international system will be shaped by the effort of India, Brazil, China, Indonesia, Turkey, and others to grapple with the tension between their search for autonomy and the actual practice of growing and profiting through the existing system. And it will be shaped by U.S. reactions to that tension.

In sum, the United States probably faces a period, likely of two or more decades, characterized by uncertainty and fluidity. Throughout this period, the United States is likely to remain the most influential actor in international politics but will have to shift the ways it wields its power. The further out in that period that we go, the more likely is it that China constitutes a genuine peer competitor—albeit without serious allies. Among the third tier of powers—Japan, Korea, India, Turkey, Brazil, Germany, and to a lesser degree the rest of the trillionaires—there is likely to be intense competition for status and influence. The United States is going to have to devote more diplomatic energy to shaping their competitive search for influence. And we should recall with concern the notion that the biggest risk lies in crisis between the second-tier powers.

The United States can influence only some of these variables—and only to some degree. It can shape growth, mostly by the exercise of its own fiscal and economic levers, but short of the crude cudgel of sanctions it cannot target that effort (say, getting India to grow and China to falter): economic ties with and between these countries are too integrated for that by now. It could try to restrict China's growth by using its global leverage to complicate China's search for energy, but this would impact China only somewhat—and at a high cost. The odds that the United States could affect the internal dynamics of states as large, complex, and sophisticated as China, India, Brazil, and Turkey are remote at best. But the United States can affect relations between the powers—mostly by creating opportunities and by shaping the international choices the powers face. This is the terrain both of specific investments and of U.S. grand strategy.

CHAPTER NINE

AMERICAN LEADERSHIP IN A FRACTURED AGE

On August 21, 2013, according to both U.S. intelligence sources and a report by a UN chemical weapons team, chemical munitions were fired from Syrian government-held territory into the small but strategically located town of Ghouta, on the outskirts of Damascus. Human rights organizations and journalists on the ground reported gruesome scenes: deaths of men, women, and children consistent with chemical attacks, possibly sarin gas.[1] More than a thousand people were estimated to have been killed, according to U.S. intelligence sources.[2]

Earlier, President Obama had declared that a significant use of chemical weapons by the Assad regime was a red line that would trigger U.S. military involvement in the conflict, an outcome Obama otherwise sought to avoid. In fact, there were several small incidents of the use of chemical weapons in 2012, but they were not deemed large enough to trigger American action. But in the wake of the August 21 attack, President Obama declared that the red line had been crossed.

If we gloss over the details of what happened next, it could look like a positive set of developments. President Obama threatened the Assad regime with an American attack; then offered a diplomatic way out, if Assad would get rid of his chemical weapons. First, Russian president Putin and then Assad himself agreed to the deal, and a UN Security Council resolution was passed authorizing the UN and the Organization for the Prohibition of Chemical Weapons (OPCW) to mount an operation to dismantle Syria's chemical stockpile. Just over two weeks later, the UN/

OPCW team was on the ground, receiving reasonable cooperation from Syria. The Obama administration strenuously asserted that the threat of force was indispensable to the UN deal.

But only a blinkered or apologist account of this episode overlooks important and troubling details, which were these. In response to the Ghouta attack, the U.S. president threatened the use of force and sought support from America's closest ally, the United Kingdom. Unfortunately, the U.K. prime minister misread his domestic politics and failed to secure a resolution in support of action. (This was not entirely Obama/Cameron's fault: they did not count on the unprincipled stance of U.K. opposition leader Ed Miliband, who chose to repay old Labour debts against Tony Blair over Iraq rather than dealing with the most significant violation of the long-standing norm against chemical weapons use since the Iran-Iraq war in 1981.) The French president did support President Obama, as did Saudi Arabia and Turkey and a handful of others, but the coalition still looked thin: for a few days, Secretary of State John Kerry was trumpeting a coalition "in the double digits" (including that military and political powerhouse Albania) in a pose reminiscent of the most tortured efforts of the Bush administration to inflate international support for the invasion of Iraq (Mongolia and Palau were singled out in 2003).

Then against the advice of his national security advisers, President Obama decided to turn to Congress for authorization. Authorization for what, exactly? It was hard to tell. It was going to be a "pinprick" strike, according to Kerry; but the U.S. military "doesn't do pinprick," according to President Obama. It was a significant hit on Syria's chemical capacity but would not weaken the regime; or, yes, it would weaken the regime but not so much that it would fall.[3] The Senate ultimately voted in favor of authorizing a strike but only after attaching the condition that the United States would up its support for the rebels, which Obama opposed. Was there a follow-on plan? More of the same, according to the administration; which was, in effect, to do very little. And within a matter of days it became evident that the administration was failing to convince the U.S. House of Representatives—and not only the Republican caucus: both Democrats and Republicans were making it clear that they could not find a strategy in the administration's message and that they wanted either more engagement or less but certainly not what the administration was proposing. By early September it was evident that Obama was heading to a no vote in Congress.

It was exactly at that moment that Secretary Kerry, seemingly flippantly, floated the idea that the Assad regime could escape the threat of force by giving up all of its chemical munitions. He then immediately dismissed the proposal as unworkable. And the White House distanced itself from the proposal—until, unexpectedly, the Russian president, Vladimir Putin, endorsed it, at which point the White House was at pains to argue that, actually, it was President Obama's proposal after all, which he had explored some two weeks earlier with Putin at the G-20 session in St. Petersburg.

At this point, President Obama addressed the nation in a prime-time TV address. He made the case for treating the use of chemical weapons as a category distinct from ongoing violence and requiring a specific response (a view I share). But he was less convincing about his decision to seek congressional approval, contrasting it with his decision not to in the case of Libya (a case in which far more military action was used than was being contemplated in Syria). And having said all this, Obama then asked for nothing. He had the option of saying, in effect, "We have a deal in hand, but I need authorization for the use of force to make its implementation credible." But he chose not to pursue that path, apparently drawing the conclusion that he was not going to win the House vote. At this stage, the threat of U.S. force was negligible.

Amidst the administration's confusion, Putin saw an opening for a triple gain. First, and I believe most important, he saw an opportunity to secure Syria's chemical weapons. Those who follow Russian policy in Syria most consistently argue that Putin's motives are dominated by his concern about the potential blowback in Chechnya and other parts of the Islamic Russian rim.[4] The idea that chemical weapons could flow from Syria into that area is a serious concern for Putin. Second, Putin saw that the deal would prop up Assad by requiring his regime's cooperation on disarmament and, more generally, by refocusing U.S. policy on his chemical weapons rather than his massive human rights abuses. Assad is both a Russian ally in the Middle East and a bulwark, in Russia's estimation, against Islamic militarism in Syria. Third—and the least important but the icing on the cake—Putin seized the opportunity to wrong-foot the Americans and project an image of Russia as a resurgent peer of the United States.

And as for the outcome: it is possible that the deal may result in most or even all of Syria's chemical weapons being removed from the theater, no minor accomplishment. But, save hope, it provides no clear path toward resolving the ongoing brutal war and humanitarian catastrophe. Whatever the outcome, this is a case study of diplomatic fumbling. But the commentary that followed was typically overwrought. Russia had reclaimed its position as a great power, it was claimed; and the entire episode was proof positive of American decline, or American retrenchment, or both.[5]

That Syria is a case of disengagement by the United States is surely true. The result, as I argue in chapter 6, has been disastrous for Syria and risks serious consequences for the region as a whole. But it is a failure of U.S. policy, not a feature of a changed order. It is probably not a worse case of disengagement than, say, American policy in Bosnia in the early 1990s, when for almost three years the United States chose to stay out of the fight and pushed the region to take the lead in resolving the crisis—at the cost of roughly 200,000 Bosnian dead—before finally agreeing to more forcefully engage through NATO. U.S. disengagement in Syria also resembles its policy in Kosovo, where the United States pursued futile diplomatic initiatives with Russia while Slobodan Milosevic's forces conducted a brutal campaign of ethnic cleansing—again, until the United States finally and belatedly agreed to act through NATO. These two episodes of prior American disengagement or failed policy came at the onset and then the peak of American unilateral hyperpower. Syria is yet another tragic episode of this phenomenon, but it is hardly, in and of itself, a harbinger of American decline. Congressional appetite for foreign intervention also is not as different as newspapers' op-ed pages would have us believe. Congress declined to authorize military action in Kosovo in 1999.[6]

Rather than treating Syria as an illustration of a coming disorder, we should instead understand Syria as an illustration of what I believe to be the iron law of multilateral action: that there is no possibility of effective collective action when U.S. policy is hesitant or partially engaged. Whatever the rationale for U.S. hesitation in Syria, it has been and will continue to be mere chimera that the UN or any other actor could tackle the problem absent substantive U.S. leadership. The United States remains indispensable to any concerted international action—and will be for the foreseeable future. As Secretary of Defense Gates said in 2008, "For any given cause or crisis, if America does not lead, then more often than not, what needs to be done simply won't get done."[7] That remains true to this day and looks set to remain true for some time to come. That Putin was able to steal some of the limelight for putting a chemical weapons team in place in Syria was a function of the diplomatic confusion of the U.S. administration. If we were to look for genuine solutions to the conflict, neither Russia nor any other power other than the United States is in a position to assemble the diplomatic coalitions or lead the kind of multinational force that could stabilize Syria. Tragically, it may now be too late for that option in Syria.

Episodes like Bosnia and Syria, in which the United States chooses not to lead, will inevitably form part of the landscape of what lies ahead. These episodes seem to epitomize the notion of a G-Zero world, where no one else can lead and America chooses not to. But these are instances of inaction, not the defining feature of the international landscape. The concept of a G-Zero world is set in opposition to alternative scenarios, like a G-1 world (in which we see the revitalization of U.S. hegemony and leadership), a G-2 world (in which we see strong U.S.-China cooperation and problem solving on global issues), a G-20 world (in which we manage complex issues through the G-20 body itself, or with those states). I broadly share the sense that these are potential leadership configurations, though I would add that a wider set of countries, not just the leading economies, can actually contribute to crisis management and global problem solving. That is, I believe that various groupings of forty (plus or minus) states will act to tackle major challenges. The configuration of states likely involved is indicated by NATO and its partners; the governing boards of the International Atomic Energy Agency and the Organization for the Prohibition of Chemical Weapons; and the membership of the Nuclear Security Summit, the Proliferation Security Initiative, and the Global Counterterrorism Forum. These G-40-like bodies are an important part of the international landscape.

Where I differ from others is in seeing these leadership configurations, not as alternatives, but rather as simultaneous features of the world we're going to be living in. There will be issues, like humanitarian interventions, in which U.S. action will be the make-or-break factor. There will be others, like Asian security and climate change, in which U.S.-China bilateral relations will be the fulcrum around which policy is organized—though policy here also involves powers like Japan and India. Decisions on much of the world's economic and financial agenda will be made primarily within the G-20 and among the G-20 members. And there will inevitably be some issues that are hamstrung by several factors: U.S. reluctance or domestic constraint, the reality that the rising players are still partial powers, and divergence of interests. We will be in a G-1, a G-2, a G-20, and a G-Zero world all at the same time. I anticipate that all of these forms of interaction will dominate the international system for some time to come.

Moreover, we have to be realistic about standards. At moments, the current debate about American leadership has seemed to invoke an idyllic period of American leadership in which the country simply stated its demands and allies and others followed unquestioningly. This idyll never was. Even when the United States guaranteed the security of Europe and the free world against the Soviet Union, America's relationships with its allies were complex and required constant negotiation and care. The brief period of American hyperpower was also challenging: the United States could project military and economic power across the globe unchecked, but that gave rise to as much resistance as respect, and many allies felt freer to ignore American pressure because they no longer needed to invoke American security guarantees.[8]

Challenges of the Coming Era

In the coming era, the account in this book suggests that American foreign policy will confront a somewhat different set of challenges than before. The options for American leadership will expand or constrict in part as a function of its allies and of the independent powers and also as a function of its performance in complex global issues like international finance and climate change. I make the case throughout this book that the emerging non-Western powers are both less threatening and more divided than is often portrayed. But I also emphasize that this good news hardly means that these powers will not be essential to the day-to-day business of the international system. If we witness a significant erosion in American relations with India, Brazil, Turkey (still formally an ally, of course), Indonesia, Mexico, and others, America's leadership options will be more complicated.

Finally, of course, the credibility of American leadership will be shaped by domestic factors. I am not going to try to address the kinds of domestic reforms—for example, to primary and secondary education, to tax policy, to infrastructure—that are necessary for the United States to sustain healthy growth, or the growing challenge of an elite that is profiting substantially from current economic trends and a middle class that is stagnating.[9] But I would stress that debates about the American economy have to take seriously the point that the U.S. economy is now firmly enmeshed in the global one. With 25 percent of its GDP dependent on trade, and growing, America cannot expect that the economic realm is hived off from broader global realities. And that realization must be integral to the country's thinking about how to retool for the period ahead.

The United States should also have the humility to be willing to learn from others as it invests in better tools to avoid new, deep, financial crises. On the positive side, U.S. administrations have so far shown the confidence and maturity to lead on International Monetary Fund reform; there, unfortunately, Congress is more blinkered so far, and American allies in Europe have allowed fairly petty national and bureaucratic stakes to get in the way of an effective European position. On the negative side, the United States has shown less willingness to learn from others about financial regulations—and the country is going to have to push deeper on global financial regulations lest some of the same challenges that undid the global financial system in 2007–09 recur, albeit perhaps in less dramatic form. As I write the final passages of this book, warning lights are starting to flash about excess debt in China. The Chinese authorities have launched an audit of debt at all levels, a step that, had the United States taken it when its domestic mortgage lending was flashing yellow in 2007, could have helped prevent or mitigate the global financial crisis that followed. In the coming period, the United States should be willing to pay attention to and learn from economies that have done a better job at growing while managing financial risk. And as noted in chapter 8, the potential threat of a U.S. debt default, if not corrected, will undermine American leadership over time.

Where I differ from some analysts is in believing that a concentrated focus on the economic underpinnings of U.S. strength and the economic foundations of a stable globalization need not deter the United States from investing in forms of action and diplomacy that can shape great-power relations in the period ahead.[10] The country is simply going to have to walk and chew gum at the same time. There is still time to shape how great-power relations evolve, but there is no time to waste.

It is still the United States that has the best chance to shape an international order that is stable and productive—that is, that avoids great-power war and fosters a stable and growing international economy. It can and should do more than that, too. It should continue to facilitate progress against civil war and poverty, helping states and peoples take advantage of the global economy and reach for their rights and for the rule of law. And it will have to grapple with the core dilemma of growing energy needs and risks to the climate.

And American foreign policy will have to learn how to achieve influence in a complex and shifting landscape—where economic competition and security rivalry play out at the same time as shared interest and cooperation; where American allies are both slumping and rising, as are foes and potential foes; where America's fate is bound to complex global negotiations; where the impulse to rivalry and the incentives for restraint are in a tense and shifting balance. But in doing this, the United States retains extraordinary assets and advantages. Two are foremost: a phalanx of allies, and a global presence.

Of course, the global presence can be seen as a complication and a drain: the other powers, it is argued, need only look after interests in their own region. But that is far from the truth. Or it is true only if we look very narrowly at traditional domains of security. It captures nothing of the economic realities that these countries confront, which are simultaneously regional and global; of the structures of global finance and information flow; and above all, of their far-flung interests in energy and resource acquisition, which give them deep stakes in the stability of regions far beyond their borders and in the transshipment routes between them. And this gives them a huge stake in our presence in these regions and our policy there; and this gives us leverage. The issues of energy resources and of globalization's networks, especially maritime trade and security, are going to be central to U.S. foreign policy in the coming era.

America as a Coalitional Power:
Foreign Policy in a Globalized Age

In doing all of this, U.S. foreign policy will have to manage four tensions.

First, U.S. foreign policy is going to have to maintain a delicate balance between strengthening its alliances and avoiding bloc formation. The breadth and range of its allies are one of America's most important sources of power, economically and strategically. Reinforcing its allies, and standing by them in need, must continue to be central to American policy. This is true whether the subject is Asian security and the role of Japan and Korea or the Middle East and the role of Israel and the United Arab Emirates. Despite the repeated frustrations of dealing with Europe within NATO, despite the tensions of the competing demands of our allies in the Middle East, despite our Asian allies' best efforts to make our lives complicated, it would be a fundamental error to allow these frustrations to dim our commitments to our alliance structure.

At the same time, if we place too much emphasis on formal alliances, we risk other policy objectives. As I argue throughout this book, the current, fluid international moment is open to being shaped, and it is the United States that has the best chance to shape it—to lead or, by implication, to lose. But many an athlete or politician has entered a race that is his or hers to lose and, by making bad choices, lost. One of the easiest ways for the United States to lose in the current moment is to adopt policies—for example, on climate change or trade—that push the emerging powers closer together.

There are two credible versions of this: one is closer Russia-China ties; the other is a genuine BRICs bloc. Unless the United States is willing to continue to see the BRICs rise economically within the system, it will undermine their incentives for restraint and cooperation. Helping the BRICs economically means creating more space for them in international financial institutions and opening up free trade, notably in agriculture and services (the issues that have long held up the Doha round of World Trade Organization talks).

Free trade is an example of an area where the United States can get caught in the tension between alliance strengthening and bloc avoidance. The U.S. push for the Trans-Pacific Partnership on trade and the Transatlantic Trade and Investment Partnership is a positive move if it bolsters broader alliance arrangements. But if the United States neglects those countries not included in either partnership—India, Brazil, Turkey, China—it will be weakening its hand in the long term, adding incentives to the BRICs to overcome their internal divisions. If an overall principle is to balance alliance maintenance with avoiding blocs, then the TTIP and TPP have to be combined with a genuine move to make progress on further trade liberalization within the WTO (especially on agriculture and government services) as well as to incorporate Turkey into the TTIP process. In 2013 Brazil gained the leadership of the WTO and looks set to put some muscle into an effort to galvanize renewed negotiations. While there are some areas (agriculture subsidies, for example) where the United States will face tough domestic politics, American strategy should not just accept but even encourage Brazilian leadership in the WTO. There are also close U.S. allies, like Australia, committed to WTO reform; the United States can also work to bolster their role. (It helps that cutting agriculture subsidies would be good for the American economy, even if tough politically.)

Of course, there are tensions between strengthening alliances and avoiding blocs of states. But tension need not be a contradiction. As long as an alliance does not focus on the containment of China, there are many ways it can promote Chinese and Indian and Brazilian and Indonesian and Mexican participation in collaborative efforts to manage a stable order. The stronger the alliances, the less China can challenge the United States for leadership and the more incentive it will have to take a restrained approach.

Second, there is a China-specific version of this balance: the challenge the United States faces between simply acceding to China's demands for changes to various international systems (such as China's now repeated demand to shift away from the U.S. dollar as a reserve currency), which would be foolhardy, and too stiffly resisting China's rise, forcing its hand toward a stance more genuinely geared to weakening the current order.

The two tensions are closely related. For example, in avoiding blocs overall, a very different kind of error would be for the United States to try, prematurely, to push countries like India and Brazil into alliance relationships—a bloc of democracies. This the autonomous powers will resist, and strongly. They have no interest in being part of a Western-dominated bloc, and they have important economic and political relationships with China that they cannot afford to lose. Now, if China presses too hard, and is too ambitious, it could force India's hand. But ironically, it is up to China to create a democratic bloc in international politics. And, for now, there is no need for one. For now at least, the United States has enough common or overlapping interests with China that it can find ways to cooperate, to deconflict interests, and to compete within boundaries. It can find myriad forms of coalitions to get things done, without forming a democratic bloc. Trying to forge one would force China's hand and set the United States on a path to a new cold war with China, an outcome it can and ought still to avoid.

More generally, when dealing with China, the United States needs to use its global position to strengthen its regional hand. This can mean facilitating Chinese interests in other parts of the world as part of broader confidence building measures, or it can mean using U.S. global strength as a source of leverage. It can mean creating openings for China in the Middle East and Central Asia and other regions in exchange for China's adherence to regimes it helps build. And it can mean using U.S. global advantages as leverage in the relationship with China. Former Australian prime minister Kevin Rudd, a close observer of China's evolving role in Asia, argued in 2013 that the subsequent five years would be critical in setting the tone in the relationship between China, the United States, and the other Asian powers.[11] In Asia, that timeline may be right. But add to that the substantial residual advantages that the United States has at the global level, including in military terms, and the time line is probably somewhat longer. Throughout, America should think of China not as a stand-alone problem or prospect but as one part of a wider transition. The United States will be in a stronger position if it deals with China in the context of a broader reality, one shaped not just by the United States but also by its core allies and, whenever possible, by other emerging powers.

Since the global financial crisis, U.S.-China relations have already gone through an important evolution. In the period from 2008 to 2010 there was probably too much enthusiasm, too much hope for a G-2-style arrangement, and too little recognition of the need to negotiate from strength. From 2010 to 2012 we saw the opposite: a sense that China could do no right, that we were already locked into a new cold war. Since 2012 and the Obama-Xi summit in Sunnylands, California, we have seen a more sound approach, focused on finding a sustainable balance between cooperation and managed competition. Chinese leaders refer to this as a "new type of great-power relations," and that is welcome, even if it suggests a closer parity between the United States and China than actually exists. The United States should not forget that it remains, and will remain for some time to come, the senior partner.

At the beginning of this chapter, I criticize the Obama administration for its handling of the Syria crisis in August-September 2013. But in the same time frame, it was undertaking an exercise in climate change negotiations that, to my mind, model precisely the kind of leadership the country is going to need in the coming period. This leadership is on what are known as short-term climate drivers—more specifically, hydrofluorocarbons (HFCs)—one of the most dangerous of carbon emissions. This collaboration began (as documented in chapter 5) as a U.S.-China bilateral agreement, placing China at the core of policymaking in a constructive manner. But it did not end there. The United States subsequently struck a parallel deal with India and then with Brazil. It then took the issue first to the MEF and then to the G-20, winning agreements from each body to take steps to cut HFCs. The result is one of the more significant steps forward on climate issues of late. And while China was present at creation for this initiative, it was the United States that took it outward, through concentric circles of action.

Concentric diplomacy is complex, but in the contemporary moment, complexity plays to the American advantage. As long as the United States is viewed by each of the major powers—established and rising—as an important part of the equation, its strategy options are open. Only the United States has the breadth of relations to manage concentric diplomacy. The minute the country starts forming rigidly aligned blocs or devising strategic arrangements to contain China, its options dramatically narrow. Of course, containment of China may ultimately prove necessary; but then the breadth and depth of U.S. alliances give the United States a strong position.

For all of these reasons, third, America is also going to have to work with diverse actors to handle crises and solve problems. It has to balance the import of direct U.S. leadership with the second sense of "ours" to lead: the notion that a broader set of actors will seek to assert leadership roles within specific issue areas and will have the capacity to succeed in this effort, at least in part. And this means balancing traditional modes of U.S. leadership with those of small groups of allies, and with wider, more multilateral or multinational, approaches.

America has already begun this balancing effort in its involvement in the Arctic, in counterpiracy in the Indian Ocean, and in the Major Economies Forum. But at present the country devotes only modest diplomatic and intellectual resources to these efforts, and there is a limited body of expertise or knowledge about these issues in the U.S. government. Jim Steinberg, as U.S. deputy secretary of state, used to stress that the United States needed to move the management of multinational coalitions for action (which he called the infrastructure for collective action) from the fringes to the core of American foreign policy.[12] He is right.

That does not mean committing the bulk of U.S. power to formal international institutions; far from it. Most of the time, the country is going to want to work through a concentric-circles approach. American interactions with allies, the emerging powers, and others have begun in time to show patterns. The essential pattern is this: we start with U.S. decision-making, which is substantially shaped by bilateral relations with a single other power, or a small handful of powers (China, or China-India-Japan, or Russia-France-Britain, or other similar combinations). Further, these decisions are taken in the context of a somewhat wider grouping (the fifteen of the UN Security Council, or the nineteen of the Major Economies Forum, or the twenty-plus of the G-20, or the twenty members and observers of the Arctic Council). In some instances, implementation will also bring in a further layer of actors—a G-40, so to speak—whether that is NATO and NATO partnership members, ASEAN members, the members of the League of Arab States, IMF board members, major troop contributors to peacekeeping operations, the members of the IAEA governing board, the governing board of the OPCW, or the Nuclear Security Summit. Learning to manage these concentric circles will become central to the skill set of U.S. diplomacy. Universal global bodies like the UN

General Assembly will have their place, too, for example in the normative debate around development issues, but rarely will they be the locus
of action or strategy or problem solving.

Fourth, and finally, the United States is going to have to find a way
to balance its focus. On the one hand, a central plank of U.S. strategy is
going to have to be a concerted, long-term effort to focus on great-power
geopolitics and geoeconomics—an effort to use its instruments of power
to shape the options that China, India, and others confront in the international system, sustaining a dynamic where there is enough on the table
for them to have incentives to participate and large enough costs to them
if they defect. On the other hand, regional crises and transnational threats
are not going to go away, and the United States will have no choice but to
continue to engage in conflict management, sometimes intervention, and a
continuing battle against various manifestations of global terrorism. The
good news is that transnational threats will be more a source of cooperation than tension with the major powers, if handled correctly.

Maritime Security: Balancing Great-Power Politics and Transnational Threats

The challenge—and opportunity—of balancing great-power tensions
with great power cooperation on transnational threats is best illustrated
by the rapidly evolving terrain of maritime security. It was for this reason
that I began each chapter of part 2 of this book with an account of the
major powers working to redefine their position or their relationships
on one of the world's oceans or seas. In earlier historic moments, naval
competition or naval arms races have been central to the dynamics of
great-power transitions, and we see similar dynamics now in the South
and East China Seas. But things are more complex than a simple arms
race or the rebalancing of military power in a contested region. As we saw
from Somalia to the Arctic to the eastern Mediterranean, there are different aspects to this game now, with different interests at play. There are
shared or at least overlapping interests in trade protection and in regional
security that are driving more cooperative approaches. And even more
important, there are overlapping interests in the stability of energy flows,
including those that flow through the Strait of Hormuz.

The United States could do much to advance its interests and to improve
the resilience of the existing order by thinking about the maritime space

at a global level, rather than region by region. One relatively straight-forward move that the United States could make is to build on existing counterpiracy efforts and trade route security. It would be wise, in doing so, to work in partnership with other committed players, like Australia and the UAE and India. There might be some value in forging a global platform for maritime security issues, building on the lessons of informal, multinational action (such as the Proliferation Security Initiative) that have been useful on nuclear safety and terrorism. A global platform could foster information and technology sharing and exchanges of best practice and, more important, set a global benchmark for joint action and disen-tanglement of interests. This last would be useful especially in framing, in global terms, the regional dynamics in the South and East China Seas.

The United States could also lead efforts to expand the kind of infor-mal, deconfliction, and conflict-avoidance arrangements that have been forged in the Arctic. It missed a major opportunity in 2013 when China and India applied for observer status in the Arctic Council. I believe that the council's response to China should have been to say, "Yes, you can have observer seats in the Arctic Council—where you have strong inter-ests in both energy and trade—the day after you sign a code of conduct to regulate behavior and to limit crises in the South China Sea." Instead, the Arctic Council allowed China to become an observer with the hope that such participation would change Chinese behavior in the South China Sea. Still, China will one day want full membership in the council, so some leverage still exists. A global maritime regime, built around some of the lessons of the Arctic, would increase the possibilities for more stable arrangements in the South and East China Seas.

The United States could also seek to spread the burdens and costs of trade route protection to others. There may be particular opportunities with India, as it builds up its navy. And off the coast of Somalia, and in other counterpiracy cases, surely there is a case for allowing others to lead joint operations.

The most complex and controversial, but also the most important, step that the United States could take in establishing a stable maritime order—and a stable order among the great powers, more generally—would be to propose to China the following basic trade: stability in the South China Sea for stability in the Gulf. Let me explain. As China con-tinues to pressure the American navy's role in the South China Sea, the (correct) American response has not been to back down but to beef up. But given the realities of constrained economic times, and the need to husband U.S. resources, this response is putting pressure on the continued U.S. military presence in the Persian Gulf. But that, in turn, makes China nervous: senior American officials visiting Beijing these days are asked much less about embargoing energy flows using America's Pacific fleet than they are about the risks of reducing America's commitment in the Gulf. The same phenomenon becomes apparent: while China is increasingly competitive with the United States in Asia, the United States still has a dominant global position—which gives it leverage.

Given that leverage, the United States should make it clear to China that America's willingness to continue to play a stabilizing role in the Gulf is increasingly going to be shaped by the question of whether it must continue to devote resources to stabilizing Asian waters. If, instead, the United States can reach a modus vivendi with China regarding Asian waters, its ability to continue to secure the Gulf is more likely to be sustainable.

What might a modus vivendi look like? I suspect that ultimately the United States and China will have to negotiate their way to something that could be called "mutually assured denial." That is, the United States will need to recognize that China is not going to give up on its quest to deny the U.S. Navy the option of choking off China's imports through the Straits of Malacca or to impede the sea lanes of communication through the South China Sea. But China, too, will need to recognize that the U.S. Navy is not going to fade quietly into the night, abandoning a presence in the western Pacific and the South China Sea that it has maintained since before the Second World War. A mutual recognition that each state will maintain enough capacity to prevent the other from closing those sea lanes could produce a stable arrangement over time. After all, the two states share a deep economic interest in keeping those sea lanes open. This is controversial and complex, and I introduce it here with some hesitation. It's an idea that warrants more than a brief paragraph. But it's the kind of proposal we need to explore as part of forging a new kind of great power relationship with China.

It's the Energy, Stupid

The complex features of the modern moment were also present in another issue that comes up again and again in part 2: energy. While energy is accorded its own subsection in chapter 5, the question of energy and other resources is also essential to the dynamics of the emerging powers' attitudes to transnational threats—as well as to crisis management and development, as more and more of the world's once war-torn states discover large reserves of natural resources. Energy is critical to the U.S.-China relationship, as just highlighted, as well as to India's economic future. And here again, the United States brings to the table substantial—and growing—strengths.

In the strategic debate about the great powers, energy and, even more so, climate change are often treated as stand-alone issues. In fact, in the emerging powers' perceptions of great-power relations and international order, energy and climate loom large and are inseparable. Balancing the emerging powers' continued thirst for energy with the intensifying pressures to find a credible climate change regime will be a major test of American leadership in the decade ahead—and beyond.[13]

It could be argued that America's growing ability to provide for its energy needs from domestic supply and from its own region (drawing on Canadian, Brazilian, and Venezuelan supplies) means that it is uncoupled from global energy insecurity. This is a very partial truth. The fact remains that should there be major disruptions to the flow of oil from the Persian Gulf, the global price of oil will rise steeply—and Americans will feel the effects of that immediately, especially in gasoline prices. And American allies, not just putative adversaries, will be badly affected. The U.S. energy position is an important fallback should relations with China or other emerging powers deteriorate. In the meantime, though, the country should use its strong energy position (coupled with its still-dominant global naval position) as a carrot, not a stick. The United States has something that all the rising powers need, and it should be willing to continue to supply it as long as the rising powers begin to deal responsibly with energy exploration and, in time, contribute to the security of energy flows.

The starting point should be using the country's increasing energy security to reinforce alliances, through approval of natural gas sales, in particular. But what should immediately follow goes beyond allies: countries like India should be high on the list of recipients of energy. And with India, there is a double reason: to solidify the relationship and to secure an ally in climate discussions.

But the United States is also going to have to take the lead in driving new arrangements for energy security at the global level, including bringing the new major consumers into a coordinating mechanism. Most proposals to deal with this suggest bringing the emerging powers into the International Energy Agency, a subsidiary body of the OECD, which in November 2013 created an "outreach mechanism" for relations with the emerging powers. However, such outreach mechanisms have been tried before, by the G-8 and the OECD, and they tend to underperform. The psychology of rise, and the instinct of these states to avoid participating in unequal treaties, means that the rising powers hesitate before engaging with a body whose rules they had no role in shaping and in which they are structurally outvoted. More likely to succeed is a forum in which Western and non-Western powers already sit together, such as the Major Economies Forum or the G-20. These bodies bring together the right countries on the right terms. There is a problem in that the domestic bureaucratic arrangements of these bodies are often staffed by the wrong parts of government (frequently environment and finance ministries, rather than energy and foreign policy ministries)—but that is comparatively easily fixed. And these bodies can draw on the existing tools of the International Energy Agency without those having to be renegotiated—as the G-20 has drawn on the technical capacities of the IMF.

When it comes to climate, the most practical thing is to pursue a back-to-basics approach, which combines a focus on natural gas (which emits carbon at roughly half the intensity of oil), efficiency, and joint investment in renewables. Here, the concentric circles start with the United States and China, where these two largest emitters can lead the way by increasing energy efficiency and reducing carbon emissions. Then the focus can shift to India (see chapter 5). Helping India navigate a pathway to clean energy growth is win-win in terms of climate and international order. More widely in Asia, the United States can play a critical role in helping the region develop a natural gas infrastructure. Long-standing tensions in the region—among China, Japan, Korea, and Russia, in particular—will impede regional cooperation; but the United States can help the region not only develop a shared gas infrastructure but also reduce carbon emissions. Beyond that small circle, the Major Economies Forum offers wider action. When there is real progress under way with the MEF, the UN can be brought in.[14]

Some climate scholars have begun to imagine alternatives for global arrangements. Strobe Talbott and William Antholis, motivated by both economic and moral concerns, propose a mechanism for free trade in clean energy instruments modeled on the General Agreement on Tariffs and Trade, which promoted global free trade after World War II.[15] Warren McKibbin, an Australian climate scholar and adviser, argues that the United States should use its dominant financial position to establish a price for carbon—and to leave it to global finance markets to figure out how to structure that into the market.[16] Others look at the critical role that cities play and the possibility that clean energy action by leading cities could happen more quickly and more effectively than at the state level. Although some of these proposals are variously based on free trade principles, subsidiarity, or monetary policy, they align on three critical points: they work in concentric circles from the most important economies outward, they require diplomatic innovation, and the United States must lead the effort to establish them.

And while grappling with new energy and maritime realities, the United States will have to continue to grapple with older challenges, like crisis in the Middle East. And here, too, it will have to find new ways to accommodate the concerns and interests of the emerging powers.

Crisis Management: A Multinational Approach

When it comes to crisis management, the American focus of late has been on NATO. That is logical, because the country has been fighting two wars in which it contributed the bulk of the fighting force and in which its most important partners were NATO members (most of the coalition in Iraq) or NATO itself (in Afghanistan and for training in Iraq). The consequence is that the bulk of U.S. attention on multinational force management has been on NATO, both in terms of learning lessons from the Iraq and Afghanistan experiences and in terms of retooling the organization to meet twenty-first-century needs.

But if in the era ahead countries like India, Brazil, Turkey (not only through NATO), Indonesia, and the Gulf states will exert more influence in crises, through financial and diplomatic means as well as through arms sales, then tools are needed that offer the option of collaboration among a wider set of actors. There is of course the option of delegating crisis management to regional organizations, but that entails letting each of the emerging powers drive crisis management in its own way. The United States will not always want to cede that much ground.

An alternative is to invest in other forms of multinational diplomacy and action, alongside NATO. There is scope for more investment in multinational crisis prevention and diplomacy. I have in mind here the kinds of mechanisms used for North Korea (the Six-Party talks) and Iran (the P5+1 process). In both cases, it has proved an asset to strategy to have both a forum for concerting the diplomatic efforts of the various states involved and a forum for deconflicting strategies—though in both cases the core of the effort remains in the hands of those with the greatest influence, and that is the United States. Specifically, in the case of Iran, I can see the value of broadening the P5+1 process to incorporate Turkey—and perhaps either Brazil or India or both, given their involvement, relationships, and (in the case of India) high stakes in the outcome. Far better to have a slightly broader conflict management tool than parallel efforts that do not align with the main thrust of strategy, as was the case in the Brazil-Turkey initiative on Iran. And as documented in chapter 6, multinational forces have proved to be a rapid, powerful, and flexible tool for response in fast-breaking and serious crises—a tool that could certainly have been used in Libya and possibly in Syria to improve outcomes.

In all of this, any administration risks criticism that it is placing too much American power in the hands of multilateral institutions. The Obama administration, for example, faced this argument during the Libya operation: critics savaged the administration's approach to Libya when a White House spokesperson described a strategy as "leading from behind."[17] By seeking Security Council authorization, and by acting through allies, or so the criticism went, the United States had weakened its own leadership and reinforced perceptions of decline. I find the argument bewildering and wrongheaded. The Arab League had broken with its traditional anti-interventionist stance and called for action. The Security Council voted to authorize the action. NATO agreed to support the action. And NATO members plus a few Arab allies agreed to share the burden, the cost, and the risks. The United States performed mission-critical functions at minimal loss of life and at minimal cost to the U.S. taxpayer (though many of these gains were squandered by not investing in even modest postconflict stabilization). And these are bad things?

One of the administration's critics used the following image to criticize U.S. policy: "Think of a marine sergeant leading a platoon in the Afghan theater of war and ask whether it is all right for him to lead from behind."[18] But a quarterback is the more appropriate analogy. Quarterbacks lead their teams: they call plays on the field, motivate team members, facilitate team members' talents, and perform essential, irreplaceable services on the field. A team can win games when any other player on the field is underperforming but not when the quarterback is. And because that is so, other teammates help block the quarterback from attacks—that is part of the arrangement. And sometimes, when it is appropriate, the quarterback steps out of the pocket, keeps the ball, and runs it down the field for yardage or for a touchdown. Winning quarterbacks must have this unilateral option in their playbook. But a quarterback who uses it too often is going to find himself knocked about, on the bench, and unable to finish the season. The unilateral option has to be used sparingly.

And there is another oddity to the lead-from-behind debate. For decades it has been a major American complaint that its allies do not carry their own weight on defense, so it is hardly consistent for Americans to complain when European powers want to play a leading role. Leadership often does involve being the guarantor of last resort, but it surely does not entail being the intervenor of first impulse or being the only country to carry costs.

In some areas, and in some crises, not only is it not a threat to U.S. interests for other states to lead, it is actively in U.S. interests that they do so—for two reasons. First, there is every financial reason for the United States to find actors to share burdens. The second reason is just as important: the more the current distribution of power endures, the more the autonomous powers will seek leadership roles. And if they do not find them, their incentives for restraint will erode in favor of their impulse to rivalry. A priority for American foreign policy should be identifying areas in which U.S. interests overlap with those of others and in which these others have the capacity to contribute and to lead.

Leadership in a Fractured Age

Given these tensions and balances, America will need to understand how to husband its resources to deploy against the most essential challenges—and to relearn the lessons of when modest investment of U.S. power can mobilize action by others. (As I believe was possible early in Syria.) At the best of times, even great powers cannot do everything; in fluid, complex times, they have to focus on what is most critical. That is very different from withdrawing from international leadership. It is very different from the argument that the United States should simply focus on its domestic situation, as second-tier powers battle it out, or that it should withdraw its naval assets from their role in the Gulf. The result of such a posture would be regional crises, mounting international tensions, and massive disruption in global trade. The argument that the United States does not have a vital stake in leading the international system neglects the fact that the American economy is deeply invested in it.

The most critical factor in deciding which of these patterns of inter-action shapes any given issue is, and for decades to come will be, U.S. policy. If the country sustains its alliance structure and invests in intensive diplomacy with the emerging powers, and if it devotes sufficient attention to forging new frameworks for joint action on critical issues—like energy and climate, maritime security, and crisis management—America will be able to sustain its critical role in the international system and secure a more or less stable order.

America is an enduring power, not a declining power. The BRICs are divided among themselves and face a complex and turbulent path ahead to the next phase of growth and influence. Each of them in its own way is torn between an impulse to competition and a deep interest in the established order, which requires cooperation—or at least an effort to keep competition within bounds. More than the BRICs are rising, too, and among the most influential states in the world there are far more U.S. allies than adversaries. The interests of the emerging powers and the United States overlap more than has commonly been depicted. And episodes of deadlock on international cooperation are no greater than they were in previous periods and are concentrated in the toughest cases, predictably; they do not illustrate a broader phenomenon. Between the impulse to rivalry and the incentives for restraint, for now and for the foreseeable future the balance tips toward restraint. There is ample space for the powers to avoid conflict and even to cooperate.

And the United States is now—and for a considerable period of time ahead is likely to be—by far and away best placed of the major actors to shape and lead the international system. In this most fundamental sense, despite challenges ahead, America can say, "It is still ours to lead."

ACKNOWLEDGMENTS

It is a truth seldom acknowledged that writing a book is at one and the same time an isolated venture and a team effort. And in this case, I was lucky to profit from not one but three teams.

The first of these is the Foreign Policy Program at the Brookings Institution. I have had the good fortune to be a senior fellow in this program, first at the suggestion of Carlos Pascual and then under the leadership of Martin Indyk, with whom I had collaborated, in a previous professional life, in the Middle East. Martin built on Carlos's successes, and under his leadership the Brookings Foreign Policy Program has been a source of incredible learning and encouragement for me. There's no part of this book that didn't profit from Martin's insights; from the enthusiasm for the topic that radiates from Brookings' indomitable leader, Strobe Talbott; and from the team of colleagues that they have assembled around them over the past several years. There can be few privileges as rewarding as working in an institution dedicated to public policy staffed by consummate professionals with vast experience of the most senior reaches of government and international life.

My colleagues in our program on international order—especially Thomas Wright, Robert Kagan, Ted Piccone, and Jeremy Shapiro—were a constant source of challenge and advice, for which I'm very grateful. Thomas, a rising star in the field, deserves particular mention for his wit and insight and support; luring him to Brookings, just as I started drafting the book, was an even better decision than I'd realized. I learned a great

215

deal also from Colin Bradford, Richard Bush, Kemal Dervis, Michael Doran, Fiona Hill, Homi Kharas, Michael O'Hanlon, Steven Pifer, Jonathan Pollack, Ken Pollack, Peter Singer, and Tamara Wittes; and I continuously profited from support and advice from Charlotte Baldwin, Gail Chalef, and Margaret Humenay. In a Washington often consumed by the latest op-ed and tweet, Brookings provides a refuge, where in-depth and independent scholarship is valued and protected, and I'm grateful to Martin and Strobe for having me there.

My time and my effort at Brookings were possible because of financial support that was generous both in scale and spirit: from the Carnegie Corporation (where I'm particularly grateful to Deana Arsenia and Steve del Rosso for their interest in the way America engages a changing world); from the MacArthur Foundation (where Barry Lowenkron and Amy Gordon understood the way energy and resources issues are playing into the changing order—and were patient as I tackled this book alongside a project on energy, which helped inform part 2 of the book); from the Rockefeller Brothers Fund (where Steve Heintz and Elizabeth Campbell saw that relations with the rising powers are going to be essential to the next phase of international peacemaking); and from the Skoll Global Threats Fund (where Bruce Lowry and Larry Brilliant have brought the best sort of intellectual ambition to the business of philanthropy). Various international consultations and conferences that informed the book were supported by the Norwegian Foreign Ministry (extraordinarily well represented in Washington at the time by my long-time friend Wegger Strommen) and by the Danish Foreign Ministry (where Ulrik Vestergaard-Knudsen lent his acute insights and network to the project). A related project on megatrends in international order was supported by the Director's Special Initiatives Fund; my thanks to Brookings Trustees David Rubenstein and Ben Jacobs, as well as the Finnish Foreign Ministry (thanks to the policy planning staff there, in particular Kari Möttölä).

At the same time, I was serving as director of the Center on International Cooperation at NYU, and there too I profited from a fabulous team. Richard Gowan, another rising star, has been my intellectual companion on a series of cognate projects in New York for nigh on a decade now, and his influence shows throughout my work. He and Jake Sherman, Molly Elgin-Cossart, Emily O'Brien, Nealin Parker, Benjamin Tortalani, and Andrew Hart were outstanding research partners and helped me run the center over the past several years, all while I simultaneously grappled with trying to understand the changing role of the United States and the multilateral system; I couldn't have done any of it without them. David Steven and Alex Evans were both a critical part of the CIC family, albeit from London and later, in Alex's case, Addis Ababa, and the chapter on energy and climate in this book reflects the fact that I have been able to piggyback on their creative and insightful efforts on both topics over the past half decade.

I learned a tremendous amount about Afghanistan and Central Asia from my colleague Barnett Rubin, who straddled the jobs of scholarship at CIC/NYU with advisory roles to Lakhdar Brahimi at the UN and then Richard Holbrooke and Marc Grossman at the U.S. State Department—a feat of unrivaled intellectual dexterity. W. P. S. Sidhu and Jim Traub were colleagues at the center in the past two years, and CIC was the better place for it. Throughout, I relied on the support of Yvonne Alonzo, without whose selfless efforts CIC would come crashing to a halt. Teresa Whitfield, Jean Arnault, Camino Kavanagh, Ian Johnstone, Elizabeth Sellwood, and Shepard Forman were also staff or fellows at the center on projects that, one way or another, informed the analysis in this book. And while the research for this book was funded out of Brookings, I'm grateful to my funders at CIC—in particular my friends and collaborators Jan Knutsson (Swedish Foreign Ministry), Kaare Aas (Norwegian Foreign Ministry), Ali Gillies (AusAID), Elissa Goldberg and Tobias Nuobaum (Canadian Department of Foreign Affairs), Michael Ungern von Sternberg and Peter Wittig (German Foreign Ministry)—for tolerating my divided focus between CIC's activities in the multilateral domain, and the United States and the emerging powers, states whose interactions will, of course, be the critical factor in shaping the multilateral system in the years to come. CIC has been my primary home now for ten years, and it couldn't have been a happier one. Thanks also to colleagues at NYU, including George Downs, John Sexton, Dick Foley, David McCaughlin, Tom Carew, Michael Gilligan, Al Bloom, Hilary Ballon, and Sujit Choudhry.

Finally, for the past five years I've been fortunate to be affiliated with Stanford University's Freeman Spogli Institute for International Affairs as a consulting professor, and in particular with its Center for International Security and Cooperation. Under the guidance of first David Holloway, then Chip Blacker, and now Tino Cuellar, FSI has emerged a premier center for the application of rigorous social science to real world security and international policy problems. My association with Stanford began through my collaboration with Steve Stedman, who in addition to being a close friend has shaped my thinking about international affairs more than any other person; to him I owe an enduring debt. Also, Lynn Eden has been a constant source of advice, inspiration, and friendship. In various jobs for the UN and NGOs I've had to stare down warlords and genocidiares and negotiate my way past checkpoints and border posts manned by terrorists, child soldiers, and untrained soldiers. None of that was quite as intimidating as giving research talks at Stanford in the presence of Stephen Krasner, sharpest but ultimately most charming of skeptics, as well as other towering scholars like Francis Fukuyama, Larry Diamond, Jim Fearon, Scott Sagan, and Steve Stedman. I'm grateful to all of them for their collaboration and collegiality. And I'm very grateful to Scott Sagan, Lynn Eden, and especially Tino Cuellar for the continuing collaboration, and to Amy Zegart, who's taken the helm at CISAC and whose own research tackles the challenge of applying theoretical debate to the real world of policymaking.

One individual, Tarun Chhabra, was connected to all three teams; he did more than any other person to help rescue me from my own entanglements. I owe him a substantial intellectual debt, as well as one of gratitude. This book would not have been completed without his advice and editorial support, offered unreservedly even where he disagreed with my views or conclusions.

Throughout, Elizabeth Cousens was a source of inspiration and insight, illustrating by example much of how the United States will have to lead in the period ahead.

In 2010 Sarah Cliffe and Nigel Roberts brought me in to the World Bank to help write the *World Development Report 2011*, on conflict, security, and development. While the research focus of that effort was on fragile states, the experience exposed me to the inner workings of the international financial institutions at a moment when reforms to deal with the growing weight of the emerging powers were under way, an experience that helped me complete the work reflected in chapter 4. I'm grateful for the opportunity and experience. Other scholars or collaborators along the way who informed my thinking include Alan Alexandroff, Scott Barrett, Dan Drezner, Jean-Marie Guehenno, Nina Hachigian, G. John Ikenberry, David Malone, Stewart Patrick, David Shorr, and Anne-Marie Slaughter. At Brookings, I'm grateful to David Nasser, head of communications, and Brookings Press staff, including Rebecca Campany, Valentina Kalk, Chris Kelaher, and Janet Walker, as well as former press director Robert Faherty. At various stages of the book process and in cognate projects I profited from research assistance from Katherine Elgin, Andrew Hart, Rob Keane, Emily O'Brien, and Ted Reinert, for which I'm very grateful. We'll be hearing more from all of them.

I'm grateful to two anonymous reviewers for insightful comments and well-timed encouragement. And, too, to Steve Stedman, Tom Wright, Richard Gowan, and Tarun Chhabra, who read the manuscript in full at an early stage and saved me from many mistakes. Those that remain are, it pains me to say, my own.

If one is lucky, books are family efforts too. In this case, that proved more than usually true when I came down with Lyme disease in the final weeks; my mother did what only a mother would do, patiently transcribing my voice recordings of the final edits. That was after my father, a retired diplomat of distinction, gave me helpful comments on an early version of the introduction. Elizabeth, my wife, not only put up with the bad humor and strange hours that invariably accompany the late phases of drafting a book, she did it all while being a highly successful policy adviser, chief of staff, ambassador, and an incredible mother to our energetic four-year-old. Talk about "leaning in."

It's to that energetic four-year-old, Wyatt, that this book is dedicated. Whenever my innate optimism was tempered by the foibles and follies of American foreign policy, or that of the other powers, his ever-present smile and gleeful wonder at everything around him reminded me why we do this work: to leave our children a more peaceful world.

NOTES

Introduction

1. Bob Corker, "Dithering While Damascus Burns," *New York Times*, April 23, 2013; Nadar Mousavizadeh, "Great-Power Myopia," *New York Times*, April 16, 2013; Naazneen Barma, Ely Ratner, and Steven Weber, "The Mythical Liberal Order," *National Interest* 124 (March/April 2013).

2. Charles Emmerson, "Eve of Disaster: Why 2013 Eerily Looks Like the World of 1913, on the Cusp of the Great War," Foreignpolicy.com, January 4, 2013.

3. Andrew Hurrell and Sandeep Sengupta, "Emerging Powers, North–South Relations and Global Climate Politics," *International Affairs* 88, no. 3 (2012).

4. On American decline: Gideon Rachman, "Think Again: American Decline. This Time It's for Real," *Foreign Policy* 184 (January/February 2011); Edward Luce, *Time to Start Thinking: America in the Age of Descent* (New York: Atlantic Monthly Press, 2012); Thomas Friedman and Michael Mandelbaum, *That Used to Be Us: How America Fell behind in the World It Invented and How We Can Come Back* (New York: Farrar, Straus, and Giroux, 2011). On the rise of the rest: Arvind Subramanian, "The Inevitable Superpower," *Foreign Affairs* 90 (September/October 2011); Kishore Mahbubani, *The New Asian Hemisphere: The Irresistible Shift of Global Power to the East* (New York: Public Affairs, 2008); Martin Jacques, *When China Rules the World: The Rise of the Middle Kingdom* (New York: Penguin, 2008). On the coming disorder and the post-Western world: Fareed Zakaria, *The Post-American World* (New York: Norton, 2008); Niall Ferguson, *Civilization: The West and the Rest* (New York: Penguin, 2012); Stephen S. Cohen and Brad de Long, *The End of Influence: What Happens When Other Countries Have the Money* (New York: Basic Books, 2010).

5. Robert Kaplan, "A World with No One In Charge," *Washington Post*, December 3, 2010.

6. Ian Bremmer and Nouriel Roubini, "A G-Zero World: The New Economic Club Will Produce Conflict, Not Cooperation," *Foreign Affairs* 90 (March/April 2011).

7. Aaron L. Friedberg, "The Future of US-China Relations: Is Conflict Inevitable?" *International Security* 30, no. 2 (2005).

8. Aaron Friedberg, "Ripe for Rivalry: Prospects for Peace in a Multipolar Asia," *International Security* 18, no. 3 (1993).

9. Barry R. Posen, "Pull Back: The Case for a Less Activist Foreign Policy," *Foreign Affairs*, 92, no. 1 (January 2013); Richard Haass, *Foreign Policy Begins at Home: The Case for Putting America's House in Order* (New York: Basic Books, 2013); Joseph M. Parent and Paul K. MacDonald, "The Wisdom of Retrenchment: America Must Cut Back to Move Forward," *Foreign Affairs* 90, no. 6 (November/December 2011).

10. The foundation for this argument has been laid persuasively by G. John Ikenberry, *Liberal Leviathan: The Origins, Crisis, and Transformation of the American World Order* (Princeton University Press, 2011).

11. Ibid.

12. For a disquisition on this line of argument, from before the current era, see Paul Kennedy, *The Rise and Fall of Great Powers* (New York: Vintage Books, 1989). For an application to the U.S. relationship with the rising powers, see Henry Kissinger, *On China* (New York: Penguin, 2011).

13. Not only was the post–cold war period not predominantly shaped by great power tensions, it was also a continuation of what has been called the long peace—the long period in modern history, from 1945 to the present, without a war between the major powers. John Lewis Gaddis named the period between 1945 and 1985 the long peace: "The Long Peace: Elements of Stability in the Postwar International System," *International Security* 10, no. 4 (1986). John Mearsheimer, in "Back to the Future," *International Security* 15, no. 1 (1990) and others believed that the end of the cold war would usher in a period of relatively anarchic multipolarity similar to the period between the two world wars, but that is not what occurred. Of course, one can argue that during the cold war the United States and the Soviet Union did engage in war— they just did it through proxies, in the Arab world and the (then-called) third world. Although these wars killed tens of millions of people each decade, still the absence of direct wars between the powers is a critically important fact of the period.

14. Andrew Mack, *Human Security Report 2012: Sexual Violence, Education, and War: Beyond the Mainstream Narrative* (Vancouver: Human Security Report Project, 2012).

15. The number of democracies in the world grew rapidly from 1990 onward; but in the last several years there have been reversals in the quality of a number of democracies. *Freedom in the World 2013: Democratic Breakthroughs in the Balance* (Washington: Freedom House, 2013) (www.freedomhouse.org/report/freedom-world/freedom-world-2013).

Chapter 1

1. "Views of the World," *Financial Times*, May 19, 2006.

2. For scholarly treatments of the question, see Christopher Layne, "The Waning of US Hegemony—Myth or Reality? A Review Essay," *International Security* 34, no. 1 (2009); Robert A. Paper, "Empire Falls," *National Interest*, no. 99 (2009); Josef Joffe, "Declinism's Fifth Wave," *American Interest* 7 (January/February 2012).

3. A foreign policy white paper issued by the Romney campaign says, "A perspective has been gaining currency, including within the high councils of the Obama administration, that regards the United States as a power in decline." Paul Ryan is quoted as

saying, "I think President Obama has placed us on a path to decline." See David Jackson, "Obama, Romney Argue about US 'decline,'" *USA Today*, September 10, 2012.

4. John McCain has said, "For the past four years, President Barack Obama has unfortunately pursued policies that are diminishing America's global prestige and influence." See John McCain, "Leading from the Front," Foreignpolicy.com, August 25, 2012.

5. Vali Nasr, *The Dispensable Nation: American Foreign Policy in Retreat* (New York: Doubleday, 2013).

6. Ian Bremmer, "America's Relative Rise," Reuters, April 19, 2013.

7. Robert Kagan, *The World America Made* (New York: Knopf, 2012); Joseph Nye Jr., "Fear Factor: The Illusion of American Decline," *World Politics Review*, October 9, 2012; Zbigniew Brzezinski, *Strategic Vision: America and the Crisis of Global Power* (New York: Basic Books, 2012); Walter Russell Mead, "The Myth of America's Decline," *Wall Street Journal*, April 9, 2012.

8. Union of Concerned Scientists, "Each Country's Share of CO_2 Emissions," August 20, 2010 (www.ucsusa.org).

9. At some point in 2014, development economists are going to proclaim that China has already overtaken the United States. This will be true only if the measure is purchasing power parity—that is, if the size of the Chinese economy is skewed to reflect differences in prices. That makes sense for looking at markets through the lens of human development. But in foreign policy terms, nominal GDP is the better measure, and there, China has some distance to go to catch up to the United States.

10. This reality looks set to continue and is at the core of China's difficulty in navigating the next wave of growth. See Michael Spence, *The Next Convergence: The Future of Economic Growth in a Multispeed World* (New York: Farrar, Straus, and Giroux, 2011); Ruchir Sharma, *Breakout Nations: In Pursuit of the Next Economic Miracles* (New York: Norton, 2012).

11. Sean Starrs, "American Economic Power Hasn't Declined—It Globalized! Summoning the Data and Taking Globalization Seriously," *International Studies Quarterly* (April 2013).

12. Ibid., p. 7.

13. Ibid.

14. When companies or countries conduct international trade, the financial exchange actually takes place at a dollar clearing house, which makes the exchange by translating their currencies into dollars and back again into their currencies. Of course, the clearinghouse takes a cut off the top. That cut translated into hundreds of billions in U.S. dollars for American financial firms in 2010.

15. Chinese senior national economic official, interview by author, Washington, June 11, 2013.

16. The following draws from Michael O'Hanlon, *Healing the Wounded Giant: Maintaining Military Preeminence While Cutting the Defense Budget* (Brookings Press, 2013).

17. SIPRI Military Expenditures Database (www.sipri.org/research/armaments/milex/milex_database).

18. Michael O'Hanlon and James Steinberg, *Strategic Reassurance and Resolve: U.S.-China Relations in the Twenty-First Century* (Princeton University Press, forthcoming).

19. Michael Mandelbaum, *The Case for Goliath: How America Acts as the World's Government in the Twenty-First Century* (New York: Public Affairs, 2005).

20. Peter Bergen, *The Longest War: The Enduring Conflict between America and al-Qaeda* (New York: Free Press, 2011).

21. Of course, the United States uses its military power selectively and not always for the common good. It was slow to act against ethnic cleansing in the Balkans in the 1990s and shamefully chose not to act against genocide in Rwanda in 1994. Its second war with Iraq, in 2003, was a war of choice that alienated all but a handful of allies. American power has also been used episodically to overthrow recalcitrant or anti-American regimes and to protect unpopular American allies, many of them dictators. All of this is part of the reality of American power and a part of its perception by states and publics worldwide.

22. Interviews by author, Delhi, October 2011 and April 2013; Beijing, October 2009 and November 2012; Brasilia, April 2011 and July 2013.

23. Interview by author, Washington, April 2007.

24. Interview by author, Beijing, April 2008.

25. See "China's Preoccupation with Asymmetric War," *Small Wars Journal,* October 15, 2009 (smallwarsjournal.com); Richard A. Clarke and Robert K. Knake, *Cyber War: The Next Threat to National Security and What to Do about It* (New York: Ecco, 2010).

26. James R. Holmes and Toshi Yoshihara, "When Comparing Navies, Measure Strength, Not Size," *Global Asia* 5, no. 4 (2010); also Andrew Davies, "Asian Military Trends and Their Implications for Australia," *Strategic Insights* 42 (2008); Rory Medcalf and Raoul Heinrichs with Justin Jones, "Crisis and Confidence: Major Powers and Maritime Security in Indo-Pacific Asia" (Sydney: Lowy Institute for Institutional Policy, 2011).

27. C. Raja Mohan, "Rising India: Partner in Shaping the Global Commons?" *Washington Quarterly* 33, no. 3 (2010).

28. A more detailed version of this discussion is given in chapter 7, capping a theme that appears throughout the book: the change in the distribution of economic and other forms of power in the international system means that China, whatever its intent, has no easy pathway to effective strategic competition with the United States.

29. Numbers for defense spending in this chapter are from SIPRI Military Expenditures Database 2012.

30. Peter Bergen, *Manhunt: The Ten-Year Search for Bin Laden—from 9/11 to Abbottabad* (New York: Crown, 2012).

31. See www.justice.gov/crt/508/report2/agencies.php.

32. Saira Kurup, "Off-Track Diplomacy?" *Times of India,* August 2, 2009.

33. Interviews by author, Brasilia, April 2011.

34. The phrase *gravitational pull* is from Bruce Jentleson and Steven Weber, *The End of Arrogance: America and the Global Competition of Ideas* (Harvard University Press, 2010), an account of the changing international system, which is likened to a Copernican revolution: the world no longer revolves around U.S. power, it argues, though the United States still exerts a strong gravitational pull on the other "planets."

35. Ted Galen Carpenter, *A Search for Enemies: America's Alliances after the Cold War* (Washington: Cato Institute, 1992); Fareed Zakaria, *From Wealth to Power: The Unusual Origins of America's World Role* (Princeton University Press, 1999).

36. Bruce D. Jones, Shepard Forman, and Richard Gowan, eds., *Cooperating for Peace and Security: Evolving Institutions and Arrangements in a Context of Changing U.S. Security Policy* (Cambridge University Press, 2010).

37. Interviews by author, Abu Dhabi, Dubai, and Doha, March 2011, July 2011, March 2012.

38. Edward Luce, *Time to Start Thinking: America in the Age of Descent* (New York: Atlantic Monthly Press, 2012).

39. Eli Lake, "Obama Stresses Nation Building at Home over Nation Building Abroad," *Daily Beast*, January 24, 2012.

40. *Global Trends 2030: Alternative Worlds* (U.S. National Intelligence Council, 2012).

41. Roger C. Altman, "The Fall and Rise of the West: Why America and Europe Will Emerge Stronger from the Financial Crisis," *Foreign Affairs* 92, no. 1 (2013).

42. Congressional Budget Office, *The 2013 Long-Term Budget Outlook*, September 2013 (www.cbo.gov).

43. Board of Governors of the Federal Reserve System, "10-Year Treasury Constant Maturity Rate," Foreignpolicy.com, October 1, 2013.

44. This view is closely associated with *New York Times* columnist Paul Krugman and with Bradford deLong, who served as Larry Summers's deputy in the Clinton administration. For an accessible account of the argument, see delong.typepad.com/sdj/2013/04/macroeconomic-overview-talk-for-umkc-mba-students-april-1-2013.html.

45. International Monetary Fund, "Mind the Gap: Narrowing Imbalances, while Maintaining Growth," IMF survey, September 13, 2013 (www.imf.org); "World Markets Reel on China Credit Concerns," *Daily Finance*, June 24, 2013 (www.dailyfinance.com).

46. In 2012–13, of the top 100 universities in the world, 47 were in the United States; there were 3 in Hong Kong and China. See "Times Higher Education World Universities Rankings 2012-2013" (www.timeshighereducation.co.uk).

47. Fareed Zakaria, "Can America Be Fixed? The New Crisis of Democracy," *Foreign Affairs* 92, no. 1 (2013).

48. Jeffrey S. Passel and D'Vera Cohn, "U.S. Population Projects: 2005–2050" (Washington: Pew Research Center for the People and the Press, 2008).

49. Congressional Budget Office, "The Economic Impact of S. 744, the Border Security, Economic Opportunity, and Immigration Modernization Act," June 18, 2013 (www.cbo.gov); President Barack Obama, "Strengthening our Economy by Passing Bipartisan Immigration Reform," Weekly Address, White House, July 13, 2013.

50. A point made by Robert Kagan in *The World America Made*; see also Robert D. Kaplan, *The Revenge of Geography: What the Map Tells Us about Coming Conflict and the Battle against Fate* (New York: Random House, 2012).

51. Vanda Felbab-Brown, *Shooting Up: Counterinsurgency and the War on Drugs* (Brookings, 2010); Shannon K. O'Neil, "Mexico Makes It: A Transformed Society, Economy, and Government," *Foreign Affairs* 92, no. 2 (2013).

52. Tight oil is oil trapped in rock formations. The old method of oil extraction relied on finding large pools of untrapped oil, which left small puddles of oil behind. New technology allows this leftover oil to be found and extracted.

53. International Energy Agency, *World Energy Outlook 2012* (Paris: November 12, 2012).

54. Sergei Rogov, "The Obama Doctrine: The Lord of Two Rings" (Russian International Affairs Council, May 15, 2013).

55. Kagan, *The World America Made*.

56. Sharma, *Breakout Nations*.

57. Ian Bremmer and David Gordon, "Powers on the Mend," *International Herald Tribune*, April 11, 2013.

58. Gideon Rachman, "Think Again: American Decline. This Time It's for Real," *Foreign Policy* (January/February 2011).

Chapter 2

1. Niall Ferguson, *Civilization: The West and the Rest* (New York: Penguin, 2011).

2. The G-20 is composed of Argentina, Australia, Brazil, Canada, China, France, Germany, India, Indonesia, Italy, Japan, the Republic of Korea, Mexico, Russia, Saudi Arabia, South Africa, Turkey, the United Kingdom, the United States of America, and the European Union.

3. Gordon Brown, *Beyond the Crash: Overcoming the First Crisis of Globalization* (New York: Free Press, 2010). Brown told me the story of the session with Brazilian president Lula when I interviewed him about his book at a public event at NYU Abu Dhabi on February 24, 2011; I later verified it with Brazilian officials.

4. Daniel W. Drezner, "The Irony of Global Economic Governance: The System Worked," working paper (New York: Council on Foreign Relations, 2012).

5. Or, more accurately, the reform of existing tools: the most important decision was the retooling of the Financial Stability Forum into the more powerful Financial Stability Board. On the details of the Financial Stability Board, see Eric Helleiner, "The Financial Stability Board and International Standards" (Waterloo, Ontario: Centre for International Governance Innovation, 2010).

6. This argument has been made most prominently by G. John Ikenberry, *Liberal Leviathan: The Origins, Crisis, and Transformation of the American World Order* (Princeton University Press, 2011).

7. Kishore Mahbubani, *The New Asian Hemisphere: The Irresistible Shift of Global Power to the East* (New York: Public Affairs, 2008).

8. Angus Maddison, "Statistics on World Population, GDP, and per Capita GDP, 1–2008AD" (www.ggdc.net/MADDISON/Historical_Statistics/vertical-file_02-2010.xls).

9. International Monetary Fund, World Economic Outlook Database, April 2013 (www.imf.org).

10. Members are as follows: United States, Russia, China, Japan, Germany, the United Kingdom, France, Italy, Canada, Spain, Brazil, Mexico, India, South Korea, Australia.

11. When the G-20 was first established as a grouping of finance ministers, in response to the Indonesian financial crisis in 1997, the rather arbitrary list that was drawn up of major financial players included Argentina, which was closer to a top-twenty ranking then than it is now.

12. Of the next twenty economies below the top twenty, a further fourteen are U.S. allies.

13. The acronym was coined by the Goldman Sachs economist Jim O'Neill in 2001. See Jim O'Neill, "Building Better Global Economic BRICs," Global Economics Paper 66 (New York: Goldman Sachs, 2001).

14. Susan L. Shirk, *China: Fragile Superpower* (Oxford University Press, 2007).

15. Brendan Taylor, "Towards Hegemony? Assessing China's Asian Ambitions," *Security Challenges* 1 (2005).

16. Shirk, *China*.

17. Rivalry and Partnership: The Struggles for a New Global Governance Leadership, Stanley Foundation conference, Princeton, January 14–15, 2011.

18. Shyam Saran, "Premature Power," *Business Standard*, March 17, 2010.

19. David Malone, *Does the Elephant Dance?: Contemporary Indian Foreign Policy* (Oxford University Press, 2011).

20. See Milan Vaishnav, "The Market for Criminality: Money, Muscle, and Elections in India," unpublished paper (2010); Arunabha Ghosh and David Steven, "India's Energy, Food, and Water Security: International Cooperation for Domestic Capacity," in *Shaping the Emerging World: India and the Multilateral Order*, edited by Waheguru Pal Singh Sidhu, Pratap Bhanu Mehta, and Bruce Jones (Brookings Press, 2013).

21. Devesh Kapur and Arvind Subramanian, "India's Unique Crisis," *Business Standard*, August 23, 2013.

22. Saran, "Premature Power."

23. Michael Beckley, "China's Century? Why America's Edge Will Endure," *International Security* 36, no. 3 (2011–12).

24. Nitin Pai, "Palpable Realism," *Economic and Political Weekly* 42, no. 3 (2007); Odd Arne Westad, *Restless Empire: China and the World since 1750* (New York: Basic Books, 2012).

25. *World Investment Report 2013* (Geneva: UNCTAD, 2013).

26. For more on securing influence through regional institutions, see Mely Caballero-Anthony, "Nontraditional Security and Multilateralism in Asia," in *Asia's New Multilateralism: Cooperation, Competition, and the Search for Community*, edited by Michael J. Green and Bates Gill (Columbia University Press, 2009); Andrew F. Hart and Bruce Jones, "How Do Rising Powers Rise?" *Survival* 52, no. 6 (2010); Andrew Hurrell, "Hegemony, Liberalism, and Global Order: What Space for Would-Be Great Powers?" *International Affairs* 82, no. 1 (2006)

27. Sharon Chen and Gopal Ratnam, "Vietnam Rises as a Middle Power at Defense Summit: Southeast Asia," *Businessweek*, August 28, 2013; C. Raja Mohan, "Facing China Threat, Vietnam Seeks American Balance," *Indian Express*, June 1, 2013.

28. Jason Fekete, "China, Canada Reach Deals on Oil, Uranium, and Air Travel," February 9, 2012 (canada.com).

29. Anne-Marie Slaughter, "The Coming Atlantic Century," *Project Syndicate*, February 21, 2013 (www.project-syndicate.org).

30. "Lost Decades: Japan's Tragedy, Cont.," *The Economist*, August 6, 2012 (www.economist.com).

31. Timothy Garton Ash, "Can Europe Survive the Rise of the Rest?" *New York Times*, September 1, 2012.

32. Jonathan Masters, "Backgrounder: The North Atlantic Treaty Organization (NATO)," Council on Foreign Relations, May 17, 2012 (www.cfr.org/nato/north-atlantic-treaty-organization-nato/p28287).

33. Thomas Wright, "Europe on a Slippery Slope," *New York Times*, April 17, 2013.

34. The difficulty of measuring the Soviet economy spawned a cold war cottage industry and still makes any figures incredibly dicey. According to the *1991 CIA World*

Factbook, the USSR had a GNP of $2.66 trillion in purchasing power parity, compared to $5.47 trillion for the United States. Russia, according to IMF data, has not quite caught up to the USSR at its peak. See "Report for Selected Countries and Subjects," World Economic Outlook Database, April 2013 (Washington: International Monetary Fund).

35. For an account of the dynamics of the Russian economy and some of its social implications, see Clifford G. Gaddy and Barry W. Ickes, *Russia's Addiction: The Political Economy of Resource Dependence* (Brookings, 2010).

36. "Top Risks 2013," Eurasia Group (www.eurasiagroup.net).

37. Nina Hachigian and Mona Sutphen, *The Next American Century: How the U.S. Can Thrive as Other Powers Rise* (New York: Simon and Schuster, 2008).

38. Secretary of State Hillary Clinton, "Delivering on the Promise of Economic Statecraft," Singapore Management University, November 17, 2012.

39. There was an easing of tensions in April 2013, when President Obama, during a trip to Israel, brokered a telephone call between Israeli prime minister Netanyahu and Turkish prime minister Erdogan, during which Netanyahu apologized for Israeli actions during the boarding of a Turkish-flagged ship seeking to break through the Israeli blockage of Gaza.

40. "Assessing Turkey's Role in Somalia" (Brussels: International Crisis Group, 2012).

41. At a conference of emerging powers I chaired in Abu Dhabi in 2010, I watched as the Gulf diplomats lambasted the Chinese participants for the wan stance on Iran and scolded them for believing they could rely on Gulf oil while failing to contribute to the Gulf states' core security challenge. The Chinese participants were pretty shocked.

42. For a largely upbeat account of Mexico's current and future trajectory, see Shannon O'Neil, *Two Nations Indivisible: Mexico, the United States, and the Road Ahead* (Oxford University Press, 2013).

43. "Asian Economic Rankings: A Game of Leapfrog," *The Economist,* April 28, 2012 (www.economist.com).

44. Kim Sung-han, "Global Governance and Middle Powers: South Korea's Role in the G20" (New York: Council on Foreign Relations, 2013).

45. "The World's Billionaires," *Forbes,* May 2013 (www.forbes.com).

46. Carol Driver, "Rise of the Son of a Poverty-Stricken Mexican Shopkeeper: £35.7bn Carlos Slim Knocks Bill Gates off Top Forbes Rich List," *Daily Mail,* March 11, 2010.

47. National Intelligence Council, *Global Trends 2030: Alternative Worlds* (2012).

48. Elisabeth Rosenthal, "Life after Oil and Gas," *New York Times,* March 23, 2013.

49. Manish Bapna, "C40 Shows How Cities Can Lead on Climate Change Solutions," *WRIInsights* (World Resources Institute), June 15, 2011 (insights.wri.org).

Chapter 3

1. This chapter draws in part on a series of conversations with political and thought leaders of the emerging powers, between 2008 and 2012. Some (especially in Beijing) requested to remain anonymous; a partial list of the rest includes (titles at time of interview), in India: Shivshankar Menon (foreign secretary); M. K. Narayanan (national security adviser); Hardeep Puri (permanent representative to the United

Nations); Manjeev Puri (deputy permanent representative to the United Nations); Lalit Mansingh (former foreign secretary); Shyam Saran (former foreign secretary); in Brazil, Antonio Patriota (foreign minister; deputy foreign minister); Celso Amorim (defense minister); Guilherme Patriota (diplomatic adviser to the president); Jose Brito de Cruz (head of policy planning); Norberto Moretti (director general for peace and security); Antonio Ramalho (director for strategic planning, Office of the President); in China, Wang Guangya (deputy foreign minister), Zheng Bijan (chair of the China Reform Forum); Wu Jiamin (president, China Foreign Affairs University); Qin Yaqing (executive vice president and professor of international studies at China Foreign Affairs University). I am particularly grateful to Burak Akçapar (Turkish ambassador to India).

2. For historical GDP data, see Angus Maddison, "Statistics on World Population, GDP, and per Capita GDP, 1–2008AD" (www.ggdc.net/MADDISON/Historical_Statistics/vertical-file_02-2010.xls).

3. I am grateful to David Malone, former Canadian ambassador to India and author of an important book on Indian foreign policy, *Can the Elephant Dance?*, for highlighting this point to me.

4. This point is made well by Ruchir Sharma, *Breakout Nations: In Pursuit of the Next Economic Miracles* (New York: Norton, 2012); and Michael Spence, *The Next Convergence: The Future of Economic Growth in a Multispeed World* (New York: Farrar, Straus, and Giroux, 2011).

5. On India, see inter alia Lawrence James, *Raj: The Making and Unmaking of British India* (New York: St. Martin's Press, 1997); and William Dalrymple, *The White Mughal: Love and Betrayal in Eighteenth-Century India* (London: HarperCollins, 2002). On China, see Odd Arne Westad, *Restless Empire: China and the World since 1750* (New York: Basic Books, 2012). For a compelling account of Western interference and noninterference in China's internal turmoil, see Stephen R. Platt, *Autumn in the Heavenly Kingdom: China, the West, and the Epic Story of the Taiping Civil War* (New York: Knopf, 2012). On the Ottoman Empire, see David Fromkin, *A Peace to End All Peace: The Fall of the Ottoman Empire and the Creation of the Modern Middle East* (New York: Henry Holt, 2009); Jason Goodwin, *Lords of the Horizons: A History of the Ottoman Empire* (London: Chatto and Windus, 1998). On the balance between internal weakness and great-power imperialism in the collapse of the Ottoman Empire, see Marian Kent, ed., *Great Powers and the End of the Ottoman Empire* (London: Routledge, 1996).

6. See in particular Jonathan Spence, *The Search for Modern China* (New York: Norton, 1990). On China's contemporary international relations, see Henry Kissinger, *On China* (New York: Penguin, 2011).

7. Yan Xuetong, *Goiji Zhengzhi yu Zhongguou* [International politics and China] (Beijing: Daxue Chubanshe, 2005).

8. Sanjaya Baru, "India in a Changing World," March 30, 2009 (livemint.com). On the term *sherpa*: modern summit diplomacy has adopted some of its terminology from actual summiteering. Thus leading officials who accompany ministers to the diplomatic heights of G-8 or G-20 summits are called *sherpas*; their assistants are called *yaks*.

9. Mark Mazower, *Governing the World: The History of an Idea* (New York: Allen Lane, 2012).

10. On China, see David Shambaugh, *China Goes Global: The Partial Power* (New York: Oxford University Press, 2013); Hui Feng, *The Politics of China's Accession to the World Trade Organization: The Dragon Goes Global* (London: Taylor and Francis,

2005). On India, see Sunil Khilnani and others, "Non-Alignment 2.0: A Foreign and Strategic Policy for India in the Twenty-First Century" (New Delhi: Centre for Policy Research, 2012); Shyam Saran, "Premature Power," *Business Standard,* March 17, 2010; Waheguru Pal Singh Sidhu, Pratap Bhanu Mehta, and Bruce Jones, eds., *Shaping the Emerging World: India and the Multilateral* Order (Brookings Press, 2013).

11. For an important discussion of this perspective, see Khilnani and others, "Non-Alignment 2.0." I was in Delhi for the launch of this report, which was attended by India's national security adviser and two of his predecessors as well as much of Delhi's strategic elite. There was a huge controversy over the name of the report, but the general thrust—that India should first and foremost act in its own interests and avoid too close an alliance with the United States (while actively preparing for potential war with China)—reflected some of the major lines of thought of Delhi's policy community.

12. For information on World Trade Organization membership dates, see www.wto.org/english/thewto_e/whatis_e/tif_e/org6_e.htm.

13. For a list of countries with McDonald's restaurants, see http://en.wikipedia.org/wiki/List_of_countries_with_McDonald's_restaurants.

14. A detailed account of this can be found in Jeffrey Sachs, "Globalization and Patterns of Economic Development," *Weltwirtschaftliches Archiv* 136, no. 4 (2000). For a take on the perspective from so-called developing countries, see Dani Rodrik, *The Globalization Paradox: Democracy and the Future of the World Economy* (New York: Norton, 2011).

15. It seems odd that a country can have a ratio of trade to GDP that exceeds 100 percent. The reason is that countries can host firms that export goods far beyond the requirements for domestic consumption. This is mostly true in small, niche operators like Singapore.

16. Shannon O'Neil, "U.S.-Latin America Economic Ties," November 16, 2012 (shannononeil.com).

17. According to Bruce Katz, this phenomenon is being driven by two major factors, free trade deals and innovation at the level of metropolitan areas, which account for the lion's share of the U.S. economy. For an overview, see Bruce Katz, "The Metropolitan Revolution," Houston, October 5, 2012 (www.brookings.edu/research/speeches/2012/10/05-metropolitan-revolution-katz).

18. For an account of Brazil's approach to this tension, see Antonio Jorge Ramalho da Rocha, "Brazil's Geopolitical Rise: Implications for US Policy in the Western Hemisphere" (Aspen: Aspen Institute, 2013).

19. "India, China Are Destined by Geography to Be Rivals: MK Naraynan," *Economic Times,* November 1, 2012. Raja Mohan, one of India's most influential thinkers, argues that Sino-Indian rivalry will be the defining feature of the Indo-Pacific area; see C. Raja Mohan, *Samudra Manthan: Sino-Indian Rivalry in the Indo Pacific* (Washington: Carnegie Endowment for International Peace, 2012).

20. The question of how to win, or at least to survive, a war with China is a major theme of a report written in 2010–11 by a group of national security scholars with ties to the government. It was launched in high-profile fashion by India's national security adviser. See Khilnani and others, "Non-Alignment 2.0."

21. Yogesh Joshi, "China Rivalry Keeping India Out of Nuclear Suppliers Group," *World Politics Review,* June 14, 2013 (www.worldpoliticsreview.com).

22. Tanvi Madan, "Premier Li Keqiang of China goes to India," *UpFront* (Brookings, 2013).

23. Barry Eichengreen, *Exorbitant Privilege: The Rise and Fall of the Dollar and the Future of the International Monetary System* (Oxford University Press, 2011).

24. World Bank data, based on 2009 figures (data.worldbank.org/indicator/EN.ATM.CO2E.PC); see also Navroz Dubash, "Climate Change," in *Shaping the Emerging World*, edited by Sidhu, Mehta, and Jones.

25. David M. Malone, *The International Struggle over Iraq: Politics in the UN Security Council 1980-2005* (Oxford University Press, 2006).

26. Robert Kagan, *Of Paradise and Power: America and Europe in the New World Order* (New York: Knopf, 2003).

27. Barnett Rubin, *Afghanistan from the Cold War through the War on Terror* (Oxford University Press, 2013).

28. Marianne Wade and Almir Maljevic, eds., *A War on Terror? The European Stance on a New Threat, Changing Laws, and Human Rights Implications* (New York: Springer, 2010); and Margaret Crahan, John Goering, and Thomas G. Weiss, eds., *Wars on Terrorism and Iraq: Human Rights, Unilateralism, and U.S. Foreign Policy* (London: Routledge, 2004).

29. Bruce Jones, "The Coming Clash? Europe and US Multilateralism under Obama," in *The Obama Moment: European and American Perspectives*, edited by Alvaro Vasconcelos and Marcin Zaborowski (Paris: European Union Institute for Security Studies, 2009).

30. "Clinton: Chinese Human Rights Can't Interfere with Other Crises," CNN, February 22, 2009 (www.cnn.com); Sophie Richardson, "Hillary Clinton's Beijing Gaffe," Human Rights Watch, February 26, 2009 (www.hrw.org).

31. I was in Tokyo in 2008 just after Hillary Clinton said that America's "relationship with China will be the most important bilateral relationship in the world in this century." See Hillary Clinton, "Security and Opportunity for the Twenty-First Century," *Foreign Affairs* 86 (2007).

32. "Remarks by President Obama to the Australian Parliament," Parliament House, Canberra, Australia, November 17, 2011 (www.whitehouse.gov).

33. Leslie H. Gelb, "The NATO Summit: What Happened to Obama's Pivot from Europe to Asia?" *Daily Beast*, May 20, 2012.

34. Michael Froman, deputy national security adviser for international economic affairs, speaking on May 16, 2012, at a Brookings event, "Previewing the G-8 and NATO Summits: An Examination of the Summits' Top Agenda Items" (www.brookings.edu).

35. China's stimulus announced in November 2008 totaled 4 trillion renminbi, or $586 billion, compared to the $787 billion package passed by the U.S. Congress in February 2009. The eurozone crisis also saw the emerging powers make sizable contributions to a European bailout fund via the IMF—another example of the fact that their interests in a stable global economy drive policy designed to shield existing economic arrangements from collapse.

36. See Thant Myint-U, *Where China Meets India: Burma and the New Crossroads of Asia* (New York: Farrar, Straus, and Giroux, 2011).

37. Interviews by author, Brasilia, Rio, summer 2013.

38. Richard Gowan, "Who Is Winning on Human Rights at the UN?" European Council on Foreign Relations, September 24, 2012 (ecfr.eu/content/entry/commentary_who_is_winning_on_human_rights_at_the_un).

39. And as Ted Piccone of the Brookings Foreign Policy program points out, the UN Human Rights Council has been much more assertive on Syria than was true of

its predecessor, the UN Human Rights Commission (www.huffingtonpost.com/ted-piccone/syria-human-rights-un_b_1868310.html?cid=em_piccone091212).

40. Specifically, it is hegemonic stability theory and a body of scholarship on power transitions. Notable contributors are Kenneth Waltz, *Theory of International Politics* (Reading, Mass.: Addison-Wesley, 1979); Paul Kennedy, *The Rise and Fall of the Great Powers: Economic Change and Military Conflict from 1500 to 2000* (New York: Random House, 1987); and, in particular, A. F. K. Organski and Jacek Kugler, *The War Ledger* (University of Chicago Press, 1980).

41. The argument is associated with the school of thought known as liberal international. The liberal internationalist argument is best encapsulated in G. John Ikenberry, *Liberal Leviathan: The Origins, Crisis, and Transformation of the American World Order* (Princeton University Press, 2011).

Chapter 4

1. "IMO Assembly Calls for Action on Piracy off Somalia," press release, International Maritime Organization, November 24, 2005.

2. UNSC Res. 1816 (2008).

3. The Charter of the United Nations, signed in San Francisco in 1945, is the operating system of the law of relations between states. The charter makes it legal for states to use force only in one circumstance: self-defense. For every other circumstance, the Security Council is the only international body that has the legal power to authorize the use of force. That gives the body a unique role in international law and politics.

4. The full list of participants has fluctuated; for details, see http://combined maritimeforces.com. At the time of this writing, participating states included Australia, Bahrain, Belgium, Canada, Denmark, France, Germany, Greece, Italy, Japan, Jordan, Republic of Korea, Kuwait, Malaysia, the Netherlands, New Zealand, Pakistan, Portugal, Saudi Arabia, Seychelles, Singapore, Spain, Thailand, Turkey, the United Arab Emirates, the United Kingdom, and the United States.

5. Details are available from EUNAVFOR (http://eunavfor.eu/).

6. Ted Galen Carpenter and Marian L. Tupy, "U.S. Defense Spending Subsidizes European Free-Riding Welfare States," *Daily Caller*, July 12, 2010.

7. It is surprisingly hard to get up-to-date details of these operations, but good accounts of them can be found in NATO reports, such as "Counter-Piracy Operations" (www.nato.int/cps/en/natolive/topics_48815.htm) and in studies of individual navies' participation. On China's, see Alison Kaufman, "Chinese Participation in Anti-Piracy Operations off the Horn of Africa: Drivers and Implications" (China News Agency, July 2009).

8. Stephen Krasner, discussion paper, Conference on Transnational Threats, Abu Dhabi, February 21–22, 2012.

9. WTO data from 2013 (www.wto.org/english/res_e/statis_e/trade_data_e.htm).

10. Navroz K. Dubash, "Of Maps and Compasses: India in Multilateral Climate Negotiations," in *Shaping the Emerging World: India and the Multilateral Order,* edited by Waheguru Pal Singh Sidhu, Pratap Bhanu Mehta, and Bruce Jones (Brookings, 2013). Also see Navroz K. Dubash, "The Politics of Climate Change in India: Narratives of Equity and Cobenefits," WIRES Climate Change, Online Library, March 15, 2013 (wires.wiley.com/WileyCDA/WiresArticle/wisId-WCC210.html).

11. I was forwarded a private copy of the original text from an official at India's Ministry for External Affairs.

12. David Shambaugh, *China Goes Global: The Partial Power* (Oxford University Press, 2013).

13. Celso Amorim, "Hardening Brazil's Soft Power," *Project Syndicate*, July 16, 2013 (www.project-syndicate.org).

14. Kenneth Lieberthal and Mikkal E. Herberg, "China's Search for Energy Security: Implications for U.S. Policy" (Seattle: National Bureau of Asian Research, 2006); Bates Gill and James Reilly, "The Tenuous Hold of China Inc. in Africa," *Washington Quarterly* 30, no. 3 (2007); Aaron L. Friedberg, "'Going Out': China's Pursuit of Natural Resources and Implications for the PRC's Grand Strategy" (Seattle: National Bureau of Asian Research, 2006).

15. Technically, Somaliland is still part of Somalia; for all intents and purposes, though, Somaliland and Puntland have, de facto, separated from Somalia—the two entities even recently signed what amounts to a nonaggression pact with one another. On land deals, see David Steven, Emily O'Brien, and Bruce Jones, *Risk Pivot: Energy, Security, and New Opportunities for New American Leadership* (Brookings Press, forthcoming); Alejandra Kubitscheck Bujones, "Mozambique in Transition and the Future Role of the UN" (New York University Center on International Cooperation, 2013).

16. Moises Naim, "Rogue Aid," *Foreign Policy* 159 (March 2007); Ali Zafar, "The Growing Relationship between China and Sub-Saharan Africa: Macroeconomic Trade, Investment, and Aid Links," *World Bank Research Observer* 22, no. 1 (2007).

17. Philip Segal, "Coming Clean on Dirty Dealing: Time for a Fact-Based Evaluation of the Foreign Corrupt Practices Act," *Florida Journal of International Law* 18 (2006).

18. *Human Security Report*, 2009, 2010, 2011, 2012 (www.hsrgroup.org).

19. The West has tried to increase cooperation with the emerging powers on this issue by bringing them into the OECD. This, they resolutely refuse to do: joining established Western clubs, where they would be latecomers and "rule takers," is not their game plan. But between 2010 and 2013, I convened and chaired a process that brought major Western and emerging-power development players together in New York. What was eminently clear from those debates was that, in formal institutions, the emerging powers retain their role as protectors of the developing world but that, in practice, they confront much the same challenges that Western aid confronts when faced with instability, corruption, and weak governance—whether in Haiti, Afghanistan, Yemen, or elsewhere. For an account of the first series of those sessions, see http://cic.es.its.nyu.edu/sites/default/files/engagement_book.pdf. For a comprehensive look at new patterns in the development policy of the emerging powers, see Sachin Chaturvedi, Thomas Fues, and Elizabeth Sidiropoulos, eds., *Development Cooperation and Emerging Powers: New Partners or Old Patterns?* (London: Zed Books, 2012).

20. This argument was a central finding in *World Development Report 2011: Conflict, Security, and Development* (Washington: World Bank, 2012).

21. "Assessing Turkey's Role in Somalia" (Brussels: International Crisis Group, 2012).

22. *Annual Review of Global Peace Operations 2013* (New York University Center on International Cooperation, 2013).

23. Joseph S. Nye Jr., Yukio Satoh, and Paul Wilkinson, *Addressing the New International Terrorism: Prevention, Intervention, and Multilateral Cooperation* (Washington: Trilateral Commission, 2003).

24. On U.S.-Russia common cause on terrorism, see Fiona Hill, "Putin and Bush in Common Cause?" *Brookings Review* 20, no. 3 (2002).

25. Brazil is notably absent from this list, but not because Brasilia refused to participate. The Global Counterterrorism Forum was established shortly after the Brazil/ Turkey mediation effort with Iran, which fell afoul of U.S. interests. The United States, as a result, decided to exclude Brazil from GCTF preparations. (Confidential interview by author, Washington, March 2011.) The United States was more forgiving of Turkey, given Turkey's vital stakes in what happens in its immediate neighborhood. Another notable absence is Israel; in putting together the coalition, the U.S. State Department had to judge whether including Israel would complicate the U.S. ability to work closely with countries like Saudi Arabia and Pakistan. The decision to exclude Israel provoked substantial criticism. See, as an example, www.investigativeproject.org/3858/us-led-global-counterterrorism-forum-excludes. For more about the Global Counterterrorism Forum, see www.state.gov/j/ct/gctf/.

26. Members are Algeria, Argentina, Armenia, Australia, Azerbaijan, Belgium, Brazil, Canada, Chile, China, Czech Republic, Denmark, Egypt, Finland, France, Gabon, Georgia, Germany, Hungary, India, Indonesia, Israel, Italy, Japan, Jordan, Kazakhstan, Lithuania, Malaysia, Mexico, Morocco, the Netherlands, New Zealand, Nigeria, Norway, Pakistan, Philippines, Poland, Republic of Korea, Romania, Russian Federation, Saudi Arabia, Singapore, South Africa, Spain, Sweden, Switzerland, Thailand, Turkey, Ukraine, United Arab Emirates, United Kingdom, United States, Vietnam. Observers are the European Union, the International Atomic Energy Agency, Interpol, and the United Nations.

27. Barnett R. Rubin and Ahmed Rashid, "From Great Game to Grand Bargain: Ending Chaos in Afghanistan and Pakistan," *Foreign Affairs* 87, no. 6 (2008); Andrew Kuchins and Thomas Sanderson, "The Northern Distribution Network and Afghanistan: Geopolitical Challenges and Opportunities" (Washington: Center for Strategic and International Studies, 2010). On the broader question of the ups and downs of NATO cooperation with Russia, see James M. Goldgeier, *The Future of NATO* (New York: Council on Foreign Relations Press, 2010).

28. Barnett R. Rubin, *Afghanistan from the Cold War through the War on Terror* (Oxford University Press, 2012).

29. Having watched American strategy in Afghanistan over the past several years, I share their doubts. The West brings to Afghanistan an approach to state building that is hopelessly unrealistic and driven more by domestic concerns than by any genuine understanding of the local dynamics of state formation, contestation, and legitimacy. The weakest part of the West's strategy is about time lines: from 2007 on, the West made the goal of building Afghan governance capacity central to overall strategy. But a World Bank study (in which I was involved) of the development of political institutions suggests that the time lines for even modest development in a place like Afghanistan should be measured in generations, not the two- or three-year timetables that characterize Western strategy. See World Bank, *World Development Report 2011*.

30. Ivo Daalder and James Goldgeier, "Global NATO," *Foreign Affairs* 85, no. 5 (2006).

31. Stephen P. Cohen and others, *The Future of Pakistan* (Brookings, 2011). For a more cautionary interpretation, see Andrew Small, "China's Caution on Afghanistan-Pakistan," *Washington Quarterly* 33, no. 3 (2010). On shared counterterrorist ties, see Ziad Haider, "Sino-Pakistan Relations and Xinjiang's Uighurs: Politics, Trade, and Islam along the Karakoram Highway," *Asian Survey* 45, no. 4 (2005).

32. I have chaired this dialogue since 2012. Its contents, though, are covered by the Chatham House rule, so I refer in various places in this book to ideas and proposals discussed in the meeting, but I do not cite or name any of the participants—who are drawn from the American and Chinese governments as well are academic institutions.

33. J. A. Roach, "Countering Piracy off Somalia: International Law and International Institutions," *American Journal of International Law* 104, no. 3 (2010); T. Treves, "Piracy, Law of the Sea, and Use of Force: Developments off the Coast of Somalia," *European Journal of International Law* 20, no. 2 (2009); Bibi van Ginkel and Frans-Paul van der Putten, eds., *The International Response to Somali Piracy: Challenges and Opportunities* (Leiden: Brill, 2010).

34. For an account of SHADE's success, see Barrett J. Smith, *NATO Regional Capacity Building: The Foundation for Success in the Counter-Piracy Campaign* (Newport: Naval War College Joint Military Operations Department, 2011).

35. In May 2012, I cochaired a meeting with the UAE on counterpiracy and Somalia, where this commitment from Dubai Ports World was announced. The logic was clear: every prior experience with piracy suggests that you cannot defeat pirates at sea—the area you have to cover is simply too large. It has been said of the CTF's efforts in the Indian Ocean that it is akin to trying to have a single police battalion patrol the whole of Europe. Ultimately, you have to defeat pirates on land, either militarily or by creating incentives for them to shift to different commercial ventures. Dubai Ports World's interest in this illustrates the UAE's global presence—it operates more than sixty-five maritime terminals on six continents.

36. International Maritime Organization, "Reports on Acts of Piracy and Armed Robbery against Ships: Annual Report, 2012," April 2, 2013 (www.imo.org).

Chapter 5

1. It is easy to forget the massive scale of the Arctic region. Nearly the size of continental Russia, the Arctic Ocean covers roughly 5,427,000 square miles. Onshore oil and gas has already been exploited by the United States, Canada, and Russia, with these fields accounting for over 15 percent of current petroleum production and almost 10 percent of the world's proven petroleum resource. But offshore fields have even greater potential, especially those within continental shelves and under less than 500 meters of water. In 2009 the U.S. Geological Survey estimated that 30 percent of the world's undiscovered gas and 13 percent of the world's undiscovered oil lies in the Arctic. See Donald L. Gautier and others, "Assessment of Undiscovered Oil and Gas in the Arctic," *Science* 324, no. 5931 (2009).

2. As Charles Ebinger and Evie Zambetakis note, "The rapidity of Arctic melt is no longer the phantasmagoria of futuristic movies but is occurring at a rate unfathomable just a few years ago." See "The Geopolitics of Arctic Melt," *International Affairs* 85, no. 6 (2009).

3. Frank Hoffman, "The Maritime Commons in the Neo-Mahanian Era," in *Contested Commons: The Future of American Power in a Multipolar World,* edited by Abraham M. Denmark and others (Washington: Center for a New American Security, 2010), 65.

4. Departments of the U.S. Marine Corps, U.S. Navy, and U.S. Coast Guard, "A Cooperative Strategy for 21st Century Seapower" (October 2007), p. 3.

5. For an upbeat account, see Daniel W. Drezner, "The Irony of Global Economic Governance: The System Worked,"working paper (New York: Council on Foreign Relations, 2012). For a more negative assessment, Kemal Dervis, "Convergence, Interdependence, and Divergence," *Finance and Development*, 49, no. 3 (September 2012).

6. For a fairly bullish account, see Michael Spence, *The Next Convergence: The Future of Economic Growth in a Multispeed World* (New York: Farrar, Straus, and Giroux, 2011); for a more bearish account, see Michael Pettis, *The Great Rebalancing: Trade, Conflict, and the Perilous Road ahead for the World Economy* (Princeton University Press, 2013). For an accessible, and convincing, detailed country-by-country assessment, see Ruchir Sharma, *Breakout Nations: In Pursuit of the Next Economic Miracles* (New York: Norton, 2012).

7. Kemal Dervis, "The Global Future of Europe's Crisis," Project Syndicate, February 14, 2012 (www.project-syndicate.org/commentary/the-global-future-of-europe-s-crisis); Spence, *The Next Convergence*.

8. Kemal Dervis and Homi Kharas, "The US Must Remain the World's Best Exporter," *UpFront*, January 14, 2011 (www.brookings.edu/blogs/up-front/posts/2011/01/14-halls-jintao); Pettis, *The Great Rebalancing*; and Spence, *The Next Convergence*, all reach this conclusion. Also see Peter Temin and David Vines, *The Leaderless Economy: Why the World Economic System Fell Apart and How to Fix It* (Princeton University Press, 2013).

9. Dervis, "The Global Future of Europe's Crisis."

10. Dervis and Kharas, "The US Must Remain the World's Best Exporter."

11. Dervis, "The Global Future of Europe's Crisis."

12. For a generally optimistic take on China and India's ability to navigate the middle-income transition, see Indermit S. Gill and Homi Kharas, "Back in the Fast Lane," *Finance and Development* 44, no. 1 (2007). For a more skeptical account, see Sharma, *Breakout Nations*. Yet even Gill and Kharas acknowledge that the transition is an extremely complicated one and point to the rule of law as an essential condition of success—no minor challenge for China.

13. Spence, *The Next Convergence*.

14. Sharma, *Breakout Nations*.

15. Gill and Kharas, "Back in the Fast Lane."

16. Ibid.

17. Minxin Pei, "Corruption Threatens China's Future," policy brief (Washington: Carnegie Endowment for International Peace, 2007); Susan L. Shirk, *China: Fragile Superpower* (Oxford University Press, 2007); David Barboza, "Politics Permeates Anti-Corruption Drive in China," *New York Times*, September 3, 2009.

18. President Obama said, "We can no longer meet the challenges of the twenty-first-century economy with twentieth-century approaches. And that's why the G-20 will take the lead in building a new approach to cooperation." Remarks at the G-20 closing press conference, Pittsburgh, September 25, 2009.

19. For an overview, see Gary Clyde Hufbauer, Jeffrey J. Schott, and Wong Foang Fong, *Figuring Out the Doha Round* (Washington: Peterson Institute for International Economics, 2010).

20. Joshua Meltzer, "The Future of Trade: A Deep-Dive Briefing on the World Trade Organization and Why It Matters," Foreignpolicy.com, April 18, 2011.

21. Kamal Nath, a controversial figure in Indian politics, was also the author of a paean to India's major new role in the global economy: *India's Century: The Age of Entrepreneurship in the World's Biggest Democracy* (New York: McGraw Hill, 2007).

22. Kevin Gallagher, "Challenging Opportunities for the Multilateral Trade Regime," in *The Future and the WTO: Confronting the Challenges*, edited by Ricardo Meléndez-Ortiz, Christophe Bellmann, and Miguel Rodriguez Mendoza (Geneva: International Centre for Trade and Sustainable Development, 2012).

23. Henry Kissinger, *On China* (New York: Penguin, 2011), makes a similar point. Also see Mireya Solis, "The Containment Fallacy: China and the TPP," *UpFront*, May 24, 2013 (www.brookings.edu).

24. Technically, China can join the TPP. But the conditions under which it would have to do so are quite tough for China to meet, and it is not clear that China would have any incentive to do so. Many commentators present the issue as if it were designed to contain China—a perception aided by the fact that it was announced as part of President Obama's "rebalancing to Asia," accompanied by his announcement of the deployment of U.S. marines to northern Australia. On this "containment fallacy," see Solis, "The Containment Fallacy."

25. For an argument that it does, see Jagdish Bhagwati, "Why the TPP Is Undermining the Doha Round," *East Asia Forum*, January 14, 2013 (www.eastasiaforum.org).

26. For an argument that the TPP can help move the WTO forward, see James Bacchus, "A Way Forward for the WTO", Bacchus notes that the TPP could be consistent with existing WTO provisions for what are known as "plurilateral trade agreements." For an account of the tensions between regional arrangements and the WTO, see Robert Lawrence, "Competing with Regionalism by Revitalizing the WTO." Both essays can be found in Meléndez-Ortiz, Bellmann, and Mendoza, *The Future and the WTO*.

27. Oliver Stuenkel, "The Politics of the BRICS Contingency Reserve Arrangement (CRA)," *Post-Western World*, May 12, 2013 (www.postwesternworld.com).

28. Pressures on exchange markets, reinforced by different growth patterns in economies like those of the United States and the emerging countries following the financial crisis, raised concerns among policymakers, and the topic of what to do about currencies took a prominent place on G-20 agendas. U.S. policy, particularly monetary easing, has had the effect of depreciating the dollar. The favorable effects for the United States in international trade came at a cost to others. The impacts of the Federal Reserve's monetary policies on exchanges rates also raised concerns in some countries about their own growth trajectories. China's major purchasing of U.S. treasuries—it is the largest holder of U.S. debt—helped fuel a massive U.S. current account deficit and a burgeoning Chinese account surplus, putting strains on the global economy. The trade imbalance has been exacerbated by Chinese authorities' policies aimed at holding the yuan far below market value. These moves have led both sides to level charges of currency manipulation and raise concerns anew about currency wars. Efforts to establish rules on global imbalances have fallen short, with leaders unlikely to agree to strictures on their fiscal policy options, particularly limits on their balance of payments. In a world where there is no fully articulated, rule-bound, monetary system, and unlike in previous eras, national governments are free to set the value of their own currency. This creates a need for a stable national currency to serve as a medium of exchange and as a reserve. The U.S. dollar unofficially played this role even after the demise of the Bretton Woods system in the early 1970s. Since the euro took off in 1999—and with the gradual shift away from New York and London as the two lead global financial hubs—doubts arose that the dollar could or would continue to play this role in the future. Here, two factors account for the declining faith in the

U.S. position. First, large macrolevel imbalances coupled with a downturn in the U.S. economy led to a concern whether dollar-denominated assets were becoming too risky. But while these concerns have been growing, with many envisioning the euro, or even the renminbi, as the future currency of last resort, there is little actual movement away from reliance on the dollar. This could, of course, change, but it is telling that it has not yet happened.

29. This matters to judgments about China's actions over the past five years. Much of the American commentary on this period takes as a given that the United States offered China a genuine opening to participate in the international system, which Beijing spurned—a perspective many in places like Delhi share (Shyam Saran, "Premature Power," *Business Standard,* March 17, 2010). Seen from Beijing's perspective, though, that offer was accompanied by the United States unilaterally pushing roughly a trillion dollars in costs onto Beijing's balance sheet; pushing harder for monitoring and verification of compliance with IMF rules that China does not as yet participate in setting; a shift in climate negotiations toward tightening carbon consumption by the emerging powers; and maintenance of its naval role in the South China Sea.

30. Barry Eichengreen, *Exorbitant Privilege: The Rise and Fall of the Dollar and the Future of the International Monetary System* (Oxford University Press, 2011).

31. In the preparations for the G-20 summit in Cannes, President Nicholas Sarkozy—the most pro-American French president in the contemporary era—argued that the time had come to renegotiate the dollar's role and to move toward an international currency regime based on a blended currency (uk.reuters.com/article/2010/12/13/uk-g20-sarkozy-idUKTRE6BC2S320101213). The United States and others objected to having the item on the agenda, and so it was taken off (www.bloomberg.com/news/2011-01-10/obama-sarkozy-say-they-are-aligned-on-economic-agenda-update1-.html). On the dynamics of the debate, see Barry Carin, Colin Bradford, and others, "Challenges and Opportunities for the French Presidency: The G20 – 2011 and Beyond," CIGI, Waterloo, March 8, 2011.

32. The only important, but modest, exception is that Brazil and China now conduct about 7 percent of their trade in their own currencies.

33. *The National Security Strategy of the United States of America* (White House, 2006), p. 41.

34. "Electricity Production from Oil, Gas, and Coal Sources (as % of Total)," HelgiLibrary (www.helgilibrary.com). British Petroleum gives numbers of a similar magnitude: oil: 33.1 percent, natural gas: 23.9 percent, coal: 29.9 percent See *BP Statistical Review of World Energy* (London: British Petroleum, June 2013).

35. International Energy Agency, *World Energy Outlook 2013* (Paris, 2013).

36. The same dynamic that drives this scramble for energy is also driving a scramble for food supplies—or more specifically for large-scale land purchases where the emerging powers can secure overseas supplies of key grains and cereals for import. This dynamic produces market and political instability, especially in less developed countries. It has not yet become a factor in relations between the major powers; David Steven and I argue elsewhere that there is a case for the United States to pay attention to the dynamic and to push for more effective regulations at the international level to limit the collateral damage of these practices. See Bruce Jones, David Steven, and Emily O'Brien, *Risk Pivot: Great Powers, International Security, and the Energy Revolution* (Brookings Press, forthcoming 2014).

37. In diplomatic terms, this notion is called "common but differentiated responsibilities"—the idea that everyone has to act against climate change but has to bear different costs, proportional to economic history and circumstances. The United States and the other major Western economies accept this idea in principle, but the devil is in the details.

38. See, for example, Kishore Mahbubani, *The Great Convergence: Asia, the West, and the Logic of One World* (New York: PublicAffairs, 2013); Charles Grant, "Multilateralism a la Carte," *New York Times*, April 16, 2012; Ian Bremmer, *Every Nation for Itself: Winners and Losers in a G-Zero World* (New York: Portfolio/Penguin, 2012); Nouriel Roubini, "It Is a G-Zero, Not a G-20 World," *New Perspectives Quarterly* 28, no. 2 (2011); Ian Bremmer and Nouriel Roubini, "A G-Zero World" (www.foreignaffairs.com/articles/67339/ian-bremmer-and-nouriel-roubini/a-g-zero-world).

39. Thomas Hale, David Held, and Kevin Young, *Gridlock: Why Global Cooperation Is Failing When We Need It Most* (Cambridge, U.K.: Polity, 2013).

40. For a detailed critique of the UN process, and a compelling alternative, see William Antholis and Strobe Talbott, *Fast Forward: Ethics and Politics in the Age of Global Warming* (Brookings Press, 2010).

41. This is highlighted by one particularly quirk of the UNFCCC process: its insistence on what can be called hard consensus. Most global bodies operate on one of two premises: either there are voting rules or they operate by consensus —which means, broadly speaking, that most of the countries present in the negotiating room have to agree on the outcome. But there are degrees of consensus. Even in a highly formalized body like the UN General Assembly, everyone understands that consensus does not mean unanimity—it does not mean that any one small country can veto progress. If a country is trying to negotiate a new arrangement of global terrorism, and it does not have the support of the United States, or Europe, or Russia, then there is no consensus. But if Venezuela or Cuba objects—well, tough beans. But for the most part, the UNFCCC does not operate this way; it takes the notion of consensus more literally, basically requiring unanimity in its proceedings. At least, it has until recently; in the Cancun session, chaired by Mexico, the very experienced Mexican chair of the process waved away some of this hard consensus rule and produced a reasonable agreement despite the opposition of a small handful of countries. Still, the idea that a package of agreements about massive changes in the energy and economic infrastructure of the world's leading economies is going to be negotiated in this inclusive fashion defies credibility.

42. The full text is available at www.state.gov/r/pa/prs/ps/2013/04/207465.htm.

43. The MEF comprises Australia, Brazil, Canada, China, the European Union, France, Germany, India, Indonesia, Italy, Japan, Korea, Mexico, Russia, South Africa, the United Kingdom, and the United States. This is basically the G-20 minus the misplaced Argentina and minus Saudi Arabia—a major energy producer, obviously, but not a major carbon emitter.

44. Arunabha Ghosh and David Steven, "India's Energy, Food, and Water Security: International Cooperation for Domestic Capacity," in *Shaping the Emerging World: India and the Multilateral Order,* edited by Waheguru Pal Singh Sidhu, Pratap Bhanu Mehta, and Bruce Jones (Brookings Press, 2013).

45. Full disclosure: At the time of these agreements, my wife, Elizabeth Cousens, was involved as the U.S. ambassador to ECOSOC in parallel negotiations on sustainable

development issues, including at the Rio+20 Summit—but not in the U.S./China or MEF outcomes.

46. International Energy Agency, *World Energy Outlook 2010* (Paris: 2010).

47. India is no longer a recipient of international development aid—it has crossed the magic threshold from low-income to middle-income status. This is a bit of a sham, actually: India's per capita income is $1,026 a year, and the World Bank set its income threshold at $1,025 (2012 figures). So India is barely over the edge. But India has grown substantially and has large numbers of middle-class and wealthy citizens. And it is no longer feasible for Western countries to justify development aid spending in India.

48. For a fuller discussion, see Andrew Hart, Bruce Jones, and David Steven, "Chill Out: Why Cooperation Is Balancing Conflict among Major Powers in the New Arctic" (Managing Global Order, Brookings, May 2012).

Chapter 6

1. The full list is Bangladesh, Belgium, Brazil, Bulgaria, Denmark, France, Germany, Greece, Indonesia, Italy, the Netherlands, Norway, Spain, Sweden, and Turkey. For more information, see unifil.unmissions.org/Default.aspx?tabid=11584&language=en-US.

2. Leon Wieseltier, "Syria Burns on Obama's Back Burner," *New Republic*, September 14, 2012; Bob Corker, "Dithering While Damascus Burns," *New York Times*, April 23, 2013.

3. Naazneen Barma, Ely Ratner, and Steven Weber, "The Mythical Liberal Order," *National Interest* (March/April 2013).

4. Kishore Mahbubani, "Syria Exposes the Decline of American Diplomacy," *Financial Times*, September 11, 2013; Timothy Garton Ash, "This crisis resolves little in Syria but says a lot about the United States: The nation is sick and tired of foreign wars and may never play its role of global anchor again. We may live to regret it," *Guardian*, September 11, 2013; Kilic Bugra Kanat, "The Syrian Crisis and American Decline (by Choice)," *Middle East Monitor*, September 19, 2013.

5. The classic study of international response to the effects of a civil war once it had crossed an international border is William Shawcross, *The Quality of Mercy: Cambodia, Holocaust, and Modern Conscience* (New York: Simon and Schuster, 1984). Equally compelling is his account of the huge changes that accompanied the entry into internal conflict by international forces: William Shawcross, *Deliver Us from Evil: Peacekeepers, Warlords, and a World of Endless Conflict* (New York: Simon and Schuster, 2000).

6. United Nations, *A More Secure World: Our Shared Responsibility* (New York: 2005).

7. Both numbers include troops and police. In 2008 there were about 80,000 troops and just over 20,000 police deployed by the UN in nineteen different peacekeeping operations.

8. Tim Witcher, "China Offers 500 Troops to UN Mali Force: Envoys," *AsiaOne*, May 23, 2013 (news.asiaone.com).

9. "Annual Review of Global Peace Operations 2013" (New York University, Center on International Cooperation, 2013).

10. That force was technically under UN command and is thus listed as a Blue Helmet rather than a multinational force operation. In fact, it was something of both. Although nominally under UN command, the various member states deployed their own forces using their own logistics, not the UN's; and they set up a separate command structure at UN headquarters, the Strategic Military Cell, to supplement normal UN command structures.

11. It is also a principle for which there were always supposed to be exceptions. Almost immediately after the principle was enshrined in the UN Charter in 1945, negotiations began on a kind of exceptions clause—the UN Convention on Genocide, which was adopted in 1948. That convention sets out the caveat that when a state is committing genocide, the international community has the right to intervene to stop it. The Genocide Convention, though it creates a right to act, does not create an *obligation* to do so; and failure to act against genocide has been a depressingly consistent theme of international politics since 1945, including in U.S. policy: it was only in 1984 that the United States signed the Genocide Convention. See Samantha Power, *A Problem from Hell: America and the Age of Genocide* (New York: Harper, 2007).

12. Ethan Bronner and David E. Sanger, "Arab League Endorses No-Flight Zone over Libya," *New York Times*, March 12, 2011.

13. Confidential interview by author, European diplomat, UN, New York, March 17, 2011.

14. "'Shame for the Failure of Our Government': Fischer Joins Criticism of German Security Council Abstention" (www.spiegel.de/international/germany/shame-for-the-failure-of-our-government-fischer-joins-criticism-of-german-security-council-abstention-a-752542.html).

15. Confidential interview by author, European diplomat, New York, March 19, 2011.

16. For example, in the wake of unrest in Mali, India's permanent representative to the UN at the time of the Libya operation has repeatedly argued that the spillover of violence from Libya to Mali undermines the West's case that action in Libya was necessary to protect civilians. In this, he is invoking a "balance of consequences" argument about R2P (responsibility to protect). For a detailed discussion, see Gareth Evans, "The Responsibility to Protect after Libya and Syria," address to the annual conference of the Castan Centre for Human Rights Law, Melbourne, July 20, 2012.

17. Gareth Evans reaches the same conclusion; see ibid.

18. Thomas Wright, "Brazil Hosts Workshop on the 'Responsibility While Protecting,'" Foreignpolicy.com, August 29, 2012.

19. For a Brazilian perspective on the debate, see Matias Spektor, "The Arab Spring, Seen from Brazil," *New York Times*, December 23, 2011.

20. During UN-mandated NATO operations in Bosnia, NATO reported to the UN Security Council once a month on its actions and on the situation on the ground. This did not impede NATO's freedom of action and did quite a lot to keep non-NATO members of the Security Council continuing to authorize the action.

21. For major arguments in this debate, see Helga Haftendorn, Robert O. Keohane, and Celeste A. Wallander, eds., *Imperfect Unions: Security Institutions over Time and Space* (Oxford University Press, 1999); Thomas M. Franck, "The Power of Legitimacy and the Legitimacy of Power: International Law in an Age of Power Disequilibrium," *American Journal of International Law*, 100, no. 1 (2006); Ian Hurd, *After Anarchy: Legitimacy and Power in the United Nations Security Council* (Princeton

University Press, 2008); Stephen D. Krasner, "Compromising Westphalia," *International Security* 20, no. 3 (1995); and Stephen Krasner and Thomas Risse, "External Actors and the Provision of Collective Goods in Areas of Limited Statehood," March 5, 2012 (iis-db.stanford.edu/docs/645/Krasner_Risse_External_Actors_Provision_Collective-Goods.pdf).

22. Fiona Hill, "The Fear that Drives Russia's Support for Syria's Assad," interview by Neal Conan, NPR, March 27, 2013 (www.npr.org).

23. American, Indian, and Saudi officials, interviews by author, Washington, New York, and Delhi.

24. See Fiona Hill, "The Real Reason Putin Supports Assad: Mistaking Syria for Chechnya," *Foreign Affairs*, March 25, 2013.

25. Bruce Jones, "The Options in Syria," Foreignpolicy.com, April 10, 2012; Michael E. O'Hanlon and Edward P. Joseph, "Bosnia May Offer Road Map for Syria," *Politico*, April 23, 2013 (www.politico.com).

26. Michael Doran and Michael O'Hanlon, "Obama Needs to Act Now on Syria," *USAToday*, June 23, 2013.

27. In that instance, Russian and American troops came close to clashing at the Kosovo airport, when American troops were ordered to attack Russian positions there; fortunately, cooler heads prevailed, the order was countermanded, and Russian and American troops patrolled in separate parts of Kosovo until Russian forces later withdrew. I was in Macedonia at the time, backstopping the UN advance team that went into Pristina two days before; they were some of the most tense hours of my life as we waited to see whether the Americans and the Russians would open fire on each other at the airport.

28. Jones, "The Options in Syria."

29. For a fuller discussion of how this might have worked, see ibid.

30. For an early account, see George Perkovich, "Dealing with Iran's Nuclear Challenge" (Washington: Carnegie Endowment for International Peace, 2003). By early in Obama's first term, the debate had moved on to strategies for dealing with Iran: see Kenneth M. Pollack and others, *Which Path to Persia? Options for a New American Strategy toward Iran* (Brookings Press, 2009). Four years later, the debate was similar: see Scott Sagan and Kenneth Waltz, *The Spread of Nuclear Weapons: An Enduring Debate* (New York: Norton, 2013).

31. Scott D. Sagan, "How to Keep the Bomb from Iran," *Foreign Affairs* 85, no. 5 (2006).

32. Kenneth Waltz, "Why Iran Should Get the Bomb," *Foreign Affairs* 91, no. 4 (2012).

33. Iran is also perhaps the first real test of cybertechnology as a tool of statecraft and warfare. Over the past few years, Iran has been subject to sophisticated cyberattacks intended to disrupt its nuclear program, the most prominent of which is Stuxnet. Developed by the United States and Israel, Stuxnet was first used during the Bush administration in cyberattacks on Iran as part of a program code named Olympic Games. The virus came to global attention when a programming error resulted in its spread from Iran's Natanz plant to computers around the world in 2010. The Obama administration stepped up the cyberattacks, which are estimated to have succeeded in temporarily crippling a fifth of the centrifuges in use to purify uranium as well as disrupting espionage operations and—presumably—covert attacks on Iranian scientists

and facilities. For more details, see David Albright, Paul Brannan, and Christina Walrond, "Stuxnet Malware and Natanz: Update of ISIS December 22, 2010 Report" (Washington: Institute for Science and International Security, 2011); and Peter W. Singer, *Wired for War: The Robotics Revolution and Conflict in the Twenty-First Century* (New York: Penguin, 2010).

34. "China Urges Calm in Strait of Hormuz," *Jerusalem Post*, December 30, 2011 (www.jpost.com); "China Warns against Shutting Strait of Hormuz," *NDTV*, January 19, 2012 (www.ndtv.com).

35. To date the Security Council has adopted six resolutions in response to Iran's nuclear program. The council first demanded that Iran suspend its uranium-enrichment-related and reprocessing activities with the adoption of Resolution 1696 in July 2006. The following three resolutions—1737, adopted in December 2006; 1747, adopted in March 2007; and 1803, adopted in March 2008—imposed incremental sanctions on Iranian persons and entities believed to have been involved in Iran's nuclear and missile programs. Resolution 1835, adopted in September 2008, reiterated the demands made in Resolution 1696, without imposing additional sanctions. The UN Security Council significantly expanded sanctions in June 2010 with the adoption of Resolution 1929.

36. The deal was that Tehran would trade its existing stocks of low-enriched uranium (which cannot be used for a weapon) for a significantly smaller quantity of highly enriched uranium (which can be), but to be used only in its research reactor. This resuscitated a "fuel-swap" proposal that had been previously backed by the UN Security Council. The point of it is that the technology to enrich uranium to weapons grade would not exist on Iranian soil but that Iran would have controlled access to its products from a third country, perhaps Russia.

37. National Security Council official's account of intercepts to author, Washington; this account was grudgingly confirmed by both Brazilian and Turkish diplomats.

38. For a highly critical take on the deal, see Fred Kaplan, "Are Brazil and Turkey Delusional or Deceptive?" *Slate*, June 11, 2010 (www.slate.com).

39. Celso Amorim, "The New Geopolitics: Emerging Powers and the Challenges of a Multipolar World," remarks, Carnegie Endowment for International Peace, Washington, November 30, 2010

40. The same point holds true for reform of the UN Security Council. This was part of the subtext of the Iran negotiations. Brazil—along with India, Japan, Germany, and less convincingly, South Africa—has made a pitch for a permanent seat on the UN Security Council. This is a matter of interests, but also of symbolism. Along with voting weights in the IMF, Security Council vetoes of the permanent members are powerful, and deeply resented, symbols of an international order dominated by older powers. For the powers aspiring to new permanent seats, though, the biggest obstacle lies not in Washington, which is ambivalent, but in Moscow and Beijing, which adamantly oppose any change—Moscow because the veto is a vital fossil of Russia's previous power, Beijing because it gives China a leg up in international security dynamics that it will not achieve by scale of military power for a decade or two to come.

41. Author interviews, Delhi, Washington. Also see "India Leads Asian Cuts in Iran Oil Imports Ahead of Waiver Review" (www.reuters.com/.../iran-sanctions-waiver-idUSL3N0DQ2N520130521).

42. Interviews by author, Turkish diplomats, April 2013.

Chapter 7

1. Gideon Rachman, "The Shadow of 1914 Falls over the Pacific," *Financial Times*, February 19, 2013; Kevin Rudd, "A Maritime Balkans of the 21st Century: East Asia Is a Tinderbox on Water," *Foreign Policy*, January 30, 2013; Anatol Lieven, "Avoiding a US-China War," *New York Times*, June 12, 2012; Charles Emmerson, "Eve of Disaster: Why 2013 Eerily Looks Like the World of 1913, on the Cusp of the Great War," *Foreign Policy,* April 1, 2013.

2. He Yafei, "The Trust Deficit: How the U.S. 'Pivot' to Asia Looks from Beijing," *Foreign Policy*, May 13, 2013.

3. Invoking the G-7 as an analog, the notion was that, given their respective sizes, if the United States and China could agree on how to cooperate on global problems, much of the rest of the world would follow. China scholars Elizabeth Economy and Adam Segal correctly referred to it at the time as "The G-2 Mirage." See *Foreign Affairs* 88, no. 3 (May/June 2009). Li Zhoaxing argued that "a G-2 framework is not consistent with China's independent foreign policy." See "What China Wants in 2012," Project Syndicate, January 12, 2012 (www.project-syndicate.org/commentary/what-china-wants-in-2012).

4. In May 2013 Chinese president Xi Jinping met with Obama's national security adviser, Tom Donilon, and told him that the American-Chinese relationship stood at a "critical juncture" and that the two countries should explore "a new type of great power relationship." Jane Perlez, "Chinese President to Seek New Relationship with U.S. in Talks," *New York Times*, May 28, 2013.

5. Aaron L. Friedberg, "The Future of U.S.-China Relations: Is Conflict Inevitable?" *International Security* 30, no. 2 (2005). Also see Joseph S. Nye Jr., "China's Rise Doesn't Mean War," *Foreign Policy* (January/February 2011). Nye gives a strong account of where historical analogies are misleading and where they provide credible warnings.

6. For an argument that China's moves in the 2010–12 period were neither as new as claimed nor as assertive as claimed, see Alastair Iain Johnston, "How New and Assertive Is China's New Assertiveness?" *International Security* 37, no. 4 (2013).

7. Dean Cheng, "Sea Power and the Chinese State: Chain's Maritime Ambitions," Backgrounder 2576 (Washington: Heritage Foundation, 2011).

8. Graham Lees, "China Seeks Burmese Route around the 'Malacca Dilemma,'" *World Politics Review*, briefing, February 20, 2007.

9. For an in-depth review of these and related incidents and issues, see in particular Richard Bush, *The Perils of Proximity: China-Japan Security Relations* (Brookings Press, 2010).

10. Clive Shofield, "Dangerous Ground: A Geopolitical Overview of the South China Sea," in *Security and International Politics in the South China Sea,* edited by Sam Bateman (New York: Routledge, 2009).

11. Edward Wong, "China's Navy Reaches Far, Unsettling Region," *New York Times*, June 14, 2011.

12. Dhruva Jaishankar, "India's Ocean: Could New Delhi's Growing Naval Force Change the Balance of Power in the Pacific?" Foreignpolicy.com, December 6, 2012.

13. U.S. Energy Information Administration, "Overview: South China Sea," February 7, 2013 (www.eia.gov.).

14. Stephen Stedman has pointed out that traditional realist scholarship (including Morgenthau) recognized that food security was an essential part of a state's

internal legitimacy and a potential driver of tensions in international security. Stedman, exchange with author, January 2013.

15. Scholars debate whether international law matters; after all, states could just ignore it. It is notable then that the United States chose not to sign the law; because it has problems with an important consequence of the UN Convention on the Law of the Sea, it has—so far—chosen not to ratify the convention.

16. Former senior U.S. Naval Institute official, interview with author, Washington, June 2012.

17. Bruce A. Ellman, "Maritime Territorial Disputes and Their Impact on Maritime Strategy: A Historical Perspective," in *Security and International Politics in the South China Sea,* edited by Sam Bateman (New York: Routledge, 2009); Shicun Wu and Keyuan Zou, eds., *Maritime Security in the South China Sea: Regional Implications and International Cooperation* (Burlington: Ashgate).

18. I am grateful to Andrew Hart for detailed research support on this section.

19. James Holmes and Toshi Yoshihara, "The Influence of Mahan upon China's Maritime Strategy," *Comparative Strategy* 24, no. 1 (2005). See also C. Raja Mohan, "Maritime Power: India and China Turn to Mahan," ISAS Working Paper 71 (National University of Singapore, 2009). Mahan himself is credited with coining the phrase *the global commons,* and U.S. strategists understand this. See Michele Flournoy and Shawn Brimley, "The Contested Commons," *Proceedings Magazine* 135, no. 7 (2009).

20. James Holmes and Toshi Yoshihara, *Red Star over the Pacific: China's Rise and the Challenge to US Maritime Security* (Annapolis: Naval Institute Press, 2010).

21. Alfred Thayer Mahan, *The Influence of Sea Power upon History: 1660–1783* (New York: Dover, 1890).

22. Mark J. Valencia, "The South China Sea: Back to the Future?" *Global Asia* 5, no. 4 (2010).

23. Roland H. Worth, *No Choice but War: The United States Embargo against Japan and the Eruption of War in the Pacific* (Jefferson, N.C.: McFarland, 1995); Irvine H. Anderson, "The 1941 De Facto Embargo on Oil to Japan: A Bureaucratic Reflex," *Pacific Historical Review* 44, no. 2 (1975).

24. David A. Shlapak and others, *A Question of Balance: Political Context and Military Aspects of the China-Taiwan Dispute* (Santa Monica; RAND, 2009).

25. Ibid. Also, for an accessible account of China's military modernization in the context of its strategy in the South China Sea, see M. Taylor Travel, "Maritime Security in the South China Sea and the Competition over Maritime Rights," in *Cooperation from Strength: The United States, China and the South China Sea,* edited by Patrick M. Cronin (Washington: Center for a New American Security, 2012).

26. However, the real impact of a technology does not have to depend on its actual effect; it can be effective if an opponent believes it might. For example, Reagan-era missile-shield technology was never proven in its impact, but it had major effects on Russian spending and strategy and, by some accounts, helped drive Russia to overspend on defense technology, accelerating its economic collapse.

27. U.S. Department of Defense, "Air-Sea Battle: Service Collaboration to Address Anti-Access & Area Denial Challenges," May 2013 (www.defense.gov).

28. Ibid.; Andrew Krepinevich, "Why AirSea Battle" (Washington: Center for Strategic and Budgetary Assessments, 2010); Bill Sweetman and Richard Fisher Jr., "AirSea Battle Concept Is Focused on China," *Aviation Week,* April 7, 2011; Richard Halloran, "AirSea Battle," *Air Force Magazine* (August 2010) (www.airforcemag.com).

29. Kurt Campbell "China Must Rein in Its Cyber Assaults," *Financial Times*, March 11, 2013.

30. For details of their estimates of Chinese nuclear forces, see www.fas.org/nuke/guide/china/nuke/index.html.

31. Thomas Fingar, "Worrying about Washington: China's Views on the U.S. Nuclear Posture," *Nonproliferation Review* 18, no. 1 (2011); M. Taylor Fravel and Evan S. Medeiros, "China's Search for Assured Retaliation: The Evolution of Chinese Nuclear Strategy and Force Structure," *International Security* 35, no. 2 (2010).

32. I am grateful to Tom Wright for bringing this dynamic to my attention.

33. Davie Shambaugh, *China Goes Global: The Partial Power* (Oxford University Press, 2013).

34. For example, see Wang Yiwei, "How to Prevent the U.S. from Declining too Rapidly?" *Global Times Online*, August 10, 2006.

35. Huang Renwei, *Zhongguo Jueqi de Shijian he Kongjian* [Time and space for China's rise] (Shanghai: Shanghai Shekeyuan Chubanshe, 2002).

36. This generation was part of the group that forged—and ardently believe in—the notion of China's "peaceful rise." See Zheng Bijian, "China's 'Peaceful Rise' to Great-Power Status," *Foreign Affairs* 84, no. 5 (2005).

37. This kind of anecdotal evidence does not tell us much, but it does illustrate themes that can be found in more detailed analytical studies. One such is David A. Ralston and others, "Doing Business in the 21st century with the New Generation of Chinese Managers: A Study of Generational Shifts in Work Values in China," *Journal of International Business Studies* 30, no. 2 (1999).

38. Andrew J. Nathan, *China's Search for Security* (Columbia University Press, 2012).

39. Aaron Friedberg, "The Future of U.S.-China Relations," concedes this point, while portraying a more worrying picture about China's intentions.

40. "Analysis: China Turns on the Charm at Regional Security Forum," *Asahi Shimbun*, June 3, 2013. National security staff, interviews with author, Washington, June 2013. Also see M. Taylor Fravel, "Xi Jinping's Overlooked Revelation on China's Maritime Disputes," *The Diplomat*, August 15, 2013,

41. A. Michael Spence, *The Next Convergence: The Future of Economic Growth in a Multispeed World* (New York: Farrar, Straus, and Giroux, 2011).

42. This is part of a broader argument about economic growth that posits that societies that have made the leap to high income levels have largely done so on the basis of "open rules" for economic management, enforced by the rule of law. See Douglass C. North, John Joseph Wallis, and Barry R. Weingast, *Violence and Social Orders: A Conceptual Framework for Interpreting Recorded Human History* (Cambridge University Press, 2009).

43. Jonathan D. Pollack, "China's Reaction to the Arab Spring," in *The Arab Awakening: America and the Transformation of the Middle East*, edited by Kenneth M. Pollack and others (Brookings Press, 2011); also see www.bloomberg.com/news/2012-05-01/leaders-in-beijing-feared-arab-spring-could-infect-china.html.

44. This is taken from Shambaugh, *China Goes Global*, p. 303.

45. Joseph S. Nye Jr. makes a similar point. See Nye, "China's Rise Doesn't Mean War."

46. Homi Kharas, who has been bullish about China's prospects for navigating the middle-income trap, has recently been more bearish on the issue. See "Developing Asia and the Middle-Income Trap," at www.brookings.edu/research/opinions/2013/08/13-developing-asia-middle-income-kharas.

47. Campbell, "China Must Rein in Its Cyber Assaults."

48. Andrew S. Erickson and Gabriel B. Collins, "China's Oil Security Pipe Dream: The Reality, and Strategic Consequences, of Seaborne Imports," *Naval War College Review* 63, no. 2 (2010) (www.andrewerickson.com).

49. *Jane's Sentinel Security Assessment: China and Northeast Asia* (Coulsdon, Surry: Jane's Information Group, 2000), p. 111.

50. William Komiss and LaVar Huntzinger, *The Economic Implications of Disruptions to Maritime Oil Chokepoints* (Alexandria, Va.: CNA, 2011) (www.cna.org).

51. Yun Sun ("Westward Ho!" Foreignpolicy.com, February 7, 2013) was among the first to report on this debate in the U.S. press, commenting in particular on an influential article by Wang Jisi, dean of the School of International Relations, Peking University. But while Yun Sun's article, and much of the reaction in Washington, treated the proposed strategy as essentially offensive, Wang Jisi explicitly talks about the shift to a focus in China's western periphery as "conducive to the establishment of more balanced Sino-US relations and promotion of Sino-US strategic mutual trust." He also talks about "strategic coordination" and "the potential of Sino-US cooperation" in investment, energy, counterterrorism, nonproliferation, and regional stability. See http://opinion.huanqin.com/opinion_world/2012-10/3193760.html.

52. Jane Perlez and Bree Feng, "China's North Korea Envoy Will Visit U.S. for Talks," *New York Times*, April 19, 2013.

53. "China Punishes North Korea for Nuclear Tests as US Asks for More," *Fox News*, March 24, 2013; "China Publicly Cuts off North Korean Bank," *Wall Street Journal*, May 8, 2013.

54. Jane Perlez, "China Ban on Items for Nuclear Use to North Korea May Stall Arms Bid," *New York Times,* September 29, 2013.

55. Ely Ratner, "Rebalancing to Asia with an Insecure China," *Washington Quarterly* 36, no. 2 (2013).

56. Chinese foreign minister Wang Yi elaborated on this concept in a major speech in Washington in September 2013. For a transcript, see www.brookings.edu/events/2013/09/20-ns-china-foreign-minister-wang yi.

57. Henry Kissinger, *On China* (New York: Penguin, 2011), examines the prospects of war between a rising China and the United States and also provides a thorough account of the argument as well as an important, if tenuous, rebuttal.

58. Other scholars who invoke the historical parallel include Yoon Young-Kwan, "Asian Power Shift Has Echoes of Prewar Failures," *Scotsman*, January 31, 2013; Emmerson, "Eve of Disaster"; John J. Mearsheimer, "The Gathering Storm: China's Challenge to US Power in Asia," *Chinese Journal of International Politics* 3, no. 4 (2010); and N. S. Sisodia, "Strategic Challenges and Risks in a Globalising World: An Indian Perspective," in *Grand Strategy for India: 2020 and Beyond,* edited by Krishnappa Venkatshamy and Princy George (New Delhi: Institute for Defence Studies and Analyses, 2012).

59. Also see Woosang Kim, "Power, Alliance, and Major Wars, 1916–1975," *Journal of Conflict Resolution* 33, no. 2 (1989); Henk W. Houweling and Jan G. Siccama, "Power Transitions as a Cause of War," *Journal of Conflict Resolution* 32, no. 1 (1988); Thomas Lemke, *Eine Kritik der Politischen Vernunft—Foucaults Analyse der modernen Gouvernementalität* (Berlin: Argument Verlag, 1997).

60. Richard Lebow and Benjamin Valentino, "Lost in Transition: A Critical Analysis of Power Transition Theory," *International Relations* 23, no. 9 (2009). There is an

oddity in that study, in that the authors do not treat China in the 1650-to-1850 period, a strange exclusion. The confrontation between an established China and a rising United Kingdom is an important episode of precisely the phenomenon that the study is attempting to measure: challenges between a lesser and a greater power. However, arguably, the China case conforms to one of the study's important findings, that great powers decline due to internal disintegration as much as to challenges from a rising power. The same could be said of India, which was already in a state of deterioration before the English defeat of the rump of the Mughal dynasty. See William Dalrymple, *White Mughals: Love and Betrayal in Eighteenth-Century India* (London: Penguin, 2002). In both cases, there was a military confrontation between England and these two aging powers but hardly a full-on war, with the full might of the rising power arrayed against the full might of the waning ones: both empires collapsed at the merest encounter with the West.

61. Also see Bruce Bueno de Mesquita, "Pride of Place: The Origins of German Hegemony," *World Politics* 43, no. 1 (1990); A. F. K. Organski and Jacek Kugler, *The War Ledger* (University of Chicago Press, 1980) use 80 percent of capability as sufficient to qualify for parity.

62. Norman Angell, *The Great Illusion: A Study of the Relation of Military Power to National Advantage* (Toronto: McClelland and Goodchild, 1912).

63. Kevin H. O'Rourke and Jeffrey G. Williamson, *Globalization and History: The Evolution of a Nineteenth-Century Atlantic Economy* (MIT Press, 2001); Dani Rodrik, *The Globalization Paradox: Democracy and the Future of the World Economy* (New York: Norton, 2012).

64. Organski and Kugler, *The War Ledger*; Lebow and Valentino, "Lost in Transition"; Robert Gilpin, *War and Change in World Politics* (Cambridge University Press, 1981); Paul Kennedy, *The Rise and Fall of Great Powers: Economic Change and Military Conflict from 1500 to 2000* (New York: Vintage, 1987). It is notable though that Lebow and Valentino find scant evidence for the notion that dominant powers tend to attack rising competitors. More frequently, according to their account, dominant powers disintegrate due to internal pressures (the Spanish Empire, the Austro-Hungarian Empire, and the Ottoman Empire all fit this pattern; and the collapse of the Soviet Union is a variant of it).

Chapter 8

1. Ruchir Sharma, *Breakout Nations: In Pursuit of the Next Economic Miracles* (New York: Norton, 2012).

2. I am grateful to Tom Wright and David Steven for this insight. For an elaboration, see Alex Evans, Bruce Jones, and David Steven, "Confronting the Long Crisis of Globalization" (Brookings Center on International Cooperation, 2010).

3. "Chinese Anger over Pollution Becomes Main Cause of Social Unrest," *Bloomberg*, March 6, 2013.

4. Jackson Diehl, "The Coming Collapse: Authoritarians in China and Russia Face an Endgame," *World Affairs* 175, no. 3 (2012).

5. Cheng Li, "The End of the CCP's Resilient Authoritarianism? A Tripartite Assessment of Shifting Power in China," *China Quarterly* 211 (September 2012).

6. Susan L. Shirk, *China: Fragile Superpower* (Oxford University Press, 2007); David Barboza and Sharon LaFraniere, "'Princelings' in China Use Family Ties to Gain Riches," *New York Times*, May 17, 2012.

7. Aaron Friedberg, "The Future of U.S.-China Relations: Is Conflict Inevitable?" *International Security* 30, no. 2 (2005).

8. Arunabha Ghosh and David Steven, "India's Energy, Food, and Water Security: International Cooperation for Domestic Capacity," in *Shaping the Emerging World: India and the Multilateral Order,* edited by Waheguru Pal Singh Sidhu, Pratap Bhanu Mehta, and Bruce Jones (Brookings Press, 2013); Matthias Williams, "Special Report: 'Coal Mafia' Stokes India's Power Crisis," Reuters, May 14, 2013.

9. This is a phenomenon vividly documented by Ellen Barry, "Russia Left Behind: A Journey through a Heartland on the Slow Road to Ruin," *New York Times*, October 13, 2013. Also see Fiona Hill and Clifford G. Gaddy, *Mr. Putin: Operative in the Kremlin* (Brookings Press, 2013).

10. I happened to be in Brasília when the revelations broke about the National Security Agency's presence in Brasília. There were tense negotiations in Rousseff's inner office over how to handle the affair, given an ongoing effort to improve U.S.-Brazil relations. Eventually, Rousseff went public, decrying the United States. Confidential interviews by author, Brasília, July 8–11, 2013.

11. Patricia Rey Mallen, "Joe Biden and Mexican President Enrique Peña Nieto Bond over Pemex, Ignore NSA Espionage," *International Business Times*, September 23, 2013.

12. For example, when I served as a UN official in the Middle East, I was alerted to the fact that UK listening stations in Cyprus would pick up every cellular phone call I had, and every e-mail, and they would be scanned for key words that would trigger closer scrutiny. At the time, I was told, the UK listening station collected millions of phone calls and e-mails per day. That was in 2001. The fact of the Cyprus listening stations was revealed in UK newspapers in August 2013, but were common knowledge among diplomatic professionals long before that. On the "revelations": Duncan Campbell, Oliver Wright, James Cusick, and Kim Sengupta, "Exclusive: UK's secret Mid-East internet surveillance base is revealed in Edward Snowden leaks," *The Independent*, August 23, 2013.

13. An illustrative example is Daniel Luzer, "This Government Shutdown Won't Be Our Last," *Pacific Standard*, October 7, 2013.

14. Christopher Chyba, "Biological Terrorism and Public Health," *Survival* 43, no. 1 (2001); "The Secretary-General's High-Level Panel Report on Threats, Challenges and Change" (United Nations, 2004); Benjamin Wittes, "Global Security," in *Megatrends in Global Interaction* (Washington: Bertelsmann Foundation, 2012).

15. On China's internal fragilities, see in particular Shirk, *China*. On the political and economic dynamics surrounding the rise of a large middle class, see Cheng Li, "The End of the CCP's Resilient Authoritarianism? A Tripartite Assessment of Shifting Power in China," *China Quarterly* 211 (September 2012).

16. Jonathan D. Spence, *Search for Modern China* (New York: Norton, 2012); Odd Arne Westad, *Restless Empire: China and the World since 1750* (New York: Basic Books, 2012).

17. Walter Russell Mead, "In the Footsteps of the Kaiser: China Boosts US Power in Asia," *American Interest,* September 26, 2010 (Via Meadia: blogs.the-american-interest.com).

18. Anne-Marie Slaughter, "The Coming Atlantic Century," *Project Syndicate*, February 22, 2013 (www.project-syndicate.org).

Chapter 9

1. United Nations Missions to Investigate Allegations of the Use of Chemical Weapons in the Syrian Arab Republic, "Report on the Alleged Use of Chemical Weapons in the Ghouta Area of Damascus on 21 August 2013" (New York: UN, 2013); "Attacks on Ghouta: Analysis of Alleged Use of Chemical Weapons in Syria" (New York: Human Rights Watch, 2013).

2. President Obama, "Weekly Address: Calling for Limited Military Action in Syria" (White House, September 7, 2013).

3. President Obama, "Remarks by the President in Address to the Nation on Syria" (White House, September 10, 2013).

4. Fiona Hill, "The Fear that Drives Russia's Support for Syria's Assad" (WNYC Radio, March 27, 2013).

5. See Lee Smith, "The Damage Done," *Weekly Standard* 19, no. 3 (2013); Timothy Garton Ash, "The End of U.S. Exceptionalism," *Los Angeles Times*, September 12, 2013; Carlo Muñoz, "House Intelligence Chief Calls Syrian Weapons Deal 'A Big Win' for Russia," *The Hill*, September 15, 2013; Ariel Cohen, "Russia Is Back," *National Interest*, September 17, 2013; Brian Michael Jenkins, "10 Reasons U.S. Influence Has Fallen in the Middle East," *Slate*, September 16, 2013; Matt K. Lewis, "Obama's Spectacularly Disastrous Syria Accomplishment," *The Week*, September 16, 2013. Also, see Vladimir Putin, "A Plea for Caution from Russia," *New York Times*, September 11, 2013.

6. "Rep. Peter King Says Bill Clinton Continued Kosovo Air Campaign after Rebuke by House," *Politifact* (www.politifact.com).

7. Robert Gates, speech, U.S. Global Leadership Campaign, Washington, D.C., July 15, 2008.

8. Ibid.

9. By 2012 inequality in the United States was at historic highs, made worse by an uneven recovery from the global financial crisis (http://elsa.berkeley.edu/~saez/saez-UStopincomes-2012.pdf).

10. Richard Haass, *Foreign Policy Begins at Home: The Case for Putting America's House in Order* (New York: Basic Books, 2013).

11. Kevin Rudd, "The Need for a New US-China Strategic Roadmap" (Brookings, 2012).

12. James Steinberg, Carnegie-State Department Dialogue Series, March 22, 2011, Brookings.

13. For more information, see the companion volume: Bruce Jones, David Steven, and Emily O'Brien, *Risk Pivot: Great Powers, International Security, and the Energy Revolution* (Brookings Press, forthcoming 2014).

14. That wider UN level is important: if the seventeen countries of the Major Economies Forum on Energy and Climate (MEF) strike a deal on carbon reductions and the next twenty medium-size economies are not part of it, those countries will have an immediate opportunity for free riding. But that does not necessarily imply that every country has to be brought into a deal from the ground up: if the seventeen members of

the MEF forge an agreement, they have more than enough diplomatic capacity to push that agreement through wider bodies like the UN Framework Convention on Climate Change (UNFCCC) and the UN summits. The real challenge here lies in sequencing. The UN has a set calendar of summits, and these are held irrespective of whether there is progress to record. In a period when the United States and China and other major powers are not acting, that may have had some merit, a kind of moral keeping of the feet to the fire—not that it produced much action. But in a period in which the major powers are acting, it is a distraction at best, a hindrance at worst. Time for a do-over.

15. William Antholis and Strobe Talbott, *Fast Forward: Ethics and Politics in the Age of Global Warming* (Brookings Press, 2010).

16. Drew Warne-Smith, "Warwick McKibbin Calls for Global Price on Carbon," *Australian*, July 8, 2010.

17. The phrase was used by an administration official in an interview with Ryan Lizza (www.newyorker.com/online/blogs/newsdesk/2011/04/leading-from-behind-obama-clinton.html).

18. Kori Schake, "Leading from Behind," Foreignpolicy.com, April 27, 2011. I'm picking on Kori, among dozens of critics, because she's one of the most thoughtful in the ranks of the Republican Party, and a friend.

INDEX